Derrida & the Political

'A remarkable book ... The first authoritative study of the political thrust of Derrida's work.'

Rodolphe Gasché
State University of New York at Buffalo

'Richard Beardsworth brilliantly performs a much needed and difficult task.'

Peggy Kamuf
University of Southern California

'Richard Beardsworth has here begun the difficult task of providing us with the markers for evaluating and thinking the meaning of deconstruction in relation to the presuppositions governing political philosophy in all its traditional guises.'

Jay Bernstein, *University of Essex*

Jacques Derrida is undoubtedly one of the most influential, controversial and complex thinkers of our time. This is the first book to consider the political implications of Derrida's philosophical project. It is a timely response to the current political focus of Continental philosophy and to Derrida's own recent shift towards the political.

Richard Beardsworth rejects readings that present Derrida's work as apolitical, relativist, liberal or tendentially anti-democratic. Rather than deducing an external political 'stance' from Derrida's writings, Beardsworth shows that deconstruction itself is inherently political: it is precisely in such central Derridean concepts as aporia that the radical political implications of Derrida's thought become most manifest.

Derrida & the Political offers students of philosophy, politics and critical theory a lucid and original account of Derrida's work as a political thinker.

Richard Beardsworth is Associate Professor of Philosophy and Literature at the American University of Paris.

Thinking the Political

General editors:
Keith Ansell-Pearson, *University of Warwick*
Simon Critchley, *University of Essex*

Recent decades have seen the emergence of a distinct and challenging body of work by a number of Continental thinkers that has fundamentally altered the way in which philosophical questions are conceived and discussed. This work poses a major challenge to anyone wishing to define the essentially contestable concept of 'the political' and to think anew the political import and application of philosophy. How does recent thinking on time, history, language, humanity, alterity, desire, sexuality, gender and culture open up the possibility of thinking the political anew? What are the implications of such thinking for our understanding of and relation to the leading ideologies of the modern world, such as liberalism, socialism and Marxism? What are the political responsibilities of philosophy in the face of the new world (dis)order?

This new series is designed to present the work of the major Continental thinkers of our time, and the political debates their work has generated, to a wider audience in philosophy and in political, social and cultural theory. The aim is neither to dissolve the specificity of 'the philosophical' into 'the political' nor to evade the challenge that 'the political' poses 'the philosophical'; rather, each volume in the series will try to show how it is only in the relation between the two that new possibilities of thought and politics can be activated.

Future volumes will examine the work of Gilles Deleuze, Luce Irigaray, Julia Kristeva, Ernesto Laclau and Chantal Mouffe, Emmanuel Levinas and others.

Derrida & the Political

Richard Beardsworth

London and New York

First published 1996
by Routledge
11 New Fetter Lane, London EC4P 4EE

Simultaneously published in the USA and Canada
by Routledge
20 West 35th Street, New York, NY 10001

© 1996 Richard Beardsworth

Typeset in Sabon by Florencetype Ltd, Stoodleigh, Devon

Printed and bound in Great Britain by
Biddles Ltd, Guildford and King's Lynn

British Library Cataloguing in Publication Data
A catalogue record for this book is available from the British Library.

Library of Congress Cataloging in Publication Data
Beardsworth, Richard, 1961–
    Derrida and the political/Richard Beardsworth.
    p.   cm. – (Thinking the political)
    Includes bibliographical references and index.
    1. Derrida, Jacques – Contributions in political science.
    2. Derrida, Jacques.   3. Deconstruction.   I. Title.   II. Series.
    JC261.D44B43   1996
    320–dc20 95–26620
    CIP

ISBN   0–415–10966–3 (hbk)
          0–415–10967–1 (pbk)

For my parents,
and in memory

The future can only be anticipated in the form of an absolute danger. It is that which breaks absolutely with constituted normality and can only be proclaimed, *presented*, as a sort of monstrosity.

J. Derrida, *Of Grammatology*

Contents

Acknowledgements   viii
Note on translations   ix
Introduction   xi

1   **From Language to Law, an Opening onto Judgement: Saussure, Kafka, Derrida**   1
• Introduction 1 • The trace, the violence of institution 6 • Law, judgement and singularity 25

2   **The Political Limit of Logic and the Promise of Democracy: Kant, Hegel, Derrida**   46
• Introduction 46 • Modernity and violence 49
• The limit of modernity 51 • The logic of Kantian morality 61 • Hegel's critique of Kant 70
• Contradiction, aporia and the fate of law 75

3   **Aporia of Time, Aporia of Law: Heidegger, Levinas, Derrida**   98
• Introduction 98 • Heidegger's thinking of aporia: a politics of authentic temporality 104 • Levinas's thinking of aporia and the fate of the ethical 122

Conclusion   145
Notes   158
Bibliography   165
Index   172

Acknowledgements

This book would not have been written in its present form without my friends Howard Caygill, George Collins, Daniel Gunn and Bernard Stiegler, and without Sylvie Vacher. My gratitude.

My thanks to David Kammerman for his demands of clarification, to students at the American University of Paris, and to the general editors of the series, Keith Ansell-Pearson and Simon Critchley, for their generous supervision of the original manuscript. I also thank the Lounsbery Foundation for offering me a small scholarship which gave me more time to write.

The initial orientation of this book was conceived for my doctoral dissertation at the University of Sussex several years ago under the supervision of Geoffrey Bennington. I would like to record my debt to him here.

Note on Translations

Page references in the text refer to the original French or German texts. They are followed by page references to the English translation, where available, for instance (Heidegger 1935: 116–17/152). Otherwise all translations are by the author.

Introduction

With regard to politics and to philosophical reflection on the political, Derrida's thinking has often been given short shrift.[1] Admired for the elegance and sophistication of its location of the undecidable in any conceptual gesture, Derrida's philosophy avoids, it is argued, problems particular to the domain and history of political and social thought – social reality, the 'logics' and formation of power, decision-making and, perhaps most interestingly, the necessity of risk. It is true that the domain of politics is not a privileged object of reflection for Derrida, although recent work of the 1990s has mobilized and reworked the term more immediately than that of the past. That said, one could easily argue that every strategy in which Derrida's thought is engaged carries political implications.

It is not my purpose here, however, simply to present an *apologia* of the political implications of deconstruction. A straightforward *apologia* of Derrida's philosophy would be, after twenty years of a culture of 'deconstruction' in the Anglo-Saxon world, uninteresting and unhelpful. Too many people, as the English expression quaintly puts it, have 'moved on'. Whatever one thinks of the speed of this house-removal, or of the terms in which it has been made, there is also too much that is shifting in our post-Cold War world for one to assume a unilateral defence of a particular set of thoughts and strategies, however complicated they are (and Derrida is complex). It is my purpose, however, to redress the misunderstandings of Derrida's thinking on the political which have themselves proved unhelpful to the task of thought and practice which lies ahead of all those who are involved in political reflection today: namely, the reinvention of political concepts to measure up to the technicization and globalization of political communities in the next century. In this respect, I believe that Derrida's itinerary concerning the political is exemplary of a certain 'style' of philosophy, or of philosophizing, from which we still have a great deal to learn – not only in terms of its conceptual decisions, but also in terms of the very way in which it reflects upon the political. One may agree or disagree with this style; one will, in turn, reflect upon the political all the better for knowing what the terms of agreement and disagreement are.

It is in this spirit that *Derrida & the Political* has been written. The twenty-first century approaches, and it is clear that our political concepts, and, therefore, the fields in which these concepts are discursively organized, acquire meaning and operate, need to be reinvented. The names of Somalia, Rwanda and Bosnia – together with the many that are already there, joining these names in the public of the electronic and digital gaze, or will join them in the future of this gaze – testify to the present paralysis of political thought and practice, caught in the increasing tension between internationalization and virtualization, on the one hand, and territorial difference and the corporal realities of human life, on the other. In this context, and given its concern with the relations between thought, time and locality, I believe that deconstruction has a telling line on how we might reinvent. Most of the book is involved with the theoretical exposition of this line, which I will introduce summarily in a moment. I also believe that this line of deconstruction is marked by a particular history – philosophical, cultural and empirical – which needs to be partly reorganized. It is not my purpose here, however, to begin this reorganization. Rather, I wish to take the reader through the political implications of the most complex negotiations of Derrida's thinking with the western tradition, concluding with several queries concerning these negotiations, queries which anticipate such a reorganization. In other words, in the context of today's political horizon – one, as I have said, of increasing technicization and globalization – I wish to suggest, with and through Derrida, *where we have come from*. Having expounded the reach of Derrida's thinking regarding the political, I will then be able to conclude – within the terms of this exposition – upon what this thinking also fails to negotiate. Not only will we have seen, consequently, the critical importance of Derrida's thought for political imagination today, but the terms in which this thought needs, in part, to be reorganized will have been negatively suggested through our very understanding of its importance. It is thus my hope that the following 'political' reading of deconstruction (re)turns the reader to Derrida's writings with a (new-found) critical respect of their complexity and contemporaneity, a critical respect which fosters debate concerning the contemporary fate of the political at a mature intellectual level, and which thereby participates, whether the reader agrees with Derrida or not, in the invention of a future which is as complex as possible. I would wish this book to be, in this sense, itself politically responsible.

As with much thought in France in recent years, Derrida's reflection upon the political is articulated through his reading of metaphysics. Following Heidegger (1924, 1926) and Derrida (1968), I understand metaphysical thought as a specific *organization* of time; one that 'disavows' time by casting an opposition between the atemporal and the temporal, the eternal and the transitory, the infinite and the finite, the transcendental and the empirical.[2] It is well known that Derrida relates all his thoughts on the political to what he calls the 'closure' of metaphysics. The power of this reflection lies consequently in his reconsideration of political thought and practice in terms of the irreducibility of time to *all* forms of organization (conceptual, logical, discursive, political, technical, etc.). In other words, the question informing this reflection is: 'What happens to politics and the concept of the political when one assumes, in one's reflection upon these fields, radical finitude?' This question is, of course, not particular to Derrida. What is often called 'contemporary French philosophy' or, more widely, 'contemporary critical theory' has distinguished itself in recent years by offering various responses to this type of question. Whatever the differences of conceptual thought, strategy and tone between, among others, the philosophies of Gilles Deleuze, Jacques Derrida, Michel Foucault, Jean-François Lyotard, Philippe Lacoue-Labarthe and Jean-Luc Nancy, there has been agreement in France that a distinction is warranted between political organization and the 'remainder' [*le reste*] of all attempts to organize politically: that is, a distinction is to be made between a political community and what necessarily exceeds this community, or is left out of account by it, in the process of its (self-)formation.

If the above distinction is consequent upon, in Derrida's terms, an understanding of the closure of metaphysics from the perspective of time, it also responds to the saturation of the political field in the last two hundred years – one which has led to Communist, Fascist and Nazi variants of 'totalitarianism', calling for a thinking of the political community which takes time and difference seriously. In both these historically immediate and philosophically more general contexts, the above distinction has, finally, often been interrogated and elaborated in recent years in terms of *écriture*, singularity and the event. Philosophers of 'writing' (most particularly Derrida, Lyotard and Nancy) witness what cannot be organized politically when they re-mark that which necessarily evades the philosophical concept, since political organization is dependent on the stability of conceptual determination in the first place. A powerful thinking has thus emerged in contemporary French thought which links the 'mourning' of metaphysical logic with a thinking of time and of singularity which exceed the politico-philosophical seizure of the 'real'. *Ecriture* is the name given to what witnesses this excess; hence French thought has often mobilized 'aesthetic' categories to articulate the above distinction between organization and remainder.

Derrida's thinking of the text, the trace, the aporetic and the event has been crucial to the formation of this intellectual constellation. This book's interpretative exposition of Derrida's negotiations with the western tradition claims that his thinking, rather than betraying a *reduction* of political possibility – a retreat onto the margins of the political community at the 'closure' of metaphysics – amounts to an *active transformation* of the political field. Hence my emphasis throughout the book on the 'inventive' side to Derrida's philosophy. The experience of the undecidable and the aporetic in Derrida's work both describes an essential limit to political logic and gives an 'account' of the very condition of decision and action. This account offers a reading, in turn, of *how* one might proceed to judge in the political domain. (The 'subjunctive' modality of the last phrase is, as we shall see, important.) Thinking the political in terms of the violence of conceptual determination, Derrida's philosophy describes the experience of aporia *qua* an experience of time in recognition of which one judges according to the 'lesser violence'. This inextricable, 'temporal' relation between aporia and judgement has been severely underestimated by both supporters and detractors of deconstruction. The underestimation has led to many misunderstandings concerning its political pertinence and force. One has often, for example, been content to stress the aporetic aspect of Derrida's thinking, its stress on the remainder of any judgment, without showing how its aporetic analysis of logic recasts at the same time the 'art' of judgment and invention, and recasts this art through an elaboration of the radical irreducibility of time. And yet, as we shall see at length, Derrida's approach to politics and the political can only be found through his 'temporal' deconstruction of the logics which inform traditional determinations of politics and the political. If one wishes, therefore, to consider the political implications of deconstruction, it is imperative to develop this approach and thereby consider the way in which it transforms our terms of political orientation. Given this, my argument is that Derrida's philosophy only makes sense politically in terms of the relation 'between' aporia and decision and neither in terms of a unilateral philosophy of aporia nor in terms of a unilateral philosophy of decision: in other words, aporia is the very locus in which the political force of deconstruction is to be found. My overall argument through the three chapters traces just how complicated this relation is and how it can best be conceived as an 'impossible' relation between the passage of time and political organization.

It is due to Derrida's attention to *écriture* that his philosophy has been most often received and expounded within departments of literature in the Anglo-Saxon world. In my first chapter 'From language to law, an opening onto judgement: Saussure, Kafka, Derrida', aware of the literary reception of Derrida's thinking, of its importance, but also of the nefarious consequences that it has had for thinking Derrida's understanding of aporia in politico-philosophical terms, I pull the common understanding of the trace and the text from its linguistic and literary framings to those of 'judgement' and 'institution'. The two texts that ironically best serve me in this endeavour are Derrida's early deconstruction of Saussurean linguistics, 'Grammatology and linguistics' (1967b) and his profound text on Kafka, 'Before the law' (1985). From a detailed consideration of these two texts within the perspective of institution and judgement the politically *transformative* nature of Derrida's aporetic thinking becomes manifest.

Chapter 2, 'The political limit of logic and the promise of democracy: Kant, Hegel, Derrida', rearticulates the conclusions of Chapter 1 in relation to political 'modernity'. Since criticisms of the political aspects of deconstruction have often come out of the modern tradition of political thought, it would seem appropriate to situate Derrida's work in relation to the modern debate about the place and limits of the political. This debate has often been poorly analysed, in particular, sadly, by those working with Derridean strategies who either have little philosophical knowledge or articulate Derrida and modernity through exclusively aesthetic categories. The debate concerns the difference between the orientation of Kant and Hegel's philosophies, a difference which forms the major axis of modern political thinking. For Derrida, both Kant and Hegel understand the political in terms of 'logics' which his thinking of aporia wishes to exceed. The chapter – long and multiple in its strategies given the stakes involved – expands Derrida's mourning of logic with regard to time into a staging of deconstruction and modernity's respective understandings of the relation between the political community and time. Derrida's underestimated work *Glas* (1974) will be central to this staging.

Chapters 1 and 2 shift our political understanding of Derrida's philosophy from literary inscription to a transformation of political modernity, rehearsing Derrida's interest in aporia from the perspective of the irreducibility of time to logic. Chapter 3 pursues the political weight of this irreducibility by showing how Derrida's understanding of the aporia of time is also one of law. Chapter 3 thereby conjoins the concerns of the previous two chapters, bringing the transformative nature of aporia to bear on recent accounts of the relation between time and human will. The conjoining is made in relation to two specific and politically crucial attempts to leave the modern tradition: the philosophies of Heidegger and of Levinas. Derrida's thinking is often aligned with both or either of these two thinkers. The alignment allows one, for example, to tar Derrida and Heidegger with the same brush (the Heidegger 'affair' of 1987) or resort to Levinas's ethical reinterpretation of ontology to salvage Derrida from his 'Heideggerianism'. Such moves simplify the complexity of Derrida's thought, particularly the *way* in which he unties time from logic. The chapter shows how his understanding of aporia in terms both of time and of law exceed the manoeuvres of either Heidegger or Levinas and, more importantly, reveal these manoeuvres to 'invert' into one another. Interestingly enough it is to here that Hegel would return, in speculative mode, as an ally of Derrida, and not as someone to whom Heidegger, Levinas and Derrida are opposed.

If I mention the last point here, it is simply because it reveals where my exposition of Derrida's thinking is *interpretative*, pushing this thinking's understanding of the aporetic into a dialogue on the political with thinkers and constellations to which it has at times taken too great a distance. The reader will judge whether this strategy of reading is effective or not.

What consistently emerges from my engagements with Saussure, Kafka, Kant, Hegel, Levinas and Heidegger is a structure of thinking and acting that Derrida has recently placed under the headings of 'double affirmation' and the 'promise' (1986a, 1987a, 1987d et al.). Following the argument of each chapter, I maintain that, for Derrida, the promise is an affirmation of the future which both renders account of and exceeds modern determinations of the future as well as 'post'-metaphysical attempts to leave or displace these determinations. The promise will be shown to summarize Derrida's deconstructions of the tradition as well as of the two philosophies (Heidegger and Levinas's) to which his work is often reduced. By the end of the third chapter we will see that the promise is essentially a rearticulation of the aporia of time and of law. In the light of this book's arguments, the promise could be considered as Derrida's specific way of developing the excess of the *politico-philosophical* organization of temporality, that is, the way in which philosophy's traditional disavowal of time *is* always already political and, therefore, immediately carries, before and in parallel with any subsequent theory of the political, political consequences. Thus, understanding what Derrida means by the promise, by tracing his work through the modern tradition and beyond, allows us also to comprehend how Derrida's recent preoccupation with 'a democracy to come' (1991a) rearticulates his overall concern, since the sixties, with deconstructing the western tradition of philosophy. As this introduction has been keen to emphasize, the key to looking at Derrida's thinking from this perspective is to consider it as an aporetic and inventive philosophy of time and law.

The promise will be seen to be the rearticulation of time in terms of the irreducibility of law and of law in terms of the irreducibility of time. Metaphysical logic reduces the passage of time to presence: its articulations of justice are consequently violent to the experience of time that constitutes the human condition. The disavowal of time in reflection upon the political has led to much injustice and violence in the field of politics. To reflect upon politics in terms of time is to endure the experience of the aporia of law (and) time. Political judgements which recognize difference according to the lesser violence are those that have endured this experience. This experience informs Derrida's non-horizonal understanding of justice and of democracy. The political resonance of deconstruction is to be located and discussed here.

This said, the question which remains for this writer is to what extent Derrida's understanding of aporia and judgment remains itself too philosophical, too conceptual, and, if so, given precisely Derrida's constant concern with the irreducibility of time to conceptuality, in what sense. I will return to this question in my conclusion where I consider, all too briefly given the stakes and complexity of the issues involved, the relation between the promise and technics. My conclusion will only be understandable, however, and perhaps challenging, once we have explored the matter of the next three chapters.

1
From Language to Law, an Opening onto Judgement

Saussure, Kafka, Derrida

> The general structure of the unmotivated trace connects within the same possibility, and they cannot be separated except by abstraction, the structure of the relationship with the other, the movement of temporalization, and language as writing.
>
> J. Derrida, *Of Grammatology*

Introduction

The first sustained reception of Derrida's thinking took place in university departments of literature. The reception of his work within the context of literary studies was understandably selective; it often led, however, to poor negotiations with the political tenor of his thought. In turn the literary aspects of Derrida's writings have deterred people with an eye on the political from reading these works carefully. My first chapter reconsiders two of Derrida's works privileged by this reception – his deconstruction of the linguistic sign and his engagements with the 'literary' – with a specific view to the political dimension of his work as a whole. My concern is not to politicize these writings, nor to derive a politics from them, one elaborated in frustration, for example, at the seeming distance which they observe to immediate political issues. It is to show how Derrida's writings regarding language and literature, *by exceeding what we normally understand by these terms*, as well as their fields of interest and influence, constitute a serious engagement with the future of thinking and acting. I demonstrate in particular that this engagement inheres in the very 'method' of deconstruction and that the political dimension of Derrida's thinking can be gauged only in respect of this 'method'. This dimension is found in his understanding of 'aporia' and 'promise'.[1]

The Fates of Deconstruction

Derrida's work on Saussure in *Of Grammatology* (1967b) and his various pronouncements on the specificity of literary writing in *Writing and Difference* (1967a) and *Dissemination* (1972a) were instrumental in the shift from the structuralist culture of the 1960s and 1970s, to its inheritor 'post-structuralism' in the anglophone world of the late 1970s and 1980s. His deconstruction of Saussure's theory of the sign was considered to be both a radical questioning of the human processes of signification and a severe rebuttal of philosophical axiomatic. Saussure had himself begun this questioning with his formal analysis of language as a differential system of values; Derrida removed the remaining philosophical nostalgia of Saussure's project by deconstructing the desire for systematicity. Through his emphasis on *écriture* Derrida both reinvented the relations and spaces between philosophy and literature and opened up a new field of inquiry into textual processes, these processes exceeding traditional distinctions between the real and the fictional, the historical and the imaginary. The above three works were crucial in promoting the emergence in the anglophone world of the discipline and institutional practice of 'literary theory', whose interest lay in the complex mechanisms of language and in procedures of reading and writing in general.

Jonathan Culler spoke well, if symptomatically, of the relation of deconstruction to literary theory in his influential *On Deconstruction: Theory and Criticism after Structuralism* (1983). He argued that the major concern of deconstruction was to read philosophy rhetorically and literature philosophically. His appraisal carried three implications. First, deconstruction was considered to be a practice of reading whose aim was to show that the philosophical *telos* of truth, reason or logic defined itself against the very writing in which this *telos* was expressed; the *telos* was undermined by the very rhetorical procedures of the writing which sustained it. Second – following this invitation to treat philosophical discourse as 'literature' – works of literature were themselves to be read in terms of their displacement of the values which philosophy promised, but necessarily denied by refusing to think the foundations of its discourse. In other words, literature could be read most fruitfully as a superior kind of 'philosophizing'. Third, Derrida's work was itself located within a tradition of thinking which included the major concerns of post-Kantian aesthetics, Nietzsche's destruction of Platonism and the writings of Paul de Man (*Blindness and Insight* (1972) and *Allegories of Reading* (1979)). Working himself from within this tradition, the author of *On Deconstruction* argued persuasively for the importance of Derrida's work for literary criticism, anticipating that literary criticism would become the avant-garde discipline of the humanities, contributing most to what came to call itself in the 1980s 'critical theory'.

This evaluation of Derrida's work characterized the reception of deconstruction until the latter part of the 1980s. In departure from it, and partly owing to increased philosophical interest in Derrida's writings, the complex 'logic' of Derrida's texts began to be untied. The works of Rodolphe Gasché (1979, 1986) and Geoffrey Bennington (1987, 1991) were particularly important in this respect. These analyses, together with the institutional history of deconstruction in the Anglo-Saxon world, made it clear that, at its intellectual best, the literary reception of Derrida's thought overplayed its rhetorical side and, at its institutional worst, made it into a practice of literary criticism, the political orientation of which was easily advertised, but poorly elaborated. It was in this intellectual and historical context that the 'affairs' of Heidegger (his profound complicity with Nazism) and de Man (his journalism in Belgium between 1940 and 1942, showing sympathies with Germany) took place in 1987.

These two events allowed those already ill-disposed towards 'deconstruction' to confirm to their public that its overall tendency was indeed reactionary (for example, Ferry and Renaut, 1988; Habermas, 1988b). However unjust the accusation, Derrida's reputation suffered through association, and the reach of his thinking was severely underestimated. In a country as culturally diverse and restless as the United States, there was a self-fulfilling desire to move on. First historicism, then multiculturalism stole front stage in North American literature departments, the work of deconstruction being for the most part recast as an intellectual gesture still working within a traditional, Eurocentric canon. The Yale school's versions of deconstruction, with its varied interests in European Romanticism, prepared for this judgement, whilst Derrida's almost exclusive references to the western European tradition of philosophy and literature fuelled it. Multiculturalism did not, of course, emerge because of the Heidegger and de Man affairs. These affairs did serve, however, as a political pretext to a broad dismissal of what had become in the meantime an institutional culture, one which often brought to texts rather repetitive procedures of interpretation through which 'deconstruction' necessarily ran the risk of being considered a *transcendental* practice of reading. It was consequently not by chance that deconstruction came to be seen in the late 1980s as constitutively incapable of articulating the historical making and unmaking of subjectivities.

The case against the institution of deconstruction is rested; but that of deconstruction's relation to its institution, and to its thinking of the institution in general, needs to be reopened. The opportunity is provided by means of a resituating of the stakes of Derrida's text on Saussure, 'Linguistics and grammatology' (1967b), and of one of his major meditations on the specificity of literature, 'Before the Law' (1985). A rereading of these works will show that the institutional culture of deconstruction fell into contradiction with the radical insights of this culture's beginnings.

If this is the fate of all thinking that inaugurates a culture – following the iterable logic of all marks, Derrida's writings lend themselves a priori to being 'misunderstood' – the complexity and implications of Derrida's thinking have been simplified by its international reception remaining unduly in the field of textual analysis. The simplification has been aggravated by a common conviction that its concerns were, if not those of language, to be worked out through language-analysis, and that this work could best be done in the 'spaces' between literature and philosophy. Whilst this is not wrong, it has, however, confined the reach of Derrida's thinking (its conceptual resources and strategies) to a debate either between the frontiers of literature and philosophy or one within their institutional confines. This debate has often proved extremely fruitful, generating questions which well exceed these frontiers, using indeed the resources of Derrida's thinking to rearticulate the very concept of 'frontier' (Derrida, 1994a; Bennington, 1994). At the same time, this textual and institutional confinement of deconstruction has heightened the prevalent scepticism or nervousness concerning the political implications of Derrida's thought.

The Method of Deconstruction

I said at the beginning of this chapter that we would be concerned with the 'method' of deconstruction and that its political dimension could be untied from this 'method'. Derrida is careful to avoid this term because it carries connotations of a procedural form of judgement. A thinker with a method has already decided *how* to proceed, is unable to give him or herself up to the matter of thought in hand, is a functionary of the criteria which structure his or her conceptual gestures. For Derrida, as we shall see at length in this book, this is irresponsibility itself. Thus, to talk of a method in relation to deconstruction, especially regarding its ethico-political implications, would appear to go directly against the current of Derrida's philosophical adventure. That said, Derrida's writings of the late 1960s and early 1970s – *Writing and Difference* (1967a), *Of Grammatology* (1967b), *Dissemination* (1972a) and *Margins of Philosophy* (1972b) – negotiate a relation between philosophy and what in France is called the 'sciences humaines' which is both characteristic of a certain style of philosophizing and carries with it and develops a clear set of intellectual, disciplinary and institutional stakes. On the one hand, Derrida wishes to show that it is impossible to dominate philosophical concepts from *outside* philosophy, since the attempt meets an essential limit in the very philosophical nature of the terms being used to dominate it (terms, for example, of propriety embedded in the discourses of anthropology, linguistics, literary studies and psychoanalysis). On the other hand, and for the same reason, philosophy is incapable of dominating the 'empiricity' or 'facticity' of these same discourses (what I will later call their 'inscription') since this empiricity and facticity inform its very gestures when it is least aware of it. As we will see with the example of linguistics, Derrida traces through this double impossibility and shows how it is both 'possible' *and* irreducible.[2] The consequent negotiation between the discourse of philosophy and the human sciences enacts a displacement and reorganization of the 'metaphysical' opposition between the transcendental and the empirical, opening up an aporetic and uncontrollable 'position', neither in philosophy (as it is traditionally organized) nor outside it, one from which the future of thinking and practice is thought.

I call this orientation the 'method' of deconstruction. My use of the term 'method' is contextually determined and strategic, motivated by a wish to press home the precise intellectual stakes of Derrida's philosophy, stakes which have often been ignored or underestimated. Thus, in distinction to writers who tend to emphasize the impossibility of the transcendental in Derrida's writings, my use of the term 'method' underscores the necessity of reinscribing the metaphysical opposition between the transcendental and the empirical. Thinking this necessity means thinking the inescapability of inscription in general – which would include the instances of history, the body, technics, politics – but it means thinking it *without* losing the inescapable gesture of the transcendental in order to do so.

Through a careful exposition of the double move of this 'method' I then emphasize that it is in the *irreducibility* of the above double-bind or aporia ('neither in philosophy nor outside it') that Derrida locates both the *necessity* of judgement and the *promise* of the future. An aporia demands decision, one cannot remain within it; at the same time its essential irreducibility to the cut of a decision makes the decision which one makes contingent, to be made again. The promise of the future (that there is a future) is located in this contingency. In this contingency of time resides the possibility of justice. In other words, the aporia of thinking which emerges from within Derrida's play between philosophy and the human sciences inaugurates a philosophy of *judgement* and a thinking of *justice* in relation to *time*. I shall argue that the ethico-political dimension of deconstruction resides in this relation between aporia and judgement.

The chapter is divided into two parts which mirror the above move from the 'method' of deconstruction and its stakes to the ensuing relations between aporia, judgement and justice. The first part elaborates the workings of deconstruction through a reading of 'Linguistics and grammatology' (1967b). The second part turns the consequences of this elaboration to an exposition of the inextricable nature of the relation in Derrida's thought between aporia and judgement, maintaining that the thinking of aporia is understood by Derrida as a thinking of law, and that this thinking, as inscribed in the literary text, is the condition and, in a sense, 'measure' of judgements, judgements which have the chance of inventing the new. Derrida's understanding of the 'promise' in terms of time – one to which considerable weight will be given, implicitly and explicitly, in Chapters 2 and 3 – will emerge through these reflections.

Let me now summarize the argument so far. The elaboration of Derrida's 'method' in his work on Saussurean linguistics serves:

- to show the way in which a political orientation to deconstruction is to be found in its location of an irreducible aporia which ensues from its reinscription of the empirico-transcendental difference. For this aporia engenders a temporal analysis of judgement.
- to show how the passage through the transcendental in Derrida's work opens up an understanding of *institutions* – I use this word to cover any act that acquires form, from institutions in the usual sense to disciplines and even broader cultural formations like religion – and an understanding of the relations between institutions and their history. These relations are violent. The necessity of the passage through the transcendental engenders an account of the irreducibility of violence (what Derrida calls 'originary violence').
- to show that the major political inflection to Derrida's manoeuvre between the transcendental and the empirical is his deconstruction of the concept and practice of *horizons* (institutional, disciplinary, temporal).[3] In his reinscription of the empirico-transcendental difference, Derrida reveals how any horizon of thinking or action is an 'ethico-theoretical decision' which denies finitude. The ethico-theoretical nature of the decision is 'political' in that, akin to politics in the common sense of the term, its demarcation of space and time is a violence predicated on disavowal. The effects of this deconstruction of horizonal thinking will then be reorganized with regard to modern political thought in Chapter 2.
- to show that each of the previous points is the same 'thesis' viewed from a different perspective.

The Trace, The Violence of Institution

The Privilege of the Sign

Before turning explicitly to 'Linguistics and grammatology' we should remind ourselves firstly of the reasons why Derrida considered the sign to be an exemplary terrain on which the deconstruction of metaphysics could be negotiated. In 'The end of the book and the beginning of writing', the introduction to *Of Grammatology* (1967b: 15–41/6–26), Derrida contends that language acquires methodological importance in

reflection upon human facticity in the same movement that puts the identity of this language in crisis. The paradox places language on the horizon
of our age, at what Derrida calls the 'closure' of metaphysics. Language
does not simply embody the paradox, however; it brings it to light in the
first place. On the one hand, the sign dominates the horizon of contemporary thinking because it is no longer regarded (the argument of
'logocentrism') as a secondary instance which represents or communicates
a prior entity (*logos*, being, God, spirit, truth, subjectivity, consciousness,
activity, intentionality); on the other hand, just when it assumes this
primary position, it moves into crisis. Since language is largely defined as
a *medium* conveying an instance prior to it, the moment this instance
withdraws, the very identity of language does as well. The sign becomes
at one and the same time both a privileged object of reflection and a
volatile object unsure of its vocation.

Three consequences follow from this paradox. First, any discipline
which prioritizes language in contradistinction to metaphysics is complicit
with metaphysics since the theory of the sign is essentially metaphysical.
Second, if writing has always been debased by this conception of language,
considered as upsetting the purity of the transmission of the prior instance,
then to address the paradox of language demands reconsidering writing.
Writing offers privileged access to the reinscription of the empirico-
transcendental difference since the sign is *the* determining instance of this
opposition for metaphysics. The very possibility of the sign is predicated
on an opposition between that which is conveyed (the signified, the *logos*,
the non-worldly) and the conveyor (the signifier, the worldly). Third,
this opposition determines *all* oppositions constituted by this difference
(infinite/finite, soul/body, nature/law, universal/particular, etc.). Derrida's
deconstruction of the sign is consequently *exemplary* for the very reason
that metaphysics is derived from the domination of a particular relation
between the ideal and the material which assumes definition in the concept
of 'sign'.

The preceding is corroborated for Derrida by a fundamental insight
achieved in the late work of Husserl, specifically *The Origin of Geometry*
(Derrida, 1962), to which Derrida refers at the beginning of the chapter
'Linguistics and grammatology' when discussing the impossibility of a
science of the *gramme*. In the context of the above argument it would be
useful to refer to it in turn. Derrida is suggesting that the condition of
truth is the possibility of writing. Rather than the inscription of writing
(mis-)reflecting the truth – the argument which sets up 'logocentrism' –
its possibility is constitutive of truth as such. Derrida writes:

> writing is not only an auxiliary means in the service of science
> – and possibly its object – but first, as Husserl in particular
> pointed out in the *Origin of Geometry*, the condition of the

> possibility of ideal objects and therefore of scientific objectivity.
> Before being its object, writing is the condition of episteme. . . .
> Historicity itself is tied to the possibility of writing; to the possi-
> bility of writing in general, beyond those particular forms of
> writing in the name of which we have long spoken of peoples
> without writing and without history. Before being the object
> of history – of an historical science – writing opens the field of
> history – of historical becoming. And the former (*Historie* in
> German) presupposes the latter (*Geschichte*).
>
> (Derrida, 1967b: 42–3/27)

The paradox of language is here radicalized to suggest, following the third
point above, that metaphysics constitutes its oppositions (here: the non-
worldly/worldly and the ideal/material) by expelling into one term of the
opposition the very possibility of the condition of such oppositions.
Derrida calls this general possibility of inscription 'arche-writing'. The
thesis puts in question, for Derrida, all frontiers between the *telos* of metaphysics and its others. It therefore puts in question those distinctions
between a transcendental approach to man (often identified with philosophy) and an empirical approach. *The question of method is thus central
to the elaboration of 'arche-writing'*. The above *telos* informs the major
values of ethical and political thinking since Plato and haunts in one way
or another the modern destructions of these values. These destructions
are crucial to the very formation of the empirical sciences. So, rather than
consider this constitutive role of writing in *rhetorical* terms, let us begin
to consider what implications it has for the ends of thinking and the
human.

Saussure's Exclusion of Writing – its Implications

'Linguistics and Grammatology' begins with a contradiction in Saussure's
method. The *Course in General Linguistics* (Saussure, 1915) argues
that linguistics is a *science* of language (that is a procedure of analysing
language which is general and universal), and yet it excludes from its
object of study the graphic sign. It is in Saussure's opening chapters that
the parameters of the object of linguistics are drawn, so founding the
discipline as a science. This institution of a human science turns on
Saussure's separation of the abstract system of *langue* – a system of distinct
signs corresponding to distinct ideas, true of all languages – from the
empirical multiplicity of languages with their linguistic, physical and physiological variations. The abstraction depends in turn on a distinction
between what is internal and essential, and what is external and accidental to the system of *langue*. Within the limits of the social conventions
which underpin the system of *langue*, Saussure argues that the essential

nature of this system is to be found in the 'union of meanings and sound-images [*l'image acoustique*]' (1915: 15/32). Despite the institutionality of *langue* – '*langue* is a pure institution' (1915: 76/110) – the sign is made up of a *natural* unity between a psychic sound or signifier and the meaning or signified that it designates. Although Saussure stresses that the psychic sound is to be distinguished from the physiological manifestation of it which one hears, the phonetic pronunciation of a word is still more 'natural' than its written inscription. It is this natural order that allows Saussure to set linguistics up as a science. The natural relation between the signified and the phonic signifier conditions in turn the 'natural' reduction of written signs to tangible forms of these sound-images, secondary representations of them, inessential to the object of linguistics.

Despite noting at the very beginning of the *Course in General Linguistics* that the only access to the matter of linguistics is through writing, Saussure considers writing's unique *raison d'être* to be the representation of speech. Indeed, whenever the question of writing turns up in Saussure's observations, it is immediately stigmatized and expelled as a 'monstrosity' which reverses the natural order between speech and writing (chapters V and VI). For example: writing is considered a tyrant (1915: 53/31) which usurps the natural phonic pronunciations of words, substituting for them their visual images. Saussure gives the example of the proper name *Lefèvre*, which written *Lefebvre* has come to be pronounced *Lefébure*, concluding, 'Such phonic deformations belong to language but do not stem from its natural functioning. They are due to an external influence. Linguistics should put them into a special compartment: they are teratological cases.' (1915: 53–4/31–2).

As Derrida observes, Saussure's reaction to what many would find somewhat amusing betrays an organizing division between the natural and the artificial, one whose implicit violence is revealed in such moments of otherwise unprofessional and unaccountable passion. The violence can be accounted for by the fact that Saussure's whole project or *telos* of linguistics is based, in its exclusive concern with the relation between phonic signifier and meaning, on the *phone*. This 'phonocentrism' is both metaphysical and violent according to the very criteria which led Saussure to the opposite conviction that linguistics is scientific – that is, general, universal, non-metaphysical and passion- or value-free. Saussurean linguistics is consequently seen to be founded on an 'ethico-theoretical decision' (1967b: 61/41) which is disguised by the apparent naturality of the object under consideration, but revealed by the obsessive insistence with which the founder of linguistics wishes to expel writing from the essence of language.

The contradictory nature of Saussure's method implies that the relation between philosophy and a human science like linguistics is much more complicated than one might at first have assumed. Saussure's wish to see a natural unity between sound and meaning is a metaphysical decision, prolonging the violence inherent in metaphysical logic. Following his analysis of the paradox of the sign and the constitutive role of writing, Derrida contends that the epoch of logocentrism is one of 'phonocentrism'. For Derrida, both the possibility and the horizon of metaphysics are predicated on the normative exclusion of writing from the procedures of truth. We have seen the pathological violence of such exclusion in Saussure's condemnation of *Lefébure*. This small, but by no means isolated, detail is extremely telling for Derrida. It shows that the procedures of truth (from the *logos* of Plato to the 'science' of linguistics) are predicated on the *disavowal* of *inscription*. It is through this disavowal that metaphysics constitutes itself in the first place. It is speech which allows for this illusion of transcending inscription because 'the system of "hearing oneself speak" through the phonic substance ... *presents itself* as the non-exterior, non-mundane therefore non-empirical or non-contingent signifier' (1967b: 17/7). In other words, the voice's apparent 'immateriality' leads to the belief that there is a qualitative difference between the non-worldly and the worldly (– for the detail of this argument see Derrida, *Speech and Phenomena*, 1967c: chapters 3 and 4). Derrida contends accordingly that the distinction between speech and writing constitutes *the* determining relation of the oppositional axiomatic of metaphysics (1967b: 20f./10f.).

Saussure repeats this determination by concentrating exclusively on the phonic signifier as the basis of *langue*. Saussure will thereby repeat exclusions specific to metaphysical logic, exclusions which follow from the disavowal of inscription, or the condition of processes of signification. The recognition of the condition of these exclusions demands a re-cognition and renegotiation of their law, and this recognition is political. To renegotiate this law means, for Derrida, to rethink the empirico-transcendental difference; inversely, to renegotiate the empirico-transcendental difference is to think the law of logic and the logic of law. At the same time, therefore, as giving a painstaking reading of Saussurean linguistics Derrida is recasting the terms in which *all institutional violence* is to be thought (we now know, however, in what sense for Derrida the question of the *phone* embraces western metaphysics; so the reading is as meticulous as its ambitions are vast). Despite its centrality to the question of the *phone*, this last 'political' aspect of the essay has often been ignored. This is because the inescapability of reinscribing the empirico-transcendental difference has not been followed through.

In order to reinscribe this opposition, Derrida must show that the very condition of the *phone* is arche-writing and that Saussure's elaboration of the *phone*'s differential value itself reveals this condition of arche-writing. In other words, Saussure's apparent phonocentrism must lead to its deconstruction, which is simultaneously the deconstruction of all empirical accounts of human facticity. The contradictions and exclusions must be accounted for from within Saussure's endeavour, and not from the imposition of an external set of criteria. Otherwise, the violence inherent to metaphysics is just repeated: the subject matter is dominated by the bringing forth of external criteria to think it. In contrast, by elaborating the violence of Saussure's discourse *from within* this discourse, Derrida allows the possibility of a different relation to law and violence to emerge.

The Contradictory Logic of Saussure's Exclusion

Having excluded writing from linguistics, Saussure's theory, Derrida argues, becomes entangled in a 'contradictory logic' (1967b: 67/46). The first contradiction ensues from the major proposition that the sign is arbitrary or unmotivated. The sign is composed of the concept, the signified, and its sound-image, the signifier: the signified 'tree' has its signifier, the sound-image, *tree*. As we have observed, for Saussure, this image is phonic, otherwise there would be no natural dimension to the unity of sound-meaning; and the phonic sign would have no priority over its graphic 'representation'. The unmotivated relation, however, between the signifier and the signified should have made Saussure think twice about the natural hierarchy which he perceives between speech and writing. For it is this notion of arbitrariness which makes of the sign an *institution*, that is, something that is not natural. To say therefore that there is a natural subordination of writing to speech – that writing is a secondary representation of a primary unity of sound and meaning – whilst propounding at the same time that all signs are arbitrary is contradictory.

The second contradiction in Saussure's argument ensues from his later statement that language is made up of differences without positive terms. For, if this is the case, the natural unit of sound-meaning – which, we recall, constituted in the first place the possibility of linguistics as a science with a phenomenally delimited object – can only be a secondary effect of the differential system of language. As a result, there is nothing natural about the phonic sign with regard to a graphic sign, and nothing secondary about a graphic sign with respect to a phonic one. Saussure betrays the contradiction between this differential account of language and his initial subordination of writing to speech when he admits that the taking of *words* as the minimum object of analysis is indeed a pragmatic decision (1915: 158/114). Without such a decision there would be no object that could appear in the phenomenal field and therefore no possibility of a science of this object. With such a decision, however, Saussure removes the very possibility of an 'objective' science which this decision at the same time institutes. His gesture is, in other words, an 'ethico-theoretical' decision which institutes the object of a 'science', but pretends to be natural whereas, *qua* a decision, and like all decisions, it is violent. The irreducibility of a decision shows that the most innocent 'theorist' is always also a legislator and policeman. It is in this sense that any statement is a judgement which carries 'political' force.

Derrida's point in locating the contradiction in the argument is not, of course, to suggest that a decision concerning the object of linguistics could or should be avoided or that all decisions are equally violent. Both suggestions – the one transcendentalist, the other empiricist – in fact repeat the desire to avoid the irreducibility of inscription. The point is rather that, firstly, a decision is always needed because there is no natural status to language, and that given this irreducibility of a decision, there are different kinds of decisions – those that recognize their legislative and executive force and those which hide it under some claim to naturality *qua* 'theory' or 'objective science'. The point is thus secondly that the acknowledgement of the prescriptive force of one's statements may make one more ready to transform the field that is posited by the nature of one's decision – given that the field, together with its frontiers, is the result of a decision and not the representation of a preceding 'real'. This is the argument of a 'lesser violence' in a general economy of violence. We will be constantly coming back to it in the following as well as in chapters 2 and 3.

In both instances of contradiction in his argument Saussure refuses to recognize that the founding of the science of linguistics is an act that exceeds the opposition of nature and institution, one which at the same time this founding institutes as 'natural'. This act is described by Derrida as one of 'originary violence'. Its force is revealed in that what it suppresses 'returns' *as* the above instances of contradiction, engendering either continued acts of violence which attempt to keep the science of linguistics coherent (the academic police) or a radical redescription of the tensions structuring Saussure's legislative decisions, in particular the effect of the initial usurpation of the natural order of speech by that of writing. Since the history of linguistics as 'phonetics' repeats this violence, Derrida is in fact describing the suppression of difference *as* history.

The Instituted Trace and Arche-Writing

Derrida's re-description of what is going on turns, first, on the contradiction concerning writing (1967b: 63–5/43–4) and, second, on that concerning the *phone*, the ultimate site and source of Saussure's contradictory logic (1967b: 78f./53f.).

With respect to the first contradiction, if all signs are unmotivated or arbitrary, Saussure cannot institute a natural hierarchy between speech and writing without himself committing an unthought violence. This violence is that through which speech is 'instituted' as 'natural' to the essence of language. Since writing is the example of the unmotivated nature of the relation between signifier and signified, and all signs are unmotivated, Saussure has in fact argued that it is writing which covers the whole field of linguistic signs, within which a secondary difference between phonic and graphic signs takes place. Writing is, therefore, both more external and more internal to speech than Saussurean linguistics would wish. Writing is not an image (graphic representation) of speech, all speech is already writing by its being unmotivated. It is only through this general understanding of writing that speech could be affected by writing (their roles reversed, etc.) in the first place. This generalization of writing permits an initial account of arche-writing as the 'instituted trace'.

> Even before it is linked to incision, engraving, drawing, or the letter, to a signifier referring in general to a signifier signified by it, the concept of the *graphie* implies the framework of the *instituted trace*, as the possibility common to all systems of signification.
>
> (Derrida, 1967b: 68/46)

The instituted trace precedes the opposition between nature and convention, allowing for their possibility; it thus takes account of and comprehends the Saussurean act of foundation elaborated on pp. 8/11 as well as its pathological refusal to include writing in the space that it founded. The instituted trace also comprehends and exceeds the instances of contradictions which emerge from this refusal. As the rewriting of the internal space of linguistics, of the exclusions which it perforce makes to institute this space, and of the contradictions which these very exclusions engender, the instituted trace accounts for these three moments: first, the foundation of a disciplinary space; second, its constitutive exclusions; and, third, the return of that which is excluded, within the disciplinary space. All three moments are effects of *arche-writing*; they together constitute what Derrida calls in 'Violence and metaphysics' an 'economy of violence' (1967a: 136, n. 1/313, n. 21). We will address this text and its argument in Chapter 3. Through the deconstruction of the sign, Derrida is writing a *genealogy* of violence, one that is explicitly taken up in the later chapter in *Of Grammatology* 'The violence of the letter: From Lévi-Strauss to Rousseau' (1967b: 149–202/ 101–140, see esp. 201–2/139–40). I will return to this chapter at the end of this section; the next chapter will reorganize this genealogy in relation to Hegel's critique of Kantian morality and his development of the inversions of 'fate', and the third chapter will rearticulate it through the philosophies of Heidegger and Levinas in terms of the aporia of time and of law.

The second case of contradiction – which emerges in Saussure's differential analysis of the *phone* – is one of the most important sites of reinscription of the empirico-transcendental difference revealed by Derrida's work. Derrida reads Saussure against himself in order to reorganize the space between philosophy and linguistics in terms of arche-writing. This reorganization shows that both philosophy and linguistics are derivatives of a movement which constitutes them, but which they disavow in order to appear as such. Derrida's description of this movement from within Saussure both accounts for the trace and accounts for its disavowal, a reinscription which is at the same time a continued reflection on the economy of violence. This is evident at the moment that Saussure develops his understanding of language as a system of differences without positive terms (1915: 'Linguistic value', 155–69/111–18). Here he abruptly acknowledges that the signifier or sound-image is *not* phonic and that, therefore, sound does *not* belong to *langue*.

> It is impossible for sound in itself, the material element, to belong to *langue*. It is only a secondary thing, substance to be put to use ... the linguistic signifier ... is not phonic but incorporeal – constituted not by its material substance but by the differences which separate its sound-image from all others.
> (Saussure, 1915: 164–5/118–19)

To justify the point, Saussure sets out the difference between the differential virtuality of phonemes and their sonorous concretization, a difference that allows for multiple pronunciations of the same phoneme and for these pronunciations to be recognized as those of the same phoneme. In his discussion of the necessary difference between the sound-image and its materialization, Saussure argues an analogy with writing. Given the importance of the passage to Derrida's elaboration of the 'quasi-transcendental' status of arche-writing I shall quote it in full. It is here that Saussure exceeds the transcendentalism of traditional philosophy without repeating its logic or oppositions. In doing so, he also contradicts the axiom of his own project of linguistics through having recourse to writing. By speaking of the reduction of the phonic substance and allowing the graphic phenomenon of writing to serve as the metaphor of this reduction, Saussure opens up a 'terrain' which is neither transcendental nor empirical, but which exceeds both philosophy and linguistics, and which permits Derrida to elaborate the quasi-concept of the trace in full:

> Since an identical state of affairs is observable in writing, another system of signs, we shall use writing to draw some comparisons that will clarify the whole issue. In fact:

1) The signs used in writing are arbitrary; there is no connection, for example, between the letter t and the sound that it designates.
2) The value of letters is purely negative and differential. The same person can write *t*, for instance, in different ways:

   t t *t*

The only requirement is that the sign for *t* is not confused in the script with the signs used for *l*, *d*, etc.
3) Values in writing function only through the reciprocal opposition within a fixed system that consists of a set number of letters. This third characteristic, though not identical to the second, is closely related to it, for both depend on the first. Since the graphic sign is arbitrary, its form matters little or rather matters only within the limitations imposed by the system.
4) The means by which the sign is produced is completely unimportant, for it does not affect the system (this also follows from characteristic 1). Whether I make the letters in white or black, raised or engraved, with pen or chisel – all this is of no importance with respect to their signification.

(Saussure, 1915: 165–6/119–20)

'Arche-writing' articulates the difference between the materialization of each phoneme or letter and the 'acoustic-sound' which they presuppose in order to be recognized as such, whatever the form of their materialization. This difference is the very difference of consciousness (of re-cognizing things 'as such'). It is transformed, with the institution of Platonism, into the *opposition* between the transcendental and the empirical, the ideal and the material, the infinite and the finite, the primary and the secondary. As a result, the simple is held to precede the complex, recognition is determined, and the human finds its vocation (yearning) and definition (organized in relation to the primary). This argument is the hinge upon which the deconstruction of such oppositions turns. As we shall see later, it *also* undercuts the arguments of those who believe that they have got behind metaphysical logic.

Derrida's move here – as in similar moments in *Writing and Difference* (1967a), *Dissemination* (1972a) and *Limited Inc* (1977) – is intimately informed by the phenomenology of Husserl. His previous radicalization of the Husserlian insight in his introduction to *Origin of Geometry* (1961), as well as his elaboration of the trace in *Speech and Phenomena* (1967c), form the background to the immense weight which Derrida attributes to Saussure's reduction of the phonic substance of the sign. Together with the question of violence, this reduction is another moment in Derrida's deconstruction of the sign which is often underestimated. Since

it organizes Derrida's deconstruction of the empirico-transcendental difference, the underestimation has contributed to major misunderstandings
concerning the reach of Derrida's reflections.

For Husserlian phenomenology the difference assumes the form of, on
the one hand, ideal objects – attained through what Husserl calls the
phenomenological reduction (or *epokhe*) of facticity (the world with all
its variations and contingencies) – and, on the other hand, the world in
its difference and empiricity. In Husserl's essay 'The Origin of Geometry'
(Derrida, 1961) this difference was radicalized when Husserl derived the
possibility of the phenomenological reduction of the world – and the
accompanying access to transcendental ideality – from writing. Writing
constitutes ideal objects by delivering them from the ties of spatio-temporal
facticity (1961: 181/186). The condition of their ideality is their repetition through time and space; this repetition depends on their inscription
on a support which transcends the empirical context. The very support
that allows for transcendence from the material world is itself material,
necessarily restricting the purity of the transcendence from the material
that is aimed at. Conversely, such repetition is not possible unless the
difference of each inscription re-marks the inscription, just as the concrete
letter 't' is re-marked in order to be recognized as such by its 'acoustic
image'. This analogy reveals that, if writing constitutes transcendence,
arche-writing comprehends the very process of constitution. This is the
reason why writing has always been the irreducible site of metaphoricity
– whatever the tradition (Arab, Christian, Greek, Jewish).

The difference between an empirical *t* and our ability to recognize it
as an instance of the letter *t* rehearses Derrida's radicalization of the
Husserlian problematic. It is here that Derrida finds the true radicality of
the Saussurean linguistic sign – all the more surprising, but telling in this
context that neither Culler (1983) nor Norris (1982, 1987) mentions this
moment in their expositions of this chapter on Saussure. Derrida insists
that the phenomenological specificity of the 'sound image' (neither in
this world nor in another, neither empirical nor transcendental) can
only be isolated *via* a passage through the phenomenological reduction
of materiality. For the 'sound-image' is not a phonic sound object but the
'difference' of each of its concretizations, that is to say it is the possibility or schema of each of its materializations. The materialization can,
of course, be *either* phonic *or* graphic; the possibility, however, can be
neither:

> The sound-image is the structure of the appearing of the sound
> (*l'apparaître du son*) which is anything but the sound appearing
> (*le son apparaissant*). . . . The sound-image is what is *heard*; not
> the sound heard but the being-heard of the sound. Being-heard
> is structurally phenomenal and belongs to an order radically

dissimilar to that of the real sound in the world. One can only divide this subtle but absolutely decisive heterogeneity by pheno-menological reduction. The latter is therefore indispensable to all analyses of being heard, whether they be inspired by linguistic, psychoanalytic, or other preoccupations.

(Derrida, 1967b: 93/63)

Derrida calls the 'being-imprinted of the imprint' (*être imprimé de l'empreinte*) *différance* (1967b: 92/63) or the 'trace'. If it allows for the articulation of difference as such (consciousness), the trace both accounts for the logic of metaphysics and exceeds it.

Articulating the living upon the non-living in general, origin of all repetition, the trace is not more ideal than real, not more intelligible than sensible, not more a transparent significa-tion than an opaque energy and *no concept of metaphysics can describe it*. As it is *a fortiori* anterior to the distinction between regions of sensibility, anterior to sound as much as to light ..., the difference in the body of the inscription is also invisible.

(1967b: 95/65)

Saussure's understanding of the 'sound-image' is thus radicalized by Derrida in order to resite the irreducibility of the 'imprint' to either tradi-tional philosophical analysis or to any analysis such as that of linguistics which presumes to supersede the originary transcendental thrust of philos-ophy. This resiting leaves the question of the graphic or phonic signifier a peripheral matter in the essay. What is important is that, for Derrida, it places us in a *middle ground*, neither suspended in the transcendental nor rooted to the empirical, neither in philosophy nor in any empirical negotiation of the world that refuses to pass through the transcendental. The refusal to pass through the transcendental condemns one to a descrip-tion of the fact of difference which is unable to take into proper account the necessity and economy of violence, its 'genealogy'. It thereby repeats the naive violence particular to the oppositional axiomatic of metaphysics.

The analogy with writing at the moment that Saussure brackets the materiality of the sound-image confirms, for Derrida, the thesis of a gener-alized writing. It also allows him to confirm that arche-writing, as an *originary structure of repetition*, constitutes the structure of the 'instituted trace' which comprehends the foundation, exclusion and contradiction of (the history of) linguistics. For a *t* to have identity as a *t*, it must be repeated. There can be no identity without repetition; and yet, this very repetition puts in question the identity which it procures, since repeti-tion is always made in difference. Absolute repetition is impossible in its possibility, for there can be no repetition without difference. The concepts of identity and difference form the precipitate of the metaphysical dissolution of an originary aporetic structure of repetition which Derrida calls 'arche-writing' or the 'trace'.

The above structure informs the science of linguistics as much as the object of which it wishes to be the science. The law of repetition essential to the ideality of the phoneme has 'always already' inscribed it in difference, accounting for the fact that 'monstrous' accidents befall it essentially. This law informs the logic of all marks whatever the nature of the idealization. The mark of an empirical institution or of a discipline is as subject to the law of repetition in difference as that of the linguistic mark. As I suggested in the introductory moves of this chapter, the opposition between speech and writing is, for Derrida, a determining one in metaphysics. He thus traces the law of this repetition, as well as the metaphysical decision to transform it into an opposition, through the linguistic mark. That said, the logic of repetition in difference is generalizable across *all* marks: all marks are only possible within this process of idealization. Because this process is irreducible, so too is the threat to its ideality. For Derrida the law of irreducible repetition is the distinction between writing and arche-writing. Irreducible repetition is in turn 'the law of contamination' (1987a: 42) to which everything, phenomenal and non-phenomenal, is subject.

'Arche-writing' brings together, therefore, the analysis of originary violence specific to the elaboration of the trace with the simultaneous reinscription by Derrida of the opposition between the transcendental and the empirical. In other words, it brings together Derrida's analysis of the institution (here, of linguistics) with his renegotiation of the frontiers between philosophy and the empirical sciences. Indeed, the one analysis cannot be separated from the other.

The 'method' of deconstruction constitutes from the beginning both a reinscription of the empirico-transcendental difference and an analysis of the irreducibility of violence in any mark.

The Double Move of Reinscription and the Political

Derrida's deduction of the traits of the trace from Saussure's reduction of the phonic substance of the acoustic image might seem a long way from political enquiry, thinking and practice. It is futile, however, to approach Derrida's philosophy in political terms unless one has 'come to terms' with the reach of his understanding of originary repetition. It is equally futile to talk of Derrida's thinking in strictly political terms, or to derive a politics from it, without arresting this thinking *within* an originary structure of repetition and contamination for which it wishes, precisely, to render an account.

What we have seen is that the 'method' of deconstruction, its reorganization of the empirico-transcendental difference, leads to a 'middle ground' which is transformed by metaphysics into an opposition between the transcendental and the empirical. This 'middle ground' – which Derrida has recently called the *khôra* (1987b) – is neither presentable nor reducible to some other instance or history. It therefore exceeds time and space, escaping any attempt to arrest it in a concept, an epoch, a place or a history. As the condition of the possibility of *all* marks as well as the condition of their essential contamination, this 'middle ground' can be neither instituted nor projected as a horizon or end of thinking or action. There can, accordingly, be no 'politics' of deconstruction. Deconstruction's concern to recognize the 'middle ground' of all marks does not, however, make it apolitical. Almost the contrary. This is the double move to be addressed when considering the 'and' between Derrida's thinking and the political.

In its affirmative refusal to advocate a politics, deconstruction forms, firstly, an account of why all political projects fail. Since the projection of any decision has ethical implications, deconstruction in fact generalizes what is meant by the political well beyond the local sense of politics. In this sense it becomes a radical 'critique' of *institutions*. I place the word critique in inverted commas because the term is being used loosely; it does not connote an instance or logic upon which the criteria of critique are made possible. I shall come back to this important point in the second part of this chapter when considering the 'measure' of decisions.

As this radical critique, deconstruction is, secondly, a 'method' of analysis which thereby accounts, without positing another horizon, for the tertiary structure of a discipline's (or institution's) foundation, its exclusions and its consequent contradictions. This tertiary structure is another way of thinking the originary law of repetition or the law of contamination. Whilst non-phenomenolizable, it allows for a certain formalization. In 'Linguistics and grammatology' it is called the trace or arche-writing, in *Limited Inc* (1977) it is called iterability, in *Glas* (1974) it is called 'stricture'. These 'quasi-transcendental' structures – 'quasi' since they open up and collapse the transcendental difference in one and the same movement – are thus as much a way of formalizing the essential contamination of any principle of thought as of accounting for the history of a principle, norm or institution. Indeed, these two ways of talking of these structures – as I observed above – come to the same thing. This is why even when Derrida is talking of the most apparently ethereal conceptual thinking (negative theology, for example: 1987d and 1987e) he is also talking of its historical and material inscription in the world.

Here emerges the political dimension to Derridean thinking – as an account of the institution as violence, and, in the recognition of necessary violence, of a transformative renegotiation of the institution in terms of a 'lesser violence' (Derrida, 1967a). In other words, Derrida's account of the mark in terms of a tertiary structure of violence recognizes the necessity of violence in such a way that the terms of this violence can be transformed. This is where, for Derrida – and without any contradiction with the above statement that there can be no politics of deconstruction – the recognition of the 'middle ground' can have an effect on political thinking and decision-making. This last point takes us to the second part of this chapter, and so I will remain at present with the first point.

The Tertiary Structure of Violence

I have spoken repeatedly of a tertiary structure to violence, specifically in relation to Saussurean linguistics. Derrida himself formalizes this structure in the later chapter of *Of Grammatology*, 'The violence of the letter: from Lévi-Strauss to Rousseau' (1967b: 149–202/101–40). Given the importance of the formalization for our overall argument, our analysis of this passage will serve as the conclusion to the concerns of the first half of this chapter: namely, the inextricable link in Derrida's writings between the reinscription of the empirico-transcendental difference and the transformation of the terms in which 'violence' is to be thought and thereby reduced.

As in his confrontation with Saussurean linguistics, Derrida's initial concern in this reading of Lévi-Strauss is to suggest how an apparent exit from philosophy through anthropology naively repeats traditional philosophical values in producing itself through schema that are complicit with the very discourses from which it wishes to wrest itself. Gathering a series of remarks and narratives from Lévi-Strauss's work, Derrida underlines how the anthropologist's 'ethico-theoretical distinction' between primitive and civilized societies depends upon a distinction between speech and writing that is derived from the concepts and values of theology and metaphysics. When least ethnocentric, Lévi-Strauss is at his most ethnocentric. The naivety of Lévi-Strauss's enterprise – his desire to posit an Other in radical distinction to European thought – can be effectively examined and deconstructed, for Derrida, through the concept of writing. Lévi-Strauss's anthropology fails to recognize the originary violence of arche-writing. His ethico-political and theoretical orientation ensue. Here we meet again Derrida's insistent and characteristic wish to pass through the transcendental in order to recognize the law of contamination and begin to think through its ethico-political consequences. The radicalization of writing in this essay picks up the earlier quotation from 'Linguistics and grammatology' (p. 8):

> Before being its object, writing is the condition of episteme....
> Historicity itself is tied to the possibility of writing; to the possi-

bility of writing in general, beyond those particular forms of writing in the name of which we have long spoken of peoples without writing and without history.

(1967b)

In distinction to Lévi-Strauss, who commits the empiricist error of only considering writing in phenomenal terms, Derrida argues:

From the moment that the proper name is erased in a system, there is writing, there is a 'subject' from the moment that this obliteration of the proper is produced, that is to say from the first appearing of the proper [*dès l'apparaître du propre*] and from the first dawn of language.

(1967b: 159/108)

It is this simultaneous appearance and disappearance of the 'proper' which is given the name of 'writing'. We are in familiar territory, since Derrida's argument is similar to the one made concerning the differential structure of the phoneme: a phoneme's identity is constituted non-phenomenally through its differences from other phonemes. Only Derrida is here rehearsing the argument in explicitly ethico-political terms. It is through the suppression of the differential structure which allows for the illusion of the 'property' of a name that the opposition between speech and writing, on which Lévi-Strauss's ethical distinction between the Same and the Other is predicated, is possible. As with Saussure's understanding of monstrosity, Lévi-Strauss's empiricist vilification of Europe depends upon a negation of an originary structure to which the passage through the transcendental gives access. This is not to deny the violence of European colonialism; it is to include it within a more embracing structure of violence which refuses the logic of opposition and, therefore, the institutional or practical politics of a proper name *opposed* to European violence. (Chapter 3 will look at the political examplarity of proper names in detail.)

A moment after the above quotation Derrida anticipates a narration given in the chapter 'On the Line' of *Tristes Tropiques* (1963) in which Lévi-Strauss recounts an incident to which he was party in his observations of the Nambikwara tribe in Brazil. Playing with the children of the tribe, in which the appellation of each member according to their proper name is forbidden, Lévi-Strauss is addressed by one of the children who has been struck by a playmate. He realizes that the child has confided to him the secret of the other child's name in an act of revenge upon her playmate, an act which is then repeated in turn by her adversary. Egging each child on against the other, the anthropologist is able to find out all the names of the children as well as of a number of the adults, before the game is put to a stop. Concerning the initial prohibition of proper names by the tribe, Derrida writes:

> Let us note that this prohibition is necessarily derivative with regard to the constitutive erasure of the proper name in what I have called arche-writing, within, that is, the play of difference. It is because the proper names are already no longer proper names, because their production is their obliteration, because the erasure and imposition of the letter are originary, because they do not supervene upon a proper inscription; it is because the proper name has never been, as the unique appellation reserved for the presence of a unique being, anything but the original myth of a transparent legibility present under the obliteration; it is because the proper name was never possible except through its functioning within a classification and therefore within a system of differences, within a writing retaining the traces of difference, that the interdict was possible, could come into play, and, when the time came ... could be transgressed ... that is to say restored to the obliteration and the non self-sameness of the origin [*non-propriété de l'origine*].
>
> (1967b: 159–60/109)

There is no relation to others, and, consequently, no community possible without a practice of writing. The distinction between law and transgression (here, the forbidding of proper names and the removal of the interdiction) are only possible on the basis of this arche-writing. The forbidding of the use of proper names in the tribe is an attempt, as violent and as powerful as the suppression of *différance* within metaphysics (it is the same gesture), to erase the play of difference and obliteration within which any proper name is inscribed in order for it to function as such. The 'radical impossibility' of a proper name in the sense of a unique appellation – what Derrida calls, with an eye towards Rousseau, the 'pure impossibility' of a 'pure idiom reserved for the unique', of 'the vocative mark' (1967b: 162/110) – forms one way of considering originary violence.

> To think the unique *within* the system, to inscribe it there, such is the gesture of arche-writing; arche-violence, loss of the proper ... in truth the loss of what has never taken place. ... Out of this arche-violence, forbidden and therefore confirmed by a second violence that is reparatory, protective, instituting the 'moral', prescribing the concealment of writing and the effacement and obliteration of the so-called proper name which was already dividing the proper, a third violence can *possibly* emerge

or not (an empirical possibility) within what is commonly called evil, war, indiscretion, rape; which consists of revealing by effraction the so-called proper-name, the originary violence which has severed the proper from its property and its self-sameness [*proprété*]. We could call this third violence one of reflection, one which unbears the native non-identity, classification as denaturation of the proper, and identity as the abstract moment of the concept. It is on this tertiary level, that of empirical consciousness, that the common concept of violence (the system of the moral law and its transgression) whose possibility remains yet unthought, should be situated. ... This last violence is all the more complex in its structure because it refers at the same time to the two inferior levels of arche-violence and law. In effect, it reveals the first nomination which was already an expropriation, but it unbears also that which since then functioned as the proper, substitute of the deferred proper, *perceived* by the *social* and *moral consciousness* as the proper, the reassuring seal of self-identity, the secret.

(1967b: 164–5/112, trans. slightly modified)

The passage is dense and demands very careful reading, deploying the argument of this whole chapter. For it brings Derrida's reinscription of the empirico-transcendental difference together with his 'genealogy' of violence, preparing for a complete rethinking of the traditional ethico-political values of peace and violence, a transformation which we will only have occasion to develop fully through chapters 2 and 3. That said, let us gloss as precisely as possible what is going on here.

In the above quotation three regions of violence are situated and inextricably wound together: first, the originary violence of the system of differences which disappropriates the proper in constituting it; second, the violence of what is commonly conceived as the attempt to put an end to violence – the institution of law – but which is revealed as a violence because of its apparent suppression of the originary difference; and third, the necessary (if empirical) possibility of phenomenal violence *as* the consequence of the inability of the law to suppress its 'illegality' in relation to originary difference. This structure makes a mockery of any attempt to arrest the meaning or conceptual coherence of the terms in play. For example, the more ethical the law attempts to be, the more unethical it becomes, the more it resembles that which it is nominally opposed to – phenomenal violence. In this sense the term 'structure' is itself inadequate since the structure is a differential economy of law. I will specifically come back to this economy – which is called 'stricture' in *Glas* (1974) – in Chapter 2. If Derrida organizes his deconstruction of Lévi-Strauss's nostalgia for a community without the violence of writing in terms of arche-writing, what ensues from this deconstruction is an economy of law which both undermines the positing of an Other outside the metaphysical tradition, in opposition or in difference to it, and opens up an analysis of law as 'repetition', one which we have already met in our exposition of the trace.

Derrida considers that this law of law (its 'economy') is formalizable. In other words, the radical 'method' of deconstruction is at the same time the formalization of the forming and unforming of law. The institution of law is necessarily violent as an effect of the 'originary violence' which exposes a being to the world and to others prior to any particular relation (ethical, political, social) which this being then entertains with them. All determined relations presuppose this originary violence of the radical impossibility of a proper name. This violence is repeated through the need of the law then instituted to maintain itself constantly *as* the law. That the law must repeat itself reveals its necessary illegality. The repetition of the law implies at the same time another repetition of the originary violence which has 'always already' accompanied the foundation and guarding of the law – that is, the breaking of it. Whatever the temporal illusion of their chronological succession (the history *of* linguistics, for example) these three 'forms of violence' arise together (hence the inadequacy of the structural description which 'spaces' them out) in the essential inability of an act of legislation to be what Derrida calls *a pure present*.

I will come back to the temporal analysis of law in Chapter 3. Here I wish to stress that the essential inability of a decision to be necessary is constitutive of law as such. The field of politics is radically contingent in this sense. Otherwise there would be no laws. Derrida calls this essential inability of the law to be the law the 'law of law' (1985: 122). The 'otherwise' of no laws is the name of absolute presence or absolute death – names for the unique proper name. As the last passage made clear, and as all Derrida's writings analyse, the desire for a reign of total freedom is the desire for that of total necessity. A kingdom (whether that of heaven, one of ends in the Kantian sense or, more simply but more profoundly, *any normative principle taken to its end*) would spell the death of man and of chance. This account of the law of law in turn accounts for and endeavours to promote the possibility of singularities and events, just as it renders an account of why neither can be pure.

Such a recognition of the structure of law opens up in turn the possibility of thinking law in terms of a 'lesser violence'. If it is only in the passage through the transcendental that the originary structure of violence is opened up (hence the resistance of philosophy to the human and social sciences), then it is in fact only through the experience of the economy of violence that judgements of lesser violence can be made. The economy of law cannot be resolved (its structure of repetition is irreducible), it will always make of one's judgements a 'fate' – hence no politics of decon-struction. It can, however, be taken into account *in such a way* that one's judgements are made in recognition of the law of contamination which at the same time exceeds them. This economy is, accordingly, to be 'experienced' as the impossible measure of one's judgements. The recog-nition of the law of contamination is, in other words, the condition of invention.

For Derrida it is *literature* which points the way to this 'impossible experience'. Literature points the way because it is itself the enactment of an *aporetic* relation between universality and singularity, as Derrida argues in 'Before the law', a long reflective essay on Kafka's remarkable tale 'Before the Law' ('Vor dem Gesetz') (1988).[4]

Law, Judgement and Singularity

Law and the 'Literariness' of Literature

The relations between law and literature in 'Before the law' can be broken down into three aspects which, although of different orders, can be brought together for the purposes of my argument. With respect to the first half of this chapter, all three aspects can be considered to contribute to a sustained reflection upon the aporia of law and on the inextricable connection between aporia and judgement. The central rela-tion in Derrida's philosophy between justice and time will emerge from the elaboration of this reflection and will be pursued in detail in the following two chapters.

The first aspect of their relation is to be located, for Derrida, in the fact that law and literature share the same conditions of possibility: the origin of law (in the phenomenal sense of a positive law) is also that of literature. Since this origin is non-originary, Derrida considers it also in terms of 'law' (in the non-phenomenal sense of what he calls the 'law of law'). Literature is necessarily concerned with the law of law.

The second aspect follows as a rigorous consequence and carries partic-ular importance when coming to terms with the interest that Derrida entertains for the relations between philosophy and literature. Literature and law (in the phenomenal sense) cross each other's paths regarding an undecidable relation between the general and the singular. This relation marks the necessary failure of law. The theme should be familiar to us by now: no law can be general enough not to be violent, not to engender exceptions or instances of counter-violence which, as the precipitate of the disjuncture between the universal law and its particular application or reality, are appropriately thought of as 'singular'. The undecidable relation between the general and the singular translates in other terms the iterability of law. For Derrida, literature – through its 'literariness' –

remarks this undecidability.[5] Kafka's tale 'Vor dem Gesetz' does so both in respect of what it narrates and with regard to its own literary status as a singular text, enshrined in its singularity by the law of copyright (with the juridical presuppositions such a law entails, notably that of an author). The tale is in this sense 'exemplary' of a certain attitude to law, one which precedes and exceeds the democratic concept of a subject before the law.

The third aspect runs on from both these arguments and concerns the specifics of literary invention. In its undecidable relation to the generality of law, the singularity of a literary text implies that the 'literariness' of literature has to do with performativity (in the sense of a performative speech act) and with rupture. As Bennington has carefully traced in 'Derridabase' (1991), a literary text may be considered in terms of law since it effects a *coup de force* in relation to the tradition which it inherits but which it does not simply repeat in order to institute itself. This *coup* reveals the structure of all founding origins (of all decisions, institutions, horizons, and politics). In this sense literature can help us to reflect upon the structure of decisions as well as upon the structure of a 'less violent' decision. Derrida's concern with the relation between literature and law becomes manifest in his description of this force of literature and it can be regarded as one with the problematic of decision and judgement. Despite Derrida's reticence in this essay over the concept of judgement (see the introductory pages to the original French text, 1985: esp. 93–6), 'Before the law' is a long reflection on the 'experience' of judgement through which one comes to judge in the recognition of the law of law, of the law of contamination. Such an experience, for Derrida, is impossible. And yet, it is from this very impossibility not only that judgement becomes necessary, but an understanding of *how one might judge* is revealed. The twist to Derrida's argument here is important and often misunderstood: I will go into it at length in the following. Impossibility is not the *opposite* of the possible: impossibility *releases* the possible.

My claim through the following reading of 'Before the law' is that these three aspects of the relations between law and literature lead to a reflection upon the 'aporetic' relation between the incalculable and calculation. I argue that this relation exercises judgement. Despite Derrida's own distance from the latter term in 'Before the law', the following suggests that the relation with which he is concerned constitutes the 'exercise' of judgement. As we shall see, judgement is neither on the side of the incalculable nor is it on the side of the calculable: it is nothing but the impossible relation between the two. I therefore maintain that the witnessing of the law of law by literature constitutes at the same time a thinking of the political in terms of judgement.

Derrida's reading of Kafka's short tale 'Vor dem Gesetz' is highly dense and detailed. Its density means that we will need to analyse at length what a non-literary account of the law implies before we are able to elaborate clearly the specificity of Kafka's text in the context of developing the above argument. Following the movement of Derrida's essay we will take Freud's account of law in 'Totem and Taboo' (1913), clarifying on the way what we mean by the aporetic nature of the 'aporia of law' through Aristotle's treatment of aporia in his *Physics*, a text of major importance to Derrida's treatment of aporia in his early essay 'Ousia and gramme: Note on a note of *Being and Time*' (1968). The detail of Derrida's essay is also one reason why Kafka's tale is quoted in its integrity at the beginning of the essay. For reasons of exposition I shall therefore summarize the 'events' of the story before proceeding to my argument.

The Law, the History of Law and the Law of Law

'Vor dem Gesetz' recounts the attempts of 'a man of the country' to gain access to the Law. Without attributes of quality, space or time, the nature of the Law is left undetermined in the text. Entrance to it is, however, figured as an opening, one which remains open throughout the story, but into which admittance is 'guarded' by a 'doorkeeper'. Both the doorkeeper and the man of the country stand – although facing in opposite directions – 'before the law [*vor dem Gesetz*]'. On the man from the country's request to gain admittance into the Law, the doorkeeper tells the man to wait, adding that he is only the first of a long line of such keepers, each one more powerful and terrifying than the last. Whilst perplexed at this attitude towards the Law, having assumed that the Law is 'accessible at all times and to everyone', the man from the country desists from attempting to enter, taking to heart the possibility of entrance in the near future. The rest of the man's life is made up of frequent attempts – each time more childish – to gain access, each attempt in turn vetoed by the doorkeeper and deferred to a later occasion. Close to death, the man beckons the doorkeeper to ask him why no one but himself has ever begged for admittance. The story closes with the doorkeeper's loud response in the old man's ear: 'No one else could ever be admitted here, since this gate was made only for you. I am now going to shut it' (Kafka, 1988: 4).

Derrida's first interest in the story turns around the relations between law and narration. In principle, the law, to have the categorical authority of law, should be exempt from narration, it should transcend the empirical, both in the sense that it should not be narratable as such (the history of a law) and in the sense that it should not engender a history (the law's history). A law with a history (a 'before' and an 'after') has not the iron measure of law. In regard to the first sense, Derrida argues:

> The law as such should never give rise to any story [*récit*]. To
> be invested with its categorical authority, the law must be
> without history, genesis or any possible derivation. Pure morality
> has no history, as Kant seems at first to remind us, no intrinsic
> history. And when one tells stories on this subject, they concern
> only circumstances, events external to the law, and at best, the
> modes of its revelation.
>
> (1985: 109/191)

As we shall see in detail in the next chapter, for Kant, the moral law is
transcendent because it transcends the sensible conditions of time and
space. Such transcendence accords it universality. All men feel respect for
the moral law, even if they do not obey it. According to Kant, for example,
a crime reveals the moral law negatively through guilt. The universality
of the moral law means that it has no history in both senses of history
alluded to above. The law is underivable, it cannot be accounted for
and therefore narrated; and it does not engender histories (of itself),
for otherwise it would not be absolute. The two senses of *histoire* – story
and history – come in fact to the same: the nonderivability of the moral
law in Kant is its ahistoricality or atemporality.

Now, it is precisely this law that modern thought has wished to narrate,
deriving it, therefore, from another instance. In nineteenth-century intellectual life, this derivation is called 'the death of God'. Following the early
Hegel's writings on law, Marx in 'On the Jewish Question' (1843b)
reduces the moral law to a configuration of bourgeois society (*bürgerliche
Gesellschaft*) and, ultimately, to modes of production; Nietzsche in *On
the Genealogy of Morals* (1887) reduces 'the cruelty of the categorical
imperative' and its attendant concepts of the sovereign individual, guilt,
conscience and responsibility to a finite economy of debts and promises
(second essay 'Guilt, "Conscience" and the Like', Sections 1–6); and
Freud in 'Totem and Taboo' reduces the categorical imperative to the
Oedipus Complex (1913: Chapter 4, 'The return of totemism in childhood'). Distinctions between the moral law in Kant and the categorical
imperative aside, all three accounts seek to give a *finite* account of the
moral law. In its complication of law and narration, Derrida's essay
'Before the law' may well look at Freud only. Given the above, the essay
should be seen, however, as a reinscription of modern thinking in terms
of 'law'. This will be confirmed in Chapter 2.

Derrida's move is twofold and should not be confused with a simple
reinstitution of the law in Kantian terms. Derrida seeks to re-relate the
law to history; and yet, in showing that Freud's genealogy of the law
presupposes the law in its very attempt to account for it, Derrida exempts
the law from any history. How are these two moves compatible?
Derrida's answer to this will be crucial for the elaboration of the exercise

of judgement. The answer is the *différance* of law. If the law is, on the one hand, unaccountable, on the other hand it is *nowhere* but *in* its inscriptions in history, whilst not being reducible *to* these inscriptions either. The nonplace of the law is analogous to that of the trace of ideality in Derrida's deconstruction of the Saussurean phoneme: neither in time or space, nor outside them. That said, the term 'analogous' is misleading since, for Derrida, they share the same structure: the trace is (also) the iterability of the law, the law of law. Derrida's deconstruction of linguistics is also a deconstruction of law (and vice versa). The point not only justifies the strategy of this chapter; it takes us to the heart of modernity, the subject of the next chapter. For Derrida's understanding of the law of law is a non-Hegelian reinscription of Kantian moral law within history, *without* this reinscription being reducible *to* history. This is what is meant when I say that the law of law is neither transcendental nor empirical. For Derrida, the law of law accounts for all histories (in the two senses above) as well as all determinations of law – moral, political, juridical, disciplinary, etc. The law of law is both radically exterior to history/ determination and is nothing but the *différance* of history/determination. Neither Freud, then, nor Kant. For Derrida, the 'literature' of Kafka's tale re-marks this trace of the law as 'fictive narrativity' (1985: 117/199).

To approach what Derrida understands by this term, I shall first elaborate the methodology of derivation and genealogy with which Derrida is concerned and 'against' which 'Before the Law' pitches the literariness of literature.

At the beginning of 'Totem and Taboo' Freud dehistoricizes the history of ethics in order to rehistoricize law by accounting for its origin in terms of one particular genealogy. 'Taboos do not differ in nature from Kant's *categorical imperative*' (1913: 93). Thus to account for the phenomena of taboos in primitive societies and in neurotics is, for Freud, to account for 'the birth of religion, morals, art and society' (219). Freud's genealogy of sin and guilt mobilizes two discourses – that of anthropology and that of psychoanalysis. Although different in their rules from one another, both are used to support each other in situating the origin of conscience in 'the story of a murder' (22). A crime is the origin of law. Following Darwin's theory of the primitive horde, Freud contends that the earliest state of social organization was made up of small communities each led by a tyrannical male who refused his sons a share in his wives. Freud concedes that this state of society (one of pure force) has never been an object of observation, the earliest group observable to empirical analysis being one made up of males with equal rights, inheritance passing through the mother (a society of law, a sort of matriarchal democracy). This does not forbid, however, an empirical derivation to the law. On two accounts: first, the psychoanalysis of the affect of guilt in neurotics suggests that neurotic disorder (the Oedipus complex) repeats an event in prehistory.

Whether the content of this disorder be real or phantasmatic (a 'primal scene' in Freudian terms), in other words whether the content of the Oedipus complex be situated in the childhood of the individual or inherited phylogenetically as an originary phantasm, for Freud, an event took place in the prehistory of the individual (phylogenetic or epigenetic) which determines his or her conscience. Neurotic guilt represents in this sense the norm for all norms of civilization. Second, the totem meal particular to both primitive and civilized societies (communion in Christianity for example) alludes to a prehistorical murder, by which society was instituted, and of which it is both the 'commemoration' and 'repetition' (1913: 203). With regard to this founding of society and its repetition, Freud continues, and these are the lines which interest Derrida:

> The tumultuous mob of brothers [was] filled with the same contradictory feelings which we can see at work in the ambivalent father-complexes of our children and of our neurotic patients. They hated their father who presented such a formidable obstacle to their craving for power and their sexual desires; but they loved and admired him too. After they had got rid of him, had satisfied their hatred and had put into effect their wish to identify themselves with him, the affect which all this time had been pushed under was bound to make itself felt. [*Note*: This fresh emotional attitude must also have been assisted by the fact that the deed cannot have given complete satisfaction to those who did it. From one point of view it had been done in vain. Not one of the sons had in fact been able to put his original wish – of taking his father's place – into effect. And, as we know, failure is far more propitious for a moral reaction than satisfaction.] It did so in the form of remorse. A sense of guilt made its appearance, which in this instance coincided with the remorse felt by the whole group. The dead father became stronger than the living one had been. ... What had up to then been prevented by his actual existence was thenceforward prohibited by the sons themselves, in accordance with the psychological procedure so familiar to us in psychoanalyses under the name of 'deferred obedience'. They revoked their deed by forbidding the killing of the totem, the substitute for their father, and they renounced its fruits by resigning their claim to the women who had now been set free. They thus created out of their filial sense of guilt the two fundamental taboos of totemism, which for that very reason corresponded to the two repressed wishes of the Oedipus complex.
>
> (Freud, 1913: 204–5)

Freud desires to derive morality from the sexual. For Derrida, any account of the moral law and its attendant affects (guilt, conscience, responsibility) necessarily makes the law finite. A story of the origin of the law makes the law non-originary, derivative of some other instance and, there-fore, finite. Whether this instance assumes the same transcendental position as the law that it accounts for is not my immediate question, although, following Derrida's understanding of the law of law, one could suspect that for deconstruction this is the case. What concerns us at present is the paradox or *aporia* into which Derrida sees Freud's account fall in its very desire to account for the law in the first place. For the anthropologico-psychoanalytic genealogy of guilt and sin narrates an event that never takes place as such. For the brothers to feel guilty for the murder of their father, the moral law would *already* have to be in place prior to the crime. To have felt remorse the brothers must have already transgressed a prior law, not produced it; otherwise their remorse is in-comprehensible. Since Freud's genealogy represents an attempt to make the affect of guilt comprehensible, his attempt ends up showing the very opposite of what it intends: it repeats the incomprehensibility of law. This repetition is not the neurotic repetition of the foundation of society, but that (clearly more radical and indeterminate in Derrida's terms) of the *aporia* of law. The aporia of law emerges from the impossibility of finding, or inventing the origin of law. The origin of law is an 'impos-sible' invention, and the condition of all inventions of law. Before we turn to Derrida's conclusions drawn from the above passage which lead to the importance of Kafka's tale, a few words of definition are now appro-priate.

Aporia, and the Law of Law as the Aporia of Law

On several occasions in this book I have used the terms 'aporia' and 'aporetic', and, specifically, 'the aporia of law'. Derrida has resorted to the term 'aporia' more and more frequently, recently publishing a text entitled *Aporias* (1994a). As Chapter 3 will argue at length through a reading of Derrida's relations to Heidegger and Levinas, this concept organizes in concentrated form the overall concerns of deconstruction, both its conceptual strategies and its understanding of tradition and the future. Although Derrida is always careful to multiply the terms of his conceptual strategies so as to prevent one term from assuming a tran-scendental position over another, I would argue that 'aporia' marks the gesture and reach of all these strategies. Consequently, as my introduc-tion to this chapter suggested, Derrida's philosophy together with its political implications can best be articulated in the form of 'aporetic thinking': that is – with respect to this chapter's negotiations – in terms of the *aporia of judgement* and the *judgement of aporia*.

As Derrida reminds his reader in *Aporias*, his first sustained consideration of the term goes back to his difficult essay on time 'Ousia and gramme: Note on a note from *Being and Time*' (1968). This essay will assume central importance for us in Chapter 3; suffice it here to regard how the concept of aporia works in this text in order to consider its inextricable relation to judgement. Aporia comes from the Greek *aporos*, which means 'without passage' or 'without issue'. An aporia is something which is impraticable. A route which is impraticable is one that cannot be traversed, it is an uncrossable path. Without passage, not treadable. For the Eleatic Zeno, who, it is generally recognized, was the first to use the term consistently, aporia implied the suspension (*epokhe*) of judgement. At the point where the path of thinking stopped, judgement was suspended. This definition of aporia was inherited by the presocratic sophists who called an aporia two contradictory sayings of equal value. The suspension of judgement was a mode of perplexity before the inability to ground either saying. Plato's battle against the sophists was one against aporia; it is a battle that informs, indeed constitutes the history of philosophy.

For Derrida, the term's crucial reappearance after the sophists is to be found in Aristotle's 'aporetic' of time in the *Physics*, Book IV (1984b: 218a). For Aristotle, following Zeno, time both is and is not. If time is thought in terms of its divisibility, it is to be thought in terms of *now*. And yet, the very *now* of time which gives it its being also robs it of any being, since *now* is always already past or future. The thinking of time is, therefore, as Aristotle puts it, an 'aporetic'. Time provokes a thinking which ends up as the aporia (without passage) of thinking (*Physics*, IV, 218a).

'Ousia and gramme', following to a certain extent Heidegger, does not stay with the terms of this aporia. This is important to us, since, if Derrida uses the concept of aporia, it is *not* within traditional sitings of the term. There are aporias and aporias: something which any philosophy of the paradox should recall before it speaks in the name of 'paradox' or which any criticism of a philosophy of aporia should remember if it wishes its criticisms to have weight. Derrida's philosophy has too often been simplified by an over-general understanding of its paradoxologies, by detractors and supporters alike. For example, aporia, for Derrida, is not, as it was for the presocratics, an oscillation between two contradictory sayings. As we recall from earlier, the condition of possibility of the ideality of the phoneme was also the condition of its impossibility. Thus the 'contradiction' applies to one and the same entity, not to two different entities. We called this, following Derrida, 'originary repetition'. It is this repetition which is aporetic, as is the originary repetition of law (what we have called the iterability of law). But Derrida's understanding of aporia *also* exceeds Aristotle's use of the term. For Aristotle, the aporia of time is that time is and is not. Although informing the *same* entity, unlike the former paradox, the aporia is still deconstructible because the solution (passage) to an understanding of it is that time has been presupposed, prejudged in terms of the *present* (Derrida, 1968: 53). The Aristotelian aporetic of time is only possible through prejudging the nature of time. Time is and is not, because it is thought in terms of 'now'. That said, Aristotle's aporia cannot be untied, as the Heidegger of *Being and Time* would wish, into an opposition between two modes of time (primordial temporality and inauthentic, 'vulgar' time, or time thought in terms of the present). The aporia *remains* impraticable for Derrida. In other words, if the terms of the aporia of time are deconstructible, the aporia of time is not; it is absolutely irreducible. For one cannot think at one and the same *time* the coimplication of *nows*, such that each now both supersedes the previous one (for time to pass) at the same time as retaining the past now and future now (for time to be recognized as the passage of time). If Derrida in this essay suggests that the concept of the 'trace' presents the way to think this coimplication, then the trace does not amount to the 'concept' of a 'thought'. For the coimplication is nothing but the impossibility of the coexistence of *nows* (1968: 63). Time constitutes this impossible possibility; or rather this impossible possibility forms the undeconstructible condition of time and space.

Let me not get diverted into the minutiae of the argument here. Chapter 3 will return to it more fully in the context of Heidegger's thought. What is important at this stage is that the aporia is constituted through the 'unthinkable' of time. (Compare here my initial argument on the *impossibility* of an exit from language as a system of signs.) *Nothing* can be *opposed* to time *qua* the originary coimplication of 'nows'. The aporia is irreducible – a central point for Derrida to which this book frequently returns. Hence in *Mémoires for Paul de Man* (1986a), as well as in many other texts of the same period which mobilize the concept of aporia, Derrida will argue that aporia is both 'undeconstructible' and the source of all deconstructions. As this source – here is the twist again – aporia does not suspend judgement, it is the latter's very condition of possibility. No judgement is possible without the experience of aporia. Whether one recognizes this experience of aporia or not, whether one takes this experience into account or not, is another matter. The difference of not doing so and doing so develops the difference between metaphysics and deconstruction. We can here return to 'Before the law'.

I argued above that Freud's genealogy prejudges, in its very account of the law, the possibility of the law. The prejudgement marks the aporia of law. If this aporia is irreducible, 'Before the law' maintains that this very *irreducibility* of the law to its account constitutes the law. The law of law is nothing but the irreducibility of law to a history of it. Hence the law of law resides nowhere other than in the failure of accounts of

the law. Freud partly admits to this in the note to the previous quotation from 'Totem and Taboo', (p. 30), suggesting that the passage (*peras*)
from nature to law, *phusis* to *nomos*, never really takes place; the passage
(*peras*) is nothing but the aporia (*aporos*) of remorse. The non-derivability
of the law is the aporia of law. Furthermore, if the dead father is more
alive when dead, the murder of the father is not only an act performed
in vain, but the aporia of law which emerges out of the inability to give
a genealogy of the son's affect of remorse constitutes at the same time
an aporia of time and of place. All these aporias are in fact the same. To
account for the law is to give the law a time and a place. The aporia of
such an account *gives*, conversely, time and space their multiplicity and
differentiality. It is this orginary difference which engenders literature, and
to which, in turn, literature gives witness by re-marking what, for example,
Freud's prejudgement only marked.

Literature, the Aporia of Law and the Promise

Derrida writes:

> The murder fails because the dead father holds even more power
> [than when he was alive]. Thus morality arises from a useless
> crime which in fact kills nobody, which comes too soon or too
> late and does not put an end to any power. . . . In fact, it inau-
> gurates nothing since repentance and morality had to be possible
> *before* the crime. Freud appears to cling to the reality of the
> event, but this event is a sort of non-event, an event of nothing
> or a quasi-event which both calls for and annuls a narrative
> account [*la relation narrative*]. For this 'deed' or 'misdeed' to be
> effective, it must be somehow spun from fiction. Everything
> happens *as if*. The guilt is none the less effective and painful for
> all that. Since the father dead is more powerful than he was
> when alive [and] more dead alive than *post mortem*, the murder
> of the father is not an event in the ordinary sense of the word.
> Nor is the origin of the law. Nobody would have encountered
> it in its proper place of happening, nobody would have faced it
> in its taking place. Event without event, pure event where nothing
> happens, the eventiality of an event which both demands and
> annuls the story [*récit*] in its fiction. Nothing new happens
> and yet this nothing new would instate the law, the two funda-
> mental prohibitions of totemism, murder and incest.
> (Derrida, 1985: 116–17/198–9)

The origin of the law is not an event; but it is not pure fiction either.
The aporia of law occupies the middle ground between reality and fiction,

opening up the distinction, but always already exceeding its terms. The aporia of law is that the origin of law does not take place and does not not take place: a crucial point to which we will return. Neither history nor phantasy, the non-origin of the origin of the law is the law, and this is the aporia of law. The non-passage between *phusis* and *nomos* is impossible *in* its possibility and possible *as* its impossibility. The father was never killed, he is more alive when dead: the father is killed all the time, and he never dies. It is this possibility as impossibility (I recall here Aristotle's aporia of time), which literature witnesses. For the aporia is *also* the law of literature.

It is here that an important part of Derrida's interest in literature is to be found. This interest is structured around an account of finitude in terms of law which literature, in distinction to other kinds of discourse that disavow the aporia of law by trying to iron it out with a history of the law, is able to re-mark. It is able to do this since it acknowledges its source of writing to be 'within' the aporia. Literature re-marks the law of law *in* and *as* the body of its text. In the case of 'Vor dem Gesetz', for example, the non-origin of the origin of the law is reinscribed as both the content of Kafka's tale – the deferment of the man of the country's access into the Law – and, as we shall see, the very 'event' of the text. The non-advent of the law is the advent of (the singular events of) a text. On the initial point, Derrida writes:

> Demanding and denying the story, this quasi-event bears the mark of fictive narrativity (fiction *of* narration as well as fiction as narration: fictive narration as the simulacrum of narration and not only as the narration of an imaginary history). It is the origin of literature at the same time as the origin of law – like the dead father, a story told, a spreading rumor, without author or end, but an ineluctable and unforgettable story.
>
> (1985: 117/199)

Law and literature come together in the immemorial impossibility of the account of the origin of law. The aporia of law, or the law of law, expresses the *différance* of law. This *différance* cannot be forgotten; whilst unaccountable, it cannot be avoided. It should initially be understood in two senses. First, as Derrida himself says of Kafka's tale:

> what is forever deferred till death is entry into the law itself, which is nothing other than that which dictates the delay. ... What *must not* and cannot be approached is the origin of *différance*: it must not be presented, represented or above all penetrated. That is the law of the law.
>
> (1985: 121/201, author's emphasis)

Second, this *différance* of law inaugurates in one single move the constant attempt to present it and the failure to do so given its aporetic impossibility. One needs to hold to both senses of *différance* at this point; otherwise one could risk turning the law of law into something outside of history, thereby losing its aporetic status. The above quotation from Derrida, with its repetition of 'must', could tempt one into interpreting Derrida in this way. As we shall see in Chapter 2 (concerning Hegelian readings of the trace), although Derrida's formulations have at times invited this risk, such an interpretation would be misguided.

This *différance* of law, its immemorial impossibility (or 'fictive narrativity', to keep the reasons for Derrida's concern with literature in our mind) is what at one moment in 'Before the law' Derrida calls the 'promise' of law (1985: 117/199). The non-presentation of the law, its aporia, is its promise. At this stage of my argument I would maintain that Derrida's more recent elaborations of the 'promise' – starting from this little remark in 'Before the law' to the major reflections on the promise in recent years from *Mémoires for Paul de Man* (1986a), *Of Spirit: Heidegger and the Question* (1987a), *The Other Heading: Reflections on Today's Europe* (1991a) to *Specters of Marx* (1993), *Aporias* (1994b) and *Politiques de l'amitié* (1994c) – remains a *refinement* of the initial elaboration of *différance* and of the trace in *Of Grammatology* (1967b), *Speech and Phenomena* (1967c)and Derrida's other writings of the 1960s and 1970s. In the Conclusion, after the negotiations of the next two chapters, I will have occasion to revise this judgement. Here, however, it is quite appropriate to maintain that the promise effects the same conceptual work, accounts for the same differential economies and opens up the same questions and aporias as does the elaboration of the trace in, for example, 'Linguistics and Grammatology'.

As Derrida argues in *Of Spirit* (1987a) and *Mémoires for Paul de Man* (1986), the promise can be seen, formally, as the remainder of the necessary undecidability of thinking and action upon which any *act* of thought (or) language (philosophical, political, juridical, literary) will fall and fail to untie. This remainder is an absolute past (it cannot be recalled in any act, being this act's very possibility) which 'gives' the 'chance' of the future. The promise which is 'always already' the memory of 'itself', constitutes consequently an *affirmation* of the future. Its immemoriality is that which returns all horizons (philosophical, ethico-political, institutional, disciplinary) to the finitude of their inauguration. One could thus recast Derrida's deconstruction of the Saussurean institution of linguistics in the following terms of the promise. The exclusions and contradictions that appear as an effect of the inaugural violence of Saussure's theory are the trace of the promise of this theory. The promise of the future of linguistics (its alterity to itself) resides in the *différance* which linguistics must disavow, but which constitutes it in the first place. The promise should thus be considered as the very law of contamination that we have been talking about in its various guises throughout this chapter. The radical structure of the immemorial promise which interrupts all horizons whilst making them possible presents the *irreducibility* of the aporia of law as the *différance* of law. To return now to Freud.

The 'Literary' Turn to the Political: the Aporia of Judgement and the Judgement of Aporia

Freud's attempt to give a genealogy of law ends in failure. Freud does not fail, however, to account for the law. Rather, just as the sons' murder of the father constitutes a non-event and failure, engendering none the less guilt and remorse, the account 'is' nothing else than the failure to account. As Derrida said above, Freud's 'story of murder' ('Totem and Taboo') is less the narration of an imaginary event than the *simulacrum of narration*. All language (and) thought are 'essentially' haunted by the spectrality of this uncanny narrativity *because* the origin or passage of law is aporetic. It is, for Derrida, the 'fictive narrativity' of literary texts which provides them with the means to re-mark this simulacrum of law.

I can here introduce my claim that literature is concerned with judgement. Literature's exemplarity is threefold: first, the 'literary' resides everywhere, although literature is only one mode of language; second, when, as in much modern literature, it remarks its 'literariness', literature is 'exemplary' of a particular awareness of the failure of law; and third, and consequently, modern literature stands out in its respect towards the law. In highly paradoxical terms, Kafka's tale offers us one way to think judgement in respect of the 'promise' of the law. The last point frames, of course, the problem of the limits of recognition concerning the law of contamination. Rather, then, than literature (or *écriture*) witnessing the end(s) of the political – as writers like Lyotard (1987), Lacoue-Labarthe (1987), and Nancy (1986) tend to stress – literature both witnesses these ends and takes us *towards* the political, although in an indeterminate sense. For it shows – inscribing this 'appearance' within its own body as the text that it is – that the aporia of law re-marks itself both as the necessity of judgement and as the necessary failure of this judgement. The aporia cannot present itself as such – otherwise it would not be impracticable: it presents itself in the effects of judgement (subjective genitive). The aporia of law is nothing else than the aporetic relation between aporia, judgement and failure. The above 'at the same time' (p. 35) therefore repeats the immemorial *non-event* of the passage from nature to law. The aporia of law constitutes the *différance* of law which can only 'appear' as *judgements* of *différance*. These judgements make up tradition. They are the decisions which institute civilization, society, law and communities – and they always fail.

How can one judge whilst respecting the inextricable structure of aporia and judgement as much as possible? How can one fail well, without failure becoming itself a principle of judgement – for a good failure is a success? Such questions concern again the nature of the *aporetic* relation between literature and the aporia of law. The judgement which is the least disrespectful of the promise of law *must* be impossible, must be the impossible, releasing possibilities in its very impossibility. The measure of judgement of interest to Derrida is the very impossibility of such a measure – impossibility *as* possibility. This 'as' provides the key to an understanding of the 'impossible' politics of deconstruction. This book will return to it three times in the concrete contexts of Hegel, Heidegger and Levinas's politics.

Literature is exemplary in the first and second sense above for reasons of indeterminacy with which we should now be familiar.

> We [can] never explain the parable of a relation called 'literary' with the help of the semantic contents originating in philosophy or psychoanalysis, or drawing on some other source of knowledge. . . . The fictitious nature of this ultimate story which robs us of every event, of this pure story, or story without story, has as much to do with philosophy, science, or psychoanalysis as with literature.
>
> (Derrida, 1985: 127/209)

In Kafka's tale the Law is silent, of it nothing is said and, like both the doorkeeper and the man from the country, we do not know what, who or where it is. In these terms we all stand before the law as members of a community who are prejudged not to know what the 'bond' of our relation is. The aporetic account of the law constitutes at the same time an aporetic account of community. The 'we' of the community (the 'we', for example, of my phrase above, 'we all stand before the law') is the impossibility of the 'we', 'we' as impossibility. No discipline can untie the aporia of law or this 'we' – but the writing called 'literature' witnesses this more than any other discipline. That said, if this is what literature witnesses, all disciplines are *also* 'literary' (even the most formal logic, the most abstract mathematics) to the extent that they betray, in their very failure to achieve their accounts of law (their disciplinary origins and horizons), the aporia of origin. My previous exposition of the 'science' of Saussurean linguistics is, of course, a good example. What I rehearsed in the first half of the chapter in terms of decisions which acknowledge their executory force and decisions that conceal themselves under the claim to naturality, all the while determining violently the space of this naturality, returns here in terms of the relative difference between the mark of the aporia of law (Freud's above prejudgement and its failure) and its re-mark in 'Vor dem Gesetz'. The 'opacity' (Salanskis: 1995) of the aporia of law is both singular to literature and informs all disciplines; but literature distinguishes itself as literature (distinguishes its 'literariness') by re-marking this opacity, rather than seeking to disavow it in its fictive narrativity and as the singular body of its text (the 'material' irreducibility that makes it a singular work).

Thus 'Vor dem Gesetz' shows with and against Kant's *Critique of Practical Reason* (1788) that there are only examples of the law, but, for this very reason, never the law itself. It therefore shows with and against Freud's 'Totem and Taboo' that the law is always more alive when dead. By showing this it is *also* an *example* before the law, although the exemplary status of 'Vor dem Gesetz' is not exemplary in the normal sense. The tale does not give the law nor, therefore, can it give an example of it or give itself as the law's example. But, through its explicit account of the impossibility of entering the law, the tale forms an 'example' *before* the law of law. In other words, the tale specifically enacts the radical absence of law of which the writing of literature is one effect. Derrida suggests the prescriptive self-reflexivity of the tale's turn upon itself in the following passage:

> The law is prohibition: this does not mean that it prohibits, but that it is itself prohibited, a prohibited place . . . one cannot reach the law, and in order to have a *rapport* of respect with it, one must not have a rapport with the law, *one must interrupt the relation* [il *faut ne pas, il ne faut pas* avoir rapport à elle, *il faut interrompre la relation*]. One *must enter into relation* [il faut n'*entrer en relation* que] only with the law's representatives, its examples, its guardians. These are interrupters [interrupteurs] as much as messengers. One must not know [*il faut ne pas savoir*] who or what or where the law is. . . . This is what *must be* the case for the *must* of the law [Voilà ce qu'*il faut* au *il faut* de la loi].
>
> (1985: 121/204, trans. slightly
> modified, author's emphasis)

The prescription 'must' comes not from the law but from the law of law. It is a meta-prescription in respect of the law of the failure of all meta-languages. The aporia of law appears as the radical impossibility of relating the story of the origin of the law. If this appearance takes form as the 'literary', it also forms the prescription to interrupt our relation to the law because we must not relate to the appearance: hence my stress on the relation *between* literature and judgement. The aporia prescribes the keeping of the aporia, the explicit *suspension* of the law. The *epokhe* of law does not constitute the suspension of judgement; on the contrary, it establishes the necessity of judgement. For judgement is nothing but the *epokhe* of law. Keeping the promise of the law as a promise (in the radical sense above), keeping the aporia as an aporia (i.e., not presenting it), judgement repeats the necessary *différance* of the promise/aporia. Hence the 'impossibility' of its 'as'. Again, the promise or aporia of law appears 'as' the necessity of judgement and 'as' the necessity of the failure of judgement. This is another way of describing the economy of violence in the last section.

In what sense, then, can this experience of aporia as the very condition of judgement help us to judge? On the one hand, we need to recognize as much as possible that the relation between the aporia of law and judgement is itself aporetic *in order to maintain the aporia*. On the other hand, no judgement can be aporetic as such if it wishes to maintain the aporetic relation. If any judgement could assume the aporia as such, there would be no aporia to 'maintain'. As a result the very impossibility of judgement is its possibility since, if the judgement were possible, and an account of the law were possible, there would be no need to judge in the first place, and therefore there would be no judgements. Any gesture of thought or language would be 'pure theory' without violence: thus the sole condition of there being a judgement is this judgement's impossibility. The experience of aporia is consequently not simply the condition of judgement, it *unfolds as* the experience of judgement, and vice versa.

This means that if Derrida actually explodes the confines of the literary by giving it a non-exemplary exemplary status concerning the witnessing of the aporia of law, he also shows that this explosion is *indefinite*. Neither literature nor politics will ever end since all theory is judgement and any judgement requires further judgements, creating thereby the space of the 'writings' of literature and politics. Thus, if we are stressing, here, the political implications of aporia given this explosion, the very way in which we are marking the political as the instance of judgement takes account at the same time of the non-account of the 'literary'. If, like literature, politics will never finish, and if this can be acknowledged within its own structure of judgement, then politics could inscribe upon its body its own indeterminacy. I do not wish, then, to politicize the 'literary'. I am showing that the 'literary' reinscribes the 'political' – in both the broad sense of any 'horizon' (the 'ethico-theoretical decision') and in the specific sense of a normative structuring of a community – in terms of the aporia of judgement. It leaves politics as it were with the problem of its own judgements. This is why literature takes us to the political, but, precisely, in an indeterminate sense. Our third instance of the exemplarity of literature comes to the fore at this juncture, drawing this chapter to a close.

Law and Singularity

In introducing my reading of Derrida's 'Before the law' I said that we would ultimately be interested in the way in which literature and the law cross as a chiasmus between the singular and the general. We can now see that this final concern of Derrida's essay is a consequence of both his exposition of the non-origin of law and of literature as an exemplary guardian of the promise of the law. This chiasmus is also another aspect of my above comments on the aporetic relation between law and judgement. What is this chiasmus and how does it relate to the aporetic relation of judgement? If the aporia of law appears as the necessity of judgement and as the failure of judgement, then this aporia 'forms' the aporetic relation between the law and the singular. Kafka's tale re-marks this both in the form of the 'events' of the 'story' and in the form of the 'event' of the text (the tale 'Vor dem Gesetz' in its difference, for example, from the inclusion of the tale in the larger narrative body, the novel *The Trial*). We recall at the end of the tale the doorkeeper's words to the man of the country: 'No one else could ever be admitted here, since this gate was made only for you. I am now going to shut it' (Kafka, 1988: 4).

How can a law to which a particular individual has no access be a law only for this individual above? Or rather how can something apparently general like the law be so specific that it is only for the singularity of one individual? Note the terms 'general', 'particular' and 'singular' – the difference between the last two is crucial. The tale ends with a paradox which is in fact another form of the aporia of law. The aporetic relation between law and singularity repeats the law of law. Only in refusing to give access to itself does the law – conceived since the modern invention of democracy in terms of 'generality' – speak, not to the particular (the fictional generality of democratic law to which all have access as particulars), but to the *singular*. Recognizing both the brutality and the promise of the aporetic ending to the tale, Derrida comments:

> [The doorkeeper] insists upon the uniqueness of this singular door; the law is neither manifold [*une multiplicité*] nor, as some believe, a universal generality. It is always an idiom; this is the sophistication of Kant's thought. Its door concerns only you – a door that is unique and singularly destined, determined (*nur für dich bestimmt*).
>
> (1985: 210/127–8)

From the previous exposition of the 'trace' we know that the condition of possibility of any identity (a law, for example) forms at the same time the condition of its impossibility. From the previous exposition of the tertiary structure of violence we know that the foundation of any law

is necessarily violent, excluding in the very move to inaugurate new possibilities of inclusion (the violence of *any* new law, let alone of a revolution).
From the same exposition we know that the law cannot in its very possibility address the individual. There is no 'pure idiom for the unique'
(Derrida, 1967b). A proper name is immediately the obliteration of the
proper. We have moreover seen that the trace, the tertiary structure of
violence, makes up the aporia of law. But here, yet again, lies the twist
of judgement. That the law can never be general in its very possibility of
being general implies, precisely, the very possibility of singularity. It is
because the law cannot address the singular that the law is destined for
the singular. Herein lies, as Derrida says, the sophistication of Kant's
thought. The sophistication develops the undecidable relation between the
general and the singular. It also develops the terms of the aporetic relation to which everything in this chapter leads. The following chapters will
show that this aporetic relation, rooted to singularity, constitutes through
the sophistication of Kantian ethics what Derrida now calls the 'promise
of democracy' (*The Other Heading* (1991a), *Specters of Marx* (1993)).
This chapter has thus shown that the concern of 'Before the law' with
the relations between philosophy and literature is nothing less than the
*radicalization of democratic thinking on the relation between law and
individuality*.

I said earlier that law and literature cross in the non-origin of the law.
I also observed that the undecidable relation between law and the
idiomatic constitutes a repetition of the aporia of law. The necessary
failure of the law to be general should be considered at the same time as
the failure of all genealogies to account for the law. If we were able to
account for the law, if our laws could achieve the status of necessity,
there would be no 'we'. The pronoun 'we' marks a community of singularities without time or place which insists in all institutions of a
community, without ever taking the *form* of a specific community. In
other words, it marks the impossibility of the experience of 'we', or, the
impossible experience of 'we'. To gather these thoughts together: the
aporia of law is nothing but the law's idiomaticity, which idiomaticity
'constitutes' the promise of law: what Derrida will call, in specific contexts,
the 'promise of democracy'. This means that the above two aspects to
the relation between law and literature are one and the same. The repetition of the aporia of law *as* the undecidable relation between law and
the singular repeats in difference the law of law. My argument has thus
shown that, for Derrida, the *différance* of aporia produces itself as the
différance of singularity. This rerelating of the two *différances* takes us,
finally, to the impossible measure of judgement.

If an aporia can never appear as such, nor can singularity. Each, in
their repetition of the other, is the ellipsis of form as such. Hence singularity and particularity must not be confused. The law is destined to the

'singular' given its ineluctable failure to articulate the 'universal' *as* the 'particular'. The singular re-marks this failure *as* the history of law, which failure 'repeats' the underivable nature of law, the law of law. In other words, due to the inability of law to lose its prescriptive status and become a pure description of the real in which the particular would be the universal and the universal the particular, particularity is always also something singular, something that escapes and/or haunts all conceptual determination. Given this, as soon as one attempts to present or represent *singularity* – that is, articulate the universal as the particular or the particular as the universal – the community of 'we' is returned to the fiction of a substantial community. The singularities of this community become what this community must exclude to live the fiction that it represents in law its members, this fiction being that all the singularities which make it up are nothing but particular examples of its universal law. The aporia of law can never be untied, nor even presented as such, without the aporia reforming silently in the suffering of another singularity. Chapter 2 on Kant and Hegel and Chapter 3 on Heidegger and Levinas respectively develop in detail the logic of this fiction and the impossible logic of singularity. There is thus no example of either the law or the singular. If literature is exemplary in its witnessing of this, it is exemplary in re-marking a radical non-exemplarity.

The aporetic relation between (the failure of) generality and (the failure of) singularity is nothing else than what I described earlier as 'the aporia of judgement' and the 'judgement of aporia'. I recall that the experience of aporia does not reside outside judgement but that judgement retraces the experience of aporia *as* an impossible experience. Aporia is impossible because one must judge: the unpresentability of the aporia releases judgements indefinitely. Inversely, because judgement cannot fail to *exclude* in the possibility of its experience of aporia, there will always be time for another judgement. Time is in this sense the *différance* of the singular. Contra Kant's understanding of the moral law time returns into the law *qua* the failure of judgement to decide the law, precipitating the advent of another singularity which will have to be judged in turn, *ad infinitum*. Thus, to resume the terms above, that there are singularities means that the particular can never be articulated as the universal *because of* the irreducibility of time. Chapter 2 will develop this major thesis at length, suggesting, rather, and following the lines of the first section of this chapter, that the universal/particular opposition is in fact formed in the first place *through* the disavowal of inscription and time.

All this implies, as these pages have suggested several times, that one cannot separate the experience of aporia from the judgement which falls upon it. For the judgement only falls upon it because it is *already* within the aporia. As I said earlier – and we can now understand the reach of Derrida's argument – aporia, for Derrida, is not an oscillation between two contradictory sayings; a form of aporia which suspends judgement for the Ancients. By the very fact that aporia constitutes and defers the same instance, judgement *must* fall. This 'must' lies behind the 'must' that Derrida speaks about in 'Before the law'. At the moment of quoting Derrida regarding this 'must', I said that the latter was a paradoxical metaprescription coming from the law of law. What we can now confirm is that this 'metaprescription', which obliges us to keep the promise, forms the paradox that the judgement one makes is without grounds, violent. Violent, it is always to come, again, as another judgement. The story of the non-origin of the law – which would seem to defy judgement – tells the story that one must judge, that one's judgement will be violent and that the singular which comes to it from the future as the non-horizonal promise 'returns' (like the repressed, like a ghost) as this judgement's very failure. The impossible aporia of law releases the possibility *of* possibility. This impossible possibility constitutes the measure by which all judgements can only fail to measure themselves. Hence the measure of judgement is nothing but the impossibility of its measure; in this impossibility the singular arrives. The tale 'Vor dem Gesetz' tells us this not simply in terms of what it says; *its very singularity as a literary text witnesses this radical lack of measure.*

Let me end this chapter with a quotation from Derrida. It comes from his more recent essay on law, 'Force of law: The "Mystical foundation of authority"' (1992b). The essay appears to reintroduce a Kantian opposition between justice and law (*droit*). Everything in this chapter has worked, however, towards showing that the 'promise of law', of which Derrida speaks in the following passage, reformulates the very method of deconstruction which exceeds all types of opposition. The chapter has also worked towards showing that this promise consitutes a non-horizonal, that is radically finite, understanding of the future. It has shown, thirdly, that the promise determines a philosophy of judgement that cannot wait; and, finally, that these three gestures are one and the same. Deconstruction's 'method' (is) the 'promise of democracy'.

> The undecidable is not merely the oscillation or the tension between two decisions; it is the experience of that which, though heterogeneous, foreign to the order of the calculable and the rule, is still obliged – it is of obligation that we must speak – to give itself up to the impossible decision, while taking account of laws and rules. A decision that did not go through the ordeal of the undecidable would not be a free decision, it would only be the programmable application or unfolding of a calculable process. It might be legal; it would not be just. ... The being 'before the law' that Kafka talks about resembles [this situation]. ...

[It is the] situation, both ordinary and terrible, of the man who cannot manage to see or above all to touch, to catch up to the law: because it is transcendent in the very measure that it is he who must found it, as yet to come, in violence. Here we 'touch' without touching this extraordinary paradox: the inaccessible transcendence of the law before which and prior to which 'man' stands fast only appears infinitely transcendent and thus theological to the extent that, so near him, it depends only on him, on the performative act by which he institutes it: the law is transcendent, violent and non-violent, because it depends only on him who is before it. . . . The law is transcendent and theological, and so always to come, always promised, because it is immanent, finite and so already past. Every 'subject' is caught up in this aporetic structure in advance.

(Derrida, 1992b: 24, 36)

Let us now uncover this aporetic structure within the modern tradition of political thought.

2
The Political Limit of Logic and the Promise of Democracy

Kant, Hegel, Derrida

_____

> The god of morality does not yield to Jupiter, the custodian of violence, for even Jupiter is still subject to fate.
>
> Kant, *Theory and Practice*

Introduction

The previous chapter uncovered within Derrida's engagements with language and literature complex issues of judgement and institution. This chapter applies the insights afforded by this uncovering to an articulation of the relation between deconstruction and modern political thought.

In the last chapter I made the point that the alogic of originary repetition caught many critiques of deconstruction out. An insistent 'political' critique of Derrida's philosophy has been that deconstruction falls back into the logic and criteria of the 'modern tradition' at the very moment that it wishes to exceed them – Dews (1987), Eagleton (1990), Ferry and Renaut (1988), Frank (1984), Habermas (1981). The critique underestimates the complexity of Derrida's understanding of the promise since it fails to consider the way in which the promise transforms the terms of modern political thinking. In other words, it does not engage with the manner in which Derrida's thinking of originary repetition and of the promise reveals the contradictions in modern democratic thought and thereby *reinvents* our relation to these contradictions according to the lesser violence. We have seen this procedure at work in Derrida's deconstruction of Saussurean linguistics. I shall now show how Derrida's deconstruction of institutional horizons in Chapter 1 can be reapplied to the liberal theory of freedom and how it resists and reorganizes in turn non-liberal readings of this theory. Derrida's understanding of the promise in terms of the 'promise of democracy' (1991a) will emerge from both analyses.

The most effective way of articulating the relation between deconstruction and the modern political tradition is to position Derrida's work with regard to its major axis – the difference between the thought of Kant and that of Hegel. It is a commonplace of contemporary philosophy that recent French thinking (from Foucault to Derrida) sets Hegel up as 'the' thinker of identity. Hegel represents almost exactly what *not* to do to be a philosopher today, that is, to articulate a thinking of difference. The judgement is somewhat precipitate and needs to be redressed.[1] I shall do this through consideration of the difference between Kant and Hegel. This difference concerns the limit between the incomprehensible and the comprehensible, the infinite and the finite; the determination of the limit's nature decides what can be articulated, negotiated and invented in this world. Put differently: how one thinks the limit between the finite and the infinite determines *the possibilities of what can be politically imagined and produced*. The nature of the limit decides, in other words, the limits of political imagination and the orientation of political invention. Thus, if deconstruction is concerned to untie aporia from logical determination, a transformation of the vectors of modern political thought *necessarily* ensues. This consequence has been oddly ignored in many readings of deconstruction. Derrida's understanding of the promise of democracy will be considered here, therefore, to be a reinvention of the contradictory relations between law and singularity through a deconstruction of Kant and Hegel's understandings of the above limit.

The breakdown of my argument goes as follows. In the first section I define what I understand by modernity, rehearsing to the reader the specific stakes involved in writing about deconstruction with respect to modernity. I then develop the central difference between Kant and Hegel concerning the limit, referring to one major Hegelian critique of deconstruction in terms of this distinction (Rose, 1984), so that the political resonance of my argument is clear. In the second section I turn to Kant, showing the way in which the 'logic' of the Idea of freedom in the Kantian sense is self-contradictory, in order to develop both the promise and the violence of the Kantian determinations of an ethical and political community. In the light of this section, the third section develops the similarities and differences between Hegel's critique of the Kantian understanding of community and deconstruction's approach. Contra much recent underestimation of Hegel's philosophy, I then elaborate what Hegel's solution to this critique as *Sittlichkeit* consists in: the 're-cognition' of the violence of civil society.[2] I then point, nevertheless, to the problems which his very solution engenders, ultimately focusing on the way in which Hegel's development of recognition ends up *also* misrecognizing actuality. The fate of Hegel's thought as totalitarian and terroristic is situated, I believe, within this inversion of Hegel's 'logic' of recognition into misrecognition. Whilst allowing us to respect the complexity of Hegel's thought, my reading foregrounds Derrida's deconstruction of this logic as a transformation of the 'formal' criteria of democracy, a transformation which avoids at the same time a 'substantial' understanding of justice.

Each section of this chapter reconfigures the initial 'limit' between the infinite and the finite which forms what I call 'the axis of modernity'. Derrida's notion of the 'promise of democracy' is thereby understood through the development of the fate of this 'limit'. Through this development Derrida both distinguishes himself from other contemporary French accounts of Hegel (which tend to ignore the complexity of the limit in their resistance to the ontologization of politics) and reaffirms the overall tendency in Hegel's philosophy to ontologize the remainder. It is here that Kant will return to haunt Hegel at the very moment that Hegel believes that he is rid of Kant's ghost. This return is a limit prior to either the Kantian limit or Hegel's *Aufhebung* of it. For Derrida, the 'limit' is where all logical determinations of the political are haunted by a 'radical other'. The non-Hegelian recognition of this radical other calls not for the mourning of the political bond, but for its reorganization given its very 'impossibility'. This other is the excess of time.

The latter half of the argument will lean heavily on Derrida's reading of Hegel in *Glas* (1974), a poorly read work which this chapter will give us the occasion to situate politically.[3] The first half presupposes Derrida's work 'Of an apocalyptic tone recently adopted in philosophy' (1981) but does not use any specific Derridean 'commentary' of Kant. Since Derrida's relation to philosophy is cast in terms of the 'closure' of metaphysics, I wish to think this closure here in terms of: a) the logics of modern political thought; b) what, for Derrida, these logics disavow; and c) what a recognition of this disavowal, beyond the terms of Hegelian recognition, implies for the modern invention of the political community. This approach means working on texts to which Derrida has not necessarily turned his attention, at least in an empirical sense.

In the context of a post-Cold War world, one which is becoming increasingly violent and 'depoliticized', Derrida's understanding of democracy is important. Whether one agrees with Derrida or not, his deconstruction of modernity should be acknowledged for what it is, and not criticized in terms which it exceeds. Future debate will otherwise be stale. This chapter presents Derrida's quasi-logic in relation to the logic of modernity, argues for its radicality, but leaves the reader to orient him or herself once the radicality of Derrida's move has been shown. Having run through my argument, and more precisely in the context of my work on Hegel, I conclude with a hesitation concerning Derrida's reinscriptions. With respect to the reinvention of politics for the next century, this hesitation concerns, again, the need to articulate Derrida's aporetic rethinking of modernity with a more precise philosophy of technology. The hesitation will be taken up more fully in the conclusion.

Modernity and Violence

I have argued that by situating Derrida between Kant and Hegel it is possible to place his philosophy in explicit relation to debates concerning 'modernity'. How, then, do I understand this term and where will Derrida's thinking emerge through it? 'Modernity' serves as a discursive term of reflection upon a period of history from the beginning of the modern epoch onwards. Its reflection concerns the how and wherefore of human freedom in an increasingly secular, technical and 'international' world. Its reflection is made in both 'temporal' terms (it deploys a political chart of the progress of the human condition) and 'spatial' terms (it concerns nation states and their internal and external relations). Modernity is accordingly a term of reflection overtly concerned with the relation between the *human* and *time*.

From the Enlightenment onwards, the concepts pertaining to philosophy, to theology and to the 'experience' of religion are rearticulated to embrace and think the condition of humanity in terms of the 'present'. Whether it be Kant defending the distinction between faith and knowledge, Hegel re-cognizing this relation as the modern divorce between state and religion, Marx, after Feuerbach, maintaining that the question of religion is the question of the political state, Baudelaire rearticulating the relation between poetic invention and urban life, or Nietzsche, in his moments of despair of articulating the relation between finitude and politics, resorting to a metaphysical politics of the 'physiological' – in each case, modern thought confronts the need to reconfigure, in a finite world, the relations between traditional human hopes and temporality. Indeed it could be argued that the ways in which the object of human thought and the end of human action are displaced from the infinite to the finite 'constitute' the field of modernity as such. It is these displacements that allow for the modern understanding of the 'political' as *an active process of self-transformation*. In doing so these displacements cannot fail, therefore, to transform the relation between the infinite and the finite since this relation determines *what* is human, *where* the human lies and *when* the human is 'truly' human.[4] The first major philosophical negotiation of this relation takes place between Kant and Hegel. Thus, in order to articulate the political implications of Derrida's philosophy, it is appropriate to elaborate the deconstruction of the empirico-transcendental difference with regard to its relation to the origin of these modern displacements. Since these displacements concern the relation between the human and time, we should already sense from Chapter 1 how Derrida's untying of the aporia of time from logic amounts to a profound engagement with these displacements as well as with the transformation of their terms.

As my introduction suggested, this transformation is engendered through a reading of the logic of the political *qua* the relation between law and violence. The limit in Kant between the infinite and the finite is one between freedom and heteronomy, determining Kant's 'regulative' distinction between ethics and politics. This limit is redetermined, in turn, by Hegel as an unthought 'middle' (*Mitte*) between the freedom of war and government and the necessity of particular wants. It is figured in socio-political terms as 'absolute ethical life' (*Sittlichkeit*). By following through this difference between Kant and Hegel, together with its complications, the reader should bear in mind the two following arguments.

First, the question of the limit in modern political philosophy is not just the question of the lesser or greater limits of a political community. What is more profoundly at stake is the relation between *rights* and *violence* (compare Caygill, 1994). I said above that Chapter 1 developed Derrida's notion of the trace as the necessary violence of any mark, and, thus, of any institution and that to consider Derrida in relation to 'modernity' is to bring this argument to bear on the modern institution of democracy. Given my definition of modernity, let me now specify why. The relation between rights and violence is exactly what the liberal notion of democracy, from Kant onwards, is constitutively unable to articulate because it makes a hard and fast distinction between the infinite and the finite, an 'abyss' which is then mediated logically by a priori principles of reason. It is in response to the lack of an immanent relation between 'faith' and 'knowledge' and rights and violence that Hegel develops his notion of *Sittlichkeit*. Modern politics *of* violence – Fascism (and racial struggle) and Marxism (and class struggle) – also constitute a response to this lack of relation in liberal democracies, as well as being a further development, and simplification, of Hegel's thought. To place the question of the 'originary violence' of the trace in relation to Hegel's response to Kant is thus to try and think the relation between rights and violence *without* ontologizing this relation (as happens in the later Hegel, Marxism and, much more obviously, Fascism). This chapter determines this relation as *aporetic* in contradistinction to Hegel's dialectical presentation of the relation. If the violence of Hegel's fates (political philosophies of the *Volk* or of class contradiction) is to be read from within this distinction, then a partial reorganization of contemporary French philosophy's understandings of Hegel with respect to the thinking of the political community is called for.

Second, I have suggested that the Derridean quasi-notion of the 'promise of democracy' is an attempt to go beyond the Kant/Hegel divide, without becoming either a philosophy of rights or that of a substantial community. Now, the debate in the United States, prior to the end of the Cold War, between liberalism and 'communitarianism'[5] repeated in displaced terms the difference between Kant and Hegel's understanding of the political. In the 1970s and 1980s political philosophy in America appeared divided between an elaboration of a 'non-foundationalist' theory of rights

– Dworkin (1977), Nozick (1974), Rawls (1972, 1980) – which reworked Kant, and an expressive understanding of community – Taylor (1979a, 1979b), MacIntyre (1981) – which reworked Aristotle and Hegel. The difference between the two conceptions of the political turned precisely around the place of rights in a political community. For the liberals, rights are the very condition of community. For the communitarians, community is the very condition of rights: the a priori concept of 'right' empties the concept of freedom of history, formation, expression and situation, confining the idea of freedom to a question of negative limits between individuals. This debate restates the Kantian-Hegelian difference, *without* rethinking, however, the relation between rights, community and violence. If, as I argue, Derrida's rearticulation of the Kantian-Hegelian difference allows us to do this, then the quasi-notion of the 'promise of democracy' also presents a major challenge to American liberal and neo-Hegelian thought.

The Limit of Modernity

The principal difference between Kant and Hegel emerges around the limit between the infinite and the finite. In this section I will develop the initial difference between Kant and Hegel with respect to this divide and trace its return in contemporary debate concerning the relation between philosophy and politics.

The Kant/Hegel Difference

Kant's *Critique of Pure Reason* (1781) and *Critique of Practical Reason* (1788) can be considered as the determining reconfiguration of philosophy at the beginning of the modern period. In the context of the growing tension between, on the one hand, value and meaning (in the form of religion and ethics), and, on the other, scientific law, Kant divides the world into two mutually compatible but ontologically exclusive realms – the phenomenal and the noumenal. This division settles, for Kant, all dispute between transcendental and empirical analysis, so installing a state of peace between tradition and the natural sciences. Knowledge pertains to the phenomenal realm alone, since it is possible only through the 'a priori forms of sensibility' of time and space. Assertions whose referents are not to be found in time and space – the beginning of the world, the soul, God, freedom – are in turn 'speculative'; they fall into the domain of speculative reason. These referents are in fact nothing but thoughts, the object of which we know nothing. Kant calls these concepts 'Ideas'. Their objects are thinkable, but unknowable. In the first *Critique* Ideas have a purely negative value, guarding the limits (*Grenzen*) of human understanding and preventing 'transcendental illusion' (the belief that one can speak knowingly about objects outside the conditions of sensibility, time and space). In the second *Critique* the Ideas are given positive determination through what Kant calls the 'moral law'. Through this double move, Kant 'saves' the value and meaning of religion and ethics from the scientific finitization of the world, whilst according science full rights to this world.

In the first *Critique* the Idea of freedom was deduced *negatively* through the feeling of 'guilt'. In feeling guilt for a deed, wishing it be 'undone' although it is irreparable, one shows that one is free. Freedom is freedom from the linear determination of *time* (1781: Second Division, Chapter 2, 'The antinomy of pure reason'). In the second *Critique* this feeling is recast *positively* as the feeling of 'respect' before the moral law, from which is deduced the idea of freedom (1788: Part 1, Book 1, Chapters 1 and 3, 'Of the deduction of the principles of pure practical reason' and 'The incentives of pure practical reason'). Since, for Kant, the moral subject takes a pure interest in the moral law, even though such interest goes against his or her sensible instincts and inclinations, he or she is free. It is crucial to Kant's enterprise of reconciliation between fact and value that the moral law is *not* known. Indeed, it is on the basis of one's inability to comprehend the moral law that the law remains moral. If one knew how to be moral, if one knew how to be free, then morality and freedom would be objects of science. To know what freedom or morality are implies removing the very condition of their possibility (compare Lyotard, 1979 and 1983).[6] This means that the relation for Kant between ethics and politics is one of 'analogical' orientation ('Perpetual peace: A philosophical sketch', 1795: 116–25). The incomprehensibility of the moral law implies a thinking of the political realm according to 'regulative' Ideas which do not determine this field, but regulate, on the basis of an analogy with natural laws, one's orientation within it. I will come to this argument in the next section. On the basis of this analogical orientation, Kant theorizes his ethical revulsion to the political terror of the French revolution ('Theory and practice', 1793: 82–7). Thus the incomprehensibility of the moral law implies, rightly, a limitation of ontological political horizons and, ambivalently, a denial of political violence.

Kant comments at the end of his prolegomena to the second *Critique, Fundamental Principles of the Metaphysics of Morals*:

> The deduction of the supreme principle of morality cannot be blamed for refusing to explain the necessity [of an unconditional practical law] by a condition, that is to say, by means of some interest assumed as a basis, since the law would then cease to be a moral law, i.e. a supreme law of freedom. And thus while we do not comprehend the practical unconditional necessity of

the moral imperative, we yet comprehend its incomprehensibility, and this is all that can be fairly demanded of a philosophy which strives to carry its principles to the very limit of human reason [*zur Grenze der menschlichen Vernunft*].

(1785: 97)

From *Faith and Knowledge* (1801/2) onwards Hegel considers this limit (*Grenze*) to be the very negation of philosophy and the beginning of faith. In this judgement many contemporary philosophers, of liberal and non-liberal persuasion, have seen the workings of a 'logic' of terror and, after the 'totalitarian' fate of Hegel's philosophy, have gone back to Kant to reorganize his understanding of law with respect to the contemporary world. As we shall see, this is too simple. For Hegel, Kant's reconciliation of value and fact does nothing but repeat their scission in the modern world. The Kantian limit, a limit which for Kant reconciles the diverse claims of human knowledge and hope by setting limits to their domains of applicability – this limit, for Hegel, turns ethics (moral law and freedom) into an *unknowable law* which deprives man of the possibility of thinking and acting freely. In the absolute separation of the infinite from the finite, law from understanding, faith from knowledge, freedom from natural causality, Kant empties practical reason of all content. He thereby leaves the world exactly where it stands, suspended, in all its bourgeois ugliness, under an incomprehensible law which resists a priori the transformative work of political imagination. Kantian ethics is unethical. For Hegel, this inversion unfolds the 'fate' of freedom when the concept of freedom is left, from the beginning, undetermined.

Kant is not only caught, however, in a contradiction which catches his own theory of ethics out. The contradiction should also be understood as the misrecognized determination of the limit. This constitutes Hegel's second move against Kant. In order to pose the limit between the finite and the infinite (to say what is comprehensible and what is not) Kant has *already* gone *beyond* the limit, thereby betraying its intellectual coherence. Kant's very demarcation of the noumenal from the phenomenal unmakes the very distinction which it is making by making it. Kantian ethics is not simply contradictory, unethical; it is *self-contradictory*. However, the contradiction remains *unarticulated*. This lack of articulation will lead, for Hegel, to the 'violence' of Kantian political philosophy, the violence of thinking politics exclusively in terms of rights. In Hegelian language, the *Aufhebung* is misrecognized (*unerkannt*), although this mediation is already the middle (*Mitte*) which allows Kant in the first place to separate ethics from cognition.

For Hegel, the 'recognition' (*Erkennen*) of the limit as a *Mitte* is truly speculative. Kant's determination of speculative reason as what is concerned with what is on the other side of the limit repeats a logic particular

to the domain of the faculty of understanding which refuses contradiction. This is a crucial point. The faculty of understanding in the first
Critique is named the faculty of 'rules'. These rules determine a priori
(that is before any particular experience) an order by which sense im-
pressions can acquire meaning for the human subject. The highest rule
of the understanding is the 'principle of contradiction' (Kant, 1781:
188–91). As the positive criterion of analytic knowledge and the negative
criterion of synthetic knowledge, it is an 'inviolable' *conditio sine
qua non* of judgement. Without conforming to it, 'judgements are in themselves, without reference to the object, null and void' (1781: 189). The
principle of contradiction constitutes nothing less than an evacuation,
from the domain of philosophy, of the problem of *time*. For, in formal
logic, A cannot be –A *at one and the same time*. Formal logic thus denies
time to constitute itself as such: it is nothing less, then, than the disavowal
of time.

Now, although Kant is careful to distinguish between the 'determining'
condition of non-contradiction with regard to analytic knowledge and
the 'formal' condition of non-contradiction for synthetic knowledge
(1781: 190–1), the principle remains 'inviolable' for *all* knowledge. This
inviolability resides in the fact that the principle is *beyond* time. Time
does not *restrict* this principle as the schemata of the categories of understanding 'restrict' these same categories to sensibility *qua* time-relations
('The schematism of the pure concepts of the understanding' (1781:
180–7)).[7] Hence, the self-contradictory nature of Kant's very move to
place ethico-political orientation under the principle of contradiction, since
ethics has nothing to do with knowledge. There is nothing more metaphysical than this move. For, in displacing the logic of non-contradiction
from the field of knowledge to the ethical and political fields – domains
which, for Kant, are precisely meant to resist the principles of knowledge
– Kant is unable to think the contradiction through between law and
time, principle and sensibility. The inability engenders in Kant's ethical
and political writings a disavowal of the inextricable, but necessary relation between rights and violence. This disavowal forms the interest of my
reading of Kant through Derrida. For Hegel, this unethical suppression is
the 'ironic' result of leaving the limit undetermined. Lack of determination leads, for Hegel, to unrecognized violence; just as for Kant, inversely,
it is determination that leads to it. To seize reason as the very process
of contradiction (as in the recognition of the determination of the limit)
prepares for the realm of speculative philosophy. For Hegel, Kant only
does this in the *Critique of Judgement* (1790) – compare Caygill's admir-
able *Art of Judgement* (1989). The delimitation of the limit, unmade in
its very making, is Hegel's determination of the above *Grenze* as *Schranke*
(the limit as 'delimitation'). The apparently natural limit between faith
and knowledge is an *active* process of unmaking on the part of human

reason. The delimitation will become, in political terms, the attempt to recognize the violence of law.

The separation of the infinite from the finite at the end of the *Fundamental Principles* is a logical way of considering the Kantian argument that the moral law is perceived by human beings as an 'ought' (see Hegel, *Science of Logic*, 1812/16: 130–3). Pure morality is impossible for finite human beings and therefore stands as an Idea, progress towards which is infinite. For Hegel, the Idea in the Kantian sense is the logical precipitate of the separation between the noumenal and phenomenal worlds and is caught in the contradiction of the limit which Kant refuses to admit. In Hegelian terms, the Idea is a 'bad infinity' (ibid.). I shall come back to this at greater length in the third section. Here I wish to stress that it is *always* the nature of the limit which is in question regarding the ethico-political difference between Kant and Hegel. The Kantian separation is what Hegel calls a 'relative identity': the misrecognition of the relation between the finite and the infinite fixes the opposition as one of constraint (*Natural Law* essay, 1802/3: 71f.). The moral subject 'should' become less sensibly affected, more dutiful, less particular, more universal, etc. The mediation of the apparent opposition is what Hegel calls, in turn, an 'absolute identity' or 'the identity of identity and difference' (ibid.). In *Faith and Knowledge* Hegel calls this differential unity the absolute identity of the 'speculative Good Friday' (1801/2: 191). The notion of the speculative Good Friday forms Hegel's response to Enlightenment universalism. Gillian Rose introduces this concept in the following terms in her major work on Hegel, *Hegel Contra Sociology*.[8]

> The abstract, pure concept or infinity in Kant and Fichte is the 'abyss of nothingness in which all being is engulfed'. The infinite is opposed to being, that is to the finite, to all determination, and hence is nothing itself. This nothingness is imposed on all being ... the individual feels abandoned by a characterless, omnipotent and hence impotent God. This experience of 'infinite grief' is re-cognized as the historical meaning of Christianity *in the present*. The feeling that God is dead or absent has always been central to Christian religious experience, because in the Christian religion the absolute is misrepresented as beyond human life, not present in it. ... How is the speculative Good Friday to take the place of the historic Good Friday? How can rationality encompass religion? Philosophy is to take the place of the older dogmatic metaphysics, of the critical philosophy and of religion in the task of creating an *idea* of absolute freedom.
>
> (Rose, 1981: 104)

This idea, in contradistinction to the Idea in the Kantian sense, structures the philosophical truth of Christianity (the 'speculative' Good Friday). The death of Christ represents in immediate, religious form both the death of God and the death of Man. For Hegel, the central experience of Christianity is, in philosophical form, the falling of the infinite into the finite and the subsumption of the finite into the infinite. Thus, grasped speculatively, the historic Good Friday is the mediation of the infinite and the finite. No other religion apart from Christianity has 're-cognized' the limit between the infinite and the finite as *mediation* (the figure and death of Christ). This is why, for Hegel, Christianity is the true religion and why Christianity can only be completed by articulating its truth in *social* and *political* form. As Rose forcefully argues, the speculative Good Friday is the heart of Hegelian philosophy (compare Derrida 1974: 44–6/31–3 and 127–35/91–6). In Christianity, although misrecognized in this religion as a *historical* religion, with its nostalgia and promises (see Hegel, *Philosophy of History*, 1821b), the Kantian realms of the finite and infinite are shown to be both the same and different from each other (the identity of identity and difference). The speculative content of Christianity thus forms the truth of Kantian morality.

Hegel's philosophy of history and his history of philosophy show how substance becomes subject, that is how the concept of God becomes the concept of modern subjectivity, and how, at the same time, the identity between these two concepts has become divorced. This divorce resides in the modern age in the split between religion and the state (Hegel's *Philosophy of Right*, 1821a: 165–72). These related points articulate the fundamental tenets of Hegel's thought. The Idea of freedom incarnated in the concept of the divine is not suspended above the limits of human knowledge as a horizon towards which we progress infinitely, it constitutes the development of the concept of freedom *in* and *as* the history of freedom (*Philosophy of Right*, Preface). The Kantian determination of faith as indeterminate is re-cognized by Hegel 'as' the philosophy of history and the history of philosophy. The *Aufhebung* of the limit is, for Hegel, the determination of philosophy as political philosophy, which philosophy apprehends the religious as the misrecognition of political freedom *in the present* (not an indefinite future like that of the Kantian Idea) (ibid.: 12). This present is *sittlich* (customs and laws) and not moral (*Moralität*). For morality describes the infinite progress of subjective rights in terms of a constantly deferred horizon. The horizon leaves the subject and freedom unreconciled *qua* 'misrecognized actualities'. For Hegel, this misrecognition is the subject of 'modern times' (1802/3: 120) inviolably free within the law, but violated in his or her concrete reality. Freedom hides unfreedom. Hegel's notion of *Sittlichkeit* constitutes an attempt to re-cognize this 'illusion' of freedom.

Contemporary Stakes Concerning the Limit

As I argued in my introductory comments, the question of this limit has returned with force in contemporary philosophical debate and has determined the terms of many politico-philosophical alliances. For those (especially philosophers of *écriture*) concerned to demarcate the limits of political thought and action, Kant has been of greater importance than Hegel, providing the basis, often with Heidegger, for a thinking of finitude and the 'unpresentable'. For those (especially social and political theorists) Hegel remains the major reference point, although their Hegel is rarely the one developed above. The most coherent and interesting attack on Derrida's philosophy of 'arche-writing' has come from Gillian Rose's reading of a non-totalistic Hegel concerned with the inversions of recognition and misrecognition.

Her provocative, if at times impatient, criticisms of Derrida's philosophy (*Dialectics of Nihilism* (1984: 131–170) and *Judaism and Modernity* (1993: 65–88)) are informed by a Hegelian wish to re-cognize and articulate the limit between what is knowable and unknowable, recognizable and unrecognizable, presentable and unpresentable. She argues that Derrida's notion of the trace cannot account for its own histories and that his philosophy, like that of Kant, consequently ends up both self-contradictory and blindly legislative and formalistic. I shall end this section by briefly elaborating her criticisms, as well as what I consider to be a Derridean response to them, in order to highlight the overall argument of this chapter: that the question of the limit offers privileged access to thinking the political implications of continental philosophy.

In *Hegel Contra Sociology* Rose argues that no separation can be made between Hegel's method and his understanding of *Sittlichkeit*.

> In Hegel's thought Spirit means the structure of recognition or misrecognition in a society. 'Objective' spirit [*Sittlichkeit*] is inseparable from absolute spirit, the meaning of history as a whole.... The absolute is not an optional extra.... Hegel's philosophy has no social import if the absolute is banished or suppressed, if the absolute *cannot be thought*.
>
> (1981: 41–2, my emphasis)

In *Dialectics of Nihilism* she accuses Derrida of making this separation when he argues, as at the beginning of *Of Grammatology*, that:

> The horizon of absolute knowledge is the effacement of writing in the logos, the retrieval of the trace in parousia; the reappropriation of difference, the accomplishment of ... the *metaphysics of the proper*. Yet all that Hegel thought within this horizon,

all, that is, except eschatology, may be reread as a meditation
on writing. Hegel is *also* the thinker of irreducible difference
... the last philosopher of the book and the first thinker of
writing.

(1967b: 26)

Summing up 'the entire philosophy of the logos' Hegel's eschatology of
parousia represents, for Derrida, 'the self-proximity of infinite subjectivity'
(ibid.: 24). Hegelian philosophy is consequently *the* example of the
incorporation of the remainder of the philosophical concept (what was
called the 'singular' in Chapter 1) given Hegel's ontological claim that the
remainder can be interiorized, conceptualized, re-cognized (grasped
[*begriffen*]). This reading of Hegel would seem to place Derrida squarely
within my initial sketch of contemporary French thought's politically
determined caricature of Hegel. For Rose, indeed, this reading of Hegelian
absolute identity is a severe reduction of Hegel's understanding of
the absolute to one of its moments – the metaphysics of subjectivity
(Rose, 1984: 139, 147). By failing to read Hegel in terms of recognition
and misrecognition, Derrida repeats the Kantian error. He makes the law
'unknowable' and, in making the law 'unknowable', he legislates without
admitting that he is legislating (the 'quasi'-transcendental concept of
'arche-writing' remains a transcendental concept for Rose). As we shall
see, Hegel's exposition of Kant attempts to show that what has been
smuggled under the Kantian determination of the moral law as 'unknowable', but universal in its 'form', is the infinite freedom of the legal concept
of 'person' particular to Roman law and specific relations of property.
The law is never beyond time and space. For Rose, Hegel's historiciza-
tion of Kantian law opens up, then, the 'between' between philosophy
and political and social thought. Hegelian exposition allows for the logic
which makes the law 'unknowable', whilst delimiting it so that it can be
re-cognized and not relegislated. 'Arche-writing', on the contrary, reproduces the illusion (*Schein*) of a 'bad infinity' à la Kant by postponing
the law indefinitely (1981: 163–5, compare 1993: 72–5). This means for
Rose (1984: 162–8; 1993: 72–5), that Derrida's quasi-transcendental structures ('trace', 'arche-writing', *différance*, and most recently, that of the
'promise') are 'unknowable absolutes' whose legal formalism betrays a
desire for mastery and a refusal of risk. Refusing to determine the excess
of conceptuality except in terms of a 'gift' that must not be accounted
for, Derrida remains master at developing the irreducible contamination
of all principles of thought and law. For Rose, he consequently ends up
unable to discriminate between these discriminations, since he is not
working from *within* their history. Quasi-transcendental logic is, precisely,
still logic; unable to give itself up to this history, Derrida's thinking of
aporia uses aporia as a tool of discrimination which allows it at the same

time to 'avoid' this very history. The 'closure' of metaphysics remains a metaphysical concept. Aware of the necessary failure of all thought and action, Derrida must end up incapable of *taking* political risks. Derrida, our contemporary Rameau's nephew.

After our reading of 'Before the law' and of the historicity of the promise we should be suspicious of this reading, although, as I argue in my conclusion, there is a particular problem in Derrida's understanding of history which Rose, I believe, partly uncovers. First, the quasi-concept of *différance* is *not* in the same position of indeterminacy and incomprehension as the moral law in Kant. This is an important point, the full weight of which will have emerged only at the end of the next chapter. Rose underestimates Derrida's understanding of the law as the *aporia of time*; that is, she underestimates the complexity of the relation between time and law in Derrida's writing of aporia. As Chapter 1 has shown, the law of *différance* is far more radical than Kant's understanding of the moral law, exceeding the metaphysical difference between the atemporality of law and that to which it is nominally opposed, history. It exceeds, in other words, form. This is what is difficult for Hegelianism to accept. Hence the trace can always be confused with Kantianism, concerned as it is with that which exceeds form (compare *Glas*, 'Seen from *Sa* [*savoir absolu*, absolute knowledge] the thought of the trace will be a jealous (finite, filial, servile, ignorant, lying, poetic) thought', Derrida, 1974: 215). Derrida is, however, interested in the moral law in Kant, since, together with Heidegger's destruction of the metaphysics of time, it offers him a more privileged access to an understanding of the finitude of the trace than does Hegel's determination of the law as an *ontology* of *contradiction*. In relation to Hegel's earlier critique of the Kantian limit, for Derrida, Hegel's 'philosophy of history' thus repeats the Kantian suppression of contradiction by itself determining the contradiction 'as' a contradiction (and not as an aporia). The paradox is the ultimate interest of the following pages. If it is here that Derrida will concentrate on the logic of contradiction in Hegel's writings, focusing on the way in which this logic determines the matter that is being thought, it ultimately means that, for Derrida, *Hegel is not a thinker of time*. The importance of this point will only be fully understood once we have considered Derrida's deconstruction of Heidegger.

Second, Derrida's resistance to Hegelian philosophy lies in his demonstration that the identity of identity and difference is a 'phantasm'. Differential unity is impossible in its impossibility; the thought of this unity constitutes in fact a desire. Since this thought is also, for Hegel, the history of this thought, this history is also phantasmatic. Thus, when Hegel thinks he is talking about history, he is not; he is talking about history as he *desires it to be* – in other words, he is writing logic. For Derrida, the speculative is libidinal in this sense: which is why, like all desires, the speculative is violent and suppressive. Hegelian recognition ends up as another example of misrecognition. This is the major argument of *Glas*. At the very moment that Hegel wishes to go beyond Kant's logic of the understanding, informed by the principle of contradiction, Derrida returns him to this logic. For *Glas* shows that the absolute identity of the speculative Good Friday *could never take place as such*. Let me formalize this argument in the context of our previous discussion:

–   Absolute identity is always deferred in Hegel's work not for empirico-historical reasons, but because it is 'impossible' as such. This impossibility has consequences for the very concept of recognition. My use of the 'category' of 'impossibility' here does not presume a logical judgement, it is a 'delayed' reaction to the aporia of time, for the aporia cannot be experienced as such. It is this aporia which restricts absolute identity to the order of the phantasmatic.
–   Absolute identity only takes place in Hegel's texts in death or *as death*. This allows for all the 'misreadings' of Hegel as subordinating sensibility to the state; and, therefore;
–   Absolute spirit, whilst not a 'methodological extra' in Hegel's thought, as Rose forcefully argues, is considered by Derrida as only possible in its impossibility, that is, as the failure of the 'speculative Good Friday'. This failure – we are in familiar territory here – is the *promise* of the speculative Good Friday, which promise remains radically external to both the philosophy of history and the history of philosophy as Hegel thinks it. For both are still determined by logic, the logic, contra Kant, *of* contradiction.

Derrida's move against Hegel is similar to Rose's against deconstruction. It is in relation to this wish to bring to light the Hegelian logic of recognition and deconstruct it that *Glas* talks not of history as the truth of the concept, but of the 'stricture' of the law of dialectic as the 'gift of time' (Derrida, 1974: 330–8, 237–42). The quasi-concept of 'stricture' constitutes for Derrida the condition of possibility and impossibility of the speculative proposition.[9] Thus at this point the accusation that Derrida's philosophy remains transcendental would first have to check if its own attempt to leave transcendental analysis does not repeat it. If it does, then the accusation is informed by the very logic it is accusing Derrida's thought of. The above would be a Derridean response to Rose. Hegel hides his own transcendentalism as 'history'. This 'illusion' needs to be thought for the finitude of violence to be developed.

    Since the speculative proposition entails a history of philosophy and a philosophy of history, one can surmise into what difficult waters the Derridean promise must take us concerning the relations between thought, law, time and violence. Since the speculative proposition is also a critique of the Idea of the republic in Kant, and since the law in Derrida wishes to reinscribe the difference between Kant's thinking of law and that of Hegel's in terms of contradiction, I can confirm the premise of my introduction. These waters imply, for Derrida, a complex reinvention of the relation between democracy and violence, with Hegel and his heritage – one made, however, in recognition of the irreducibility of time to logic. To see this, let us turn, first, to Kant.

The Logic of Kantian Morality

In this section I look at the way in which the Idea of freedom (in the Kantian sense) is self-contradictory. This deconstruction of the Idea of freedom both reveals the violence of democratic law and gives testimony to this violence (its act and consequences). My argument focuses on the 'universality of law' in Kant. Kant determines through the universality of 'form' the way in which the moral law, whilst unknowable, orients the 'matter' of political judgement's maxims according to the principle of universality. A deconstruction of the universality of form suspends the universalist aspirations of Kantian ethics, pinpoints the contradictions in Kant's ensuing determinations of law and violence and transforms these determinations with a view to lesser violence. A comparison of Hegel's and Derrida's readings of law will then be possible.

The Inversions of Kantian Universality and the Temporal Suspension of the Idea

I recall that Kant separates the moral law from cognition and understanding. It is this 'incomprehensibility' of the moral law that allows Kant to keep freedom out of scientific law and calculation. From the anteriority of this law both the Idea of freedom is negatively deduced and the 'regulative' use of the Idea in the political domain is developed. The Idea is articulated in terms of the 'form' of 'universality'. The articulation takes the principle of contradiction from the realm of knowledge and applies it to the 'regulative' procedure of the moral law. The articulation is made despite the fact that, in Kant's very understanding of ethics, the moral law, as the origin of this Idea, must be resistant to these principles of knowledge to remain moral. This inconsistency in Kant's thinking is already latent in the delimitation of the limit between the ethical and the cognitive. It is repeated and explicitly revealed in the form and content of the Kantian Idea of freedom. Let us see how.

For Kant, our interest in the moral law is undetermined. The idea of freedom can be deduced from the law but only negatively. If one feels 'respect' for the law, whether one obeys it or not, this is a negative sign of one's freedom from natural causality. It is thus moral to know when to stop and where to draw the *limit* between the ethical and the cognitive. Reason, for Kant, has nothing to say about our interest in, and respect before, the moral law. However, both the *Fundamental Principles of the Metaphysics of Morals* (1785) and the second *Critique* (1788) have to be *written* in the first place, in order for Kant to delimit the realm of pure practical interest and then abolish human claims upon the purity of this interest. Kant never says anything of this prior move – the date and signature of his texts. Rather, as in the Preface to the first *Critique* (1781), the critical delimitation is made in the name of Reason which, as Reason, stands *outside* time and space. And yet Kant's very 'signature' betrays the fact that he must have crossed the limit of the ethical *in order to* place it as such, keep it from cognitive determination and declare, in an act of unwitting hypocrisy, that the limit between ethics and understanding is 'natural'. His very need to demarcate the ethical realm from the cognitive realm shows, as Hegel argues, that the limit is in itself divisible. This delimitation of the limit has consequences which pick up all the hesitations and ambivalence of Kant's ethical and political tracts concerning the end of morality and the moral relation to political violence.

It is only by presuming from the start ethics to be something like knowledge that they can then be separated out. This implies that the limit is not natural as Kant would retrospectively wish, so disavowing his own writing in the name of an ahistorical Reason which humanity essentially betrays. Rather, the limit is *forced* and *institutional*, and thus, like any frontier, this limit must be maintained in violence. Kant's claim to 'defend' a limit which precedes his own act of legislation represents a classic gesture of 'liberal' rationality which disavows its own force under the cover of naturality. As we shall see, this disavowal cannot fail, like all democratic thought, to place violence *outside* the law. The violence in maintaining the limit as natural is revealed as/in the *contradictions* of Kant's thought.[10]

The next contradiction is that of the regulative form of the law. It follows on from the first contradiction. Given his failure to develop the delimitation of the limit, Kant can do nothing but *posit* what the form of law should be. He argues that the law, as unconditioned condition, implies what a good performance of the law should be. This is a law that has the 'form of law' (1788: 35). Law is that which is universalizable, applicable to each particular will, *as if* it were a universal law of nature. Kant reinvites a relation between the two realms of freedom and nature, ethics and cognition which the drawing of the limit had wished to separate. The 'form of law' throws a bridge across the limit that allows for ethical action to be possible. This becomes clear in the formulations of the categorical imperative. For example: 'Act as if the maxims of your will should serve at the same time as the universal law of all rational beings' or 'Act as if the maxim of your action were to become through your will a universal law of nature' (1785: 56–7).

What is important to Kant is that this bridge is only analogical. The move from the moral law to the principle of universality through the notion of *form* permits the regulative Idea of the sovereignty of the 'general will'. The object of moral orientation in the political domain is *not* to institute popular sovereignty (universality). Its 'end' is the concept of sovereignty or the pure concept of right which limits a priori the very condition of politics. As a limiting Idea, sovereignty is *regulative*. One should think of law as if its pure concept was sovereignty, but not make the object or end of one's political judgements pure sovereignty, at the risk of instituting terror. Lyotard has insistently stressed this regulative value to the Idea in the Kantian sense in opposition to post-Kantian political violence (see J.-F. Lyotard, 1979, 1983, 1993). Whilst Kant's analogical understanding of politics is made in the name of a lesser violence, one should nevertheless recall that what regulates this fictional orientation is the principle of contradiction, the condition of universality. For this logical determination of the Idea's form both reintroduces the problem of cognition and, more importantly, confirms the lack of a relation in Kantian thought between the a priori concept of right and violence.

Kant argues that the form of law is a necessary consequence of the incomprehensibility of the law. In the chapter 'Of the type of pure practical reason' in the *Critique of Practical Reason* (1788: 70–3) the argument goes as follows. That the moral law can be moral only if it *immediately* determines the will means that the determination of the will by objects is always particular and contingent. What remains, then, in order for one to think how to judge ethically can only be the *form* of law as such and not its *matter*, the objects of a particular maxim. Since matter for Kant is particularity, differing in its determinations from one person to the next, maxims of action which have a particular object in view are technical or empirical (maxims, for example, of happiness). Maxims which remain faithful to one's interest in the law can only be those which imply that the object to be realized can be applied universally, can acquire, that is, 'the form of law'. Hence 'the legislative form, in so far as it is contained in the maxims, is the only thing which can constitute a determining ground of the will' (1788: 51). It is a short move from the unconditional universality of the moral law's determination of the will to the 'schema' of law provided by the understanding's 'form of lawfulness' in general. Judgement serves practical reason by applying analogically this form of lawfulness to the way in which the will should conduct itself morally. For example, one judges negatively that it is not moral to deceive because, if everybody deceived, there would be no point in deceiving in the first place. The prescription 'You should not deceive' is *regulative*; it is not the case that if x deceives, y will deceive.

Thus, for Kant, the analogy established between ethical and natural causality allows one to determine one's maxims according to the form of universality which the unconditioned value of the moral law invites. As a result of the principle of contradiction, the universal form of law is made a rule of ethical judgement – one in the very realm in which Kant had nevertheless argued that the law was *incalculable*, because it was incomprehensible. What does this inconsistency imply? As I have mentioned, Kant criticizes Enlightenment understandings of law for their terroristic possibilities, safeguarding the law from cognitive determination by determining it as an Idea of freedom. At the same time, however, he argues that the content of this Idea necessarily finds form in the 'form of universality'. This form also reduces ethical orientation to an easily rehearsed programme of judgement. By making the principle of ethics universality, Kant banishes, in the name of ethics, the *risk* of ethical judgement. Chapter 1 showed that judgement according to its very concept can only be a risk. Kantian ethics therefore abolishes judgement, the very condition of ethical orientation.

This last point does not just ensue from the specific argument of the form of law, as Levinas and Lyotard have nevertheless rightly asserted (Levinas, 1961: 191–4/215–20; Lyotard, 1979: 73–84/37–43). The principle of contradiction forms the very idea of the Idea of the sovereign will. According to the same logic as above, this principle makes the Idea contradictory within its own terms. Universalist ethics are not undone by empirico-historical realities, as our common, and essentially religious, understanding would have it. To believe in the horizon as such, to believe in its 'promise', whatever the empirico-historical failings of the inscriptions of this promise in the world, is, as Derrida has recently put it, 'messianist' (1993). The promissory horizon of Kantian ethics is unethical *within its own terms*, before any demarcation between the transcendental and the empirical. As Chapter 1 stressed, the constitutive aporia of *any* horizon is *différance*. Ethical horizonality in politics must, accordingly, be suspended to remain ethical; or, more clearly put, the promise of democracy must be suspended to remain a *promise*. Therefore, in the very name of democracy, one cannot affirm the principles of democracy to their end, that is, *all* the *time*. To be a democrat, one cannot be a democrat. The promise of democracy (in the Derridean sense) resides in this 'temporal' suspension of the undemocratic logic of the democratic promise. The development of the Kantian Idea of autonomy shows why.

In paragraph 8 of the second *Critique* (1788) Kant states the positive transformation of 'respect' of the law, its subjective effect, into the law of autonomy:

The *autonomy* of the will is the sole principle of all moral laws and of the duties conforming to them; *heteronomy* of choice, on the other hand, not only does not establish any obligation but is opposed to the principle of duty and to the morality of the will. The sole principle of morality consists in the independence from all material of the law (i.e., a desired object) and in the accompanying determination of choice by the mere form of giving universal law which a maxim must be capable of having. That independence, however, is freedom in the negative sense, while this intrinsic legislation [*Gesetzgebung*] of pure and thus practical reason is freedom in the positive sense. Therefore, the moral law expresses nothing else than the autonomy of pure practical reason, i.e., freedom. This autonomy of freedom is itself the formal condition of all maxims, under which alone they can all agree with the supreme practical law.

(1788: 33–4)

The feeling of respect reveals to the passive receiver of the law a self who is active and practical, a moral subject. The moral subject is a pure sovereign, unaffected in its legislative acts by the ends of sensibility. Moral freedom lies in the determination of respect as autonomy. The moral subject invents the law which it obeys. Freedom is the law which we prescribe to ourselves. The will is not merely subject to the law, obeying it out of interest – fear of punishment, desire for success or pathological love of the law, all incentives that make our relation to the law one of 'legality' or 'heteronomy' – it is only subject to the law if it invents the law, it is subject to the law *only because* it invents the law. This idea of sovereignty informs the pure concept of right which is the ethical and negative condition of modern politics (Kant, 1793 and 1795). Now, in terms of what I said above, this law of rights, if taken to its end as a principle, will be fated to become the very opposite of that which it intended. The opposite of rights is the state of nature, a state of violence (at worst a state of war) against which the concept of right was first forged. How does this inversion of moral intent take place in Kant?

The Kantian Idea of sovereignty is riven by an ambiguity that symptomatically organizes – in Freudian terms, represses and simultaneously reveals in displaced form – the contradiction of the principle of contradiction. On the one hand, Kant conceives of morality in terms of a pure moral will, what he calls a 'holy will'. Only the holy will is moral and it thereby serves as an ideal for rational sensible beings like ourselves. On the other hand, morality is to be found only in rational sensible beings, since morality can be understood in terms of 'respect' and 'duty' alone. Anything on the other side of the limit has no moral interest in the law, since the law does not interest it, rather it informs its very being. It is because a finite will is not holy, not sovereign, that it is 'interested' in the law, that is, that there is something like morality. The Kantian horizon of a holy will confuses the very limit (*Grenze*) between ethics and knowledge which the ethical Idea of a holy will is supposed to sustain. The contradiction confirms our earlier suggestion that it is ethical *not to pose a hard and fast limit between ethics and knowledge*, that to pose such a limit is in fact *unethical*. It suggests, in other words, that it is more ethical to think the 'between' between ethics and knowledge than to think ethics *tout court*.[11] An analysis of the practical will in the Kantian sense bears this out: ethics, to be ethical, must be contradictory and *aporetic*.

> A rational being belongs to the realm of ends as member [*Untertan*] when he gives universal laws in it while also subject to these laws. He belongs to it as sovereign [*Oberhaupt*] when he, as legislating, is subject to the will of no other. The rational being must regard himself always as legislative in a realm of ends possible through the freedom of the will, whether he belongs to it as member or as sovereign. He cannot maintain the latter position merely through the maxims of his will. ... If the maxims (of the rational agent's will) do not by their nature already necessarily conform to this objective principle of rational beings as universally lawgiving, the necessity of acting according to that principle is called practical constraint, i.e., duty. Duty pertains not to the sovereign in the realm of ends but rather to each member, and to each in the same degree.
>
> (Kant, 1785: 52)

The passage implies that the principle of republican sovereignty as an 'Idea' is itself self-limiting. First, no one can pretend to the position of the Sovereign since that position has – in Hegelian language – rights but no duties. Enjoying all the benefits of the social contract, the sovereign has at the same time no duties to others. This position of total narcissism should be considered, ultimately, as one of suicide. The very principle of the democratic 'separation' of powers emerges from this fact, although Kant only misrecognizes it symptomatically, in the contradictions that his discourse breeds, in order not to face up fully to the violence which freedom entails. The legislative is not simultaneously the executive because full sovereignty – what Rousseau in the *Social Contract* calls 'true democracy' in which the governed are also the governors (1762: III, Chapter IV) – would mean the end of the relation to the other. If one has no duties to others, then the social relation has come to an end. The logical and historical consequence is the non-recognition of the other (whether this be in the form of ignorance, forgetting or murder). *True democracy* is thus *the death of democracy*. Kant's Idea of Sovereignty both testifies to the possible terror of its direct application in determinant judgement and fails to see that those terrors still inform the very end of the Idea of sovereignty. Full sovereignty is nothing less than the arbitrariness of the monarchic despot.

The point is equally applicable to the holy will, reconfiguring and re-cognizing our fantasies of utopia and paradise as sites of absolute violence and death. To follow Derrida's 'Violence and metaphysics', peace would be 'absolute violence' (1967a: 171–2/116–17). In Kantian terms, the holy will, which has no consciousness of, nor interest in the law, but is its very embodiment, has no consciousness of the distinction between the universal and the particular, and, therefore, is a contradiction in terms, since it has no need to will. Outside time and space, it is the pure destruction of time and space. Willing is a mark of finitude upon which the very distinction between ethics and politics is possible and as a result of which this distinction must also collapse. A holy will is both a *despot* and is *perfect*. There is no choice here. The aporetic 'logic' with which we are here engaged exceeds human intention and will. Pure heteronomy in Kantian terms is nothing but pure autonomy, and inversely. The *horizon* of the holy will for rational sensible beings amounts to the same horizon as that in relation to which the Idea of the autonomous will was invented in the first place and against which it set itself – the realm of nature in which all act according to their will, what post-Renaissance thinking from Hobbes to Hegel calls 'a state of war'. Kant's description of humanity's asymptotic progress to the 'Highest Good' is at the same time an asymptotic regress to a pure realm of nature.[12]

Thus the application of the principle of non-contradiction to the realm of ethics, if a logic by which Kant actually seeks an exit out of the realm of nature, is one which, taken to its end, returns Kant squarely to it. In taking the transcendental distinction *between* ethics and knowledge to its end, in fixing the difference between faith and knowledge, ethics and politics, morality and legality as a *limit*, critique works contrary to the very limit which it wishes to lay down. This aporetic 'logic' into which the 'logics' of critique must be reinscribed implies several things.

First, the letter of the law must carry an unethical stamp in order not to arrive at its destination; that is, the Idea must be suspended to keep the 'promise' that it holds out but which it contradicts in thinking through this promise to its end. The promise of democracy should, first, be understood in this strictly *logical* sense. The logic of non-contradiction suppresses the very promise that it bears as the Idea of sovereignty; the (quasi-)logic of this logic retains the promise as a promise *so that* it remains a promise. In the very name of democracy one must suspend the Idea of autonomy. In other words, the explicit formulation of the *différance* of the Idea *as* a 'promise' re-cognizes that the very attempt to place the limit is the gesture by which the limit will go on to confuse the terms it served to separate out.

Second, for Derrida, the puncturing of the logic of the Idea cannot be reduced to a hyper-logic, a criticism of Derrida's quasi-transcendentals which we met in Rose's critique of deconstruction. It shows, rather, that the very *idea* of sovereignty at the basis of our democratic understanding of law and subjectivity, is itself a *violent decision* which excludes as much as it promises. This violence is to be recognized. The puncturing of the logic of the Idea in the Kantian sense both acknowledges the importance of the Idea and acknowledges the seriousness of its exclusions consequent upon the logic of its very promise. Both these recognitions are to be held together. For Derrida, this is an impossible logic and this impossibility is also what bears the promise. This contradictory impossibility is, to use Derrida's phrase of 'Before the Law', the 'sophistication of Kant' that the deconstruction of the Idea in the Kantian sense effects. Recognition both of the law of right and of the law of right's exclusions is impossible at one and the same time, thereby imploding the principle of contradiction which would allow a horizon or Idea to 'efface' time. The setting back of the Idea of a rational community onto its 'promise' neither denies, then, nor affirms the horizon of democracy unilaterally. The Derridean promise of democracy amounts to both the affirmation of the Idea and the acknowledgement of the violence of this very affirmation. In this sense, the promise is the affirmation both of the universality of the general will and of the singular which emerges in the necessary discrepancy between universal (holy) and particular (rational sensible) wills.

Third, the reinscription of the a priori concept of right into an aporetic logic (the memory of the promise of sovereignty and the mourning of this promise's exclusions) amounts to the recognition that *time is irreducible to the history of an idea or to a logic*. It is in this sense that the political implications of the deconstruction of horizon ensue from its reflections upon the relation between time and violence. Inversely, any thinking of time as that which will always resist and call forth logic necessarily engenders reflection upon the political. Aporetic responsibility is the recognition, in the political domain, of finitude.

Fourth, aporetic responsibility concerning the political therefore implies the reinvention of political categories according to the lesser violence. I said earlier that the limit between the finite and the infinite offers privileged access to thinking the political implications of continental philosophy. This reinvention starts, here, with Kant and with his ethical idea of democratic autonomy. Tracing through the relation between the aporias of this Idea and Kant's violent determination of the limit between the knowable and the unknowable as a 'natural' frontier, this reinvention concerns the transformation of the terms in which one thinks *both* the limit between the finite and the infinite *and* the categories themselves of the finite and the infinite on either side of the limit. This transformation amounts to a reorganization of the 'contradictions' of ethico-political thinking which ensue from the disavowal of time and of violence. The reorganization is made, therefore, in something like the name of lesser violence.

An Aporetic Understanding of Revolt

There is a famous conundrum in Kantian political philosophy which turns around the nature of the relation between the juridical concept of right and violence 'outside' the law. Kant argues in several of his political tracts that rebellious acts against the existing sovereign are unjust. The right to resistance is not a right, because it is self-contradictory and, therefore, immoral. This argument is, for many, *the* formulation of reformism, one which disavows violence. The problem of the last two centuries of non-reformist political thought has been that it has tended, in opposition to the non-recognition of violence, to *ontologize* violence by making it a *principle* itself of political action. The above deconstruction of the Idea in the Kantian sense in terms of an aporetic promise offers another direction, one which will be confirmed in our reading of the similarities and differences between Hegel and Derrida. The absoluteness of Kant's principle that rebellion is a priori unjust derives from the principle of contradiction informing the terms and logic of Kant's political vision. One has no right to rebel against an existing government, however unjust it is, because the gesture taken to its end as a principle would contradict itself. To make rebellion universal invalidates the very constitution which one is rebelling for. For Kant, accordingly, change can only take place slowly through the public domain of critical reason, a domain which, to be public, must hold no secrets ('Theory and practice', 1793: 82–5). Kant's argument repeats the logic of the Idea of freedom. It is a logic to which Kant returns *whenever* he is faced with the contradiction between law and history. Kantian philosophy is unable to develop the contradiction, because law and reason as universal subjects must lie outside the time of violence and the violence of time.

Hence the ambivalence of Kantian political philosophy. In the very name of less violence (the regulative Idea of freedom as a horizon to time and space), Kant ends up being violent by refusing a necessary relation between law and violence. For Derrida, this ambivalence is not to be resolved. It is to be thought *aporetically*. Hence, in the clearest terms possible, the political weight of Derrida's use of aporia. I have argued in this section that the Derridean quasi-notion of the promise of democracy, in suspending the Idea of freedom and sovereignty, *also* recognizes the violence that this Idea engenders in its very logic. In other words, as a philosophy of time, Derrida's thinking works between the universal and the singular, never happy with either, refusing the ontologization of both. To confirm the particularity of this thought – to confirm that it is a

thought, however 'restrictive', of political invention – we need now
to read Hegel's critique of Kant and his concomitant elaboration of
Sittlichkeit. For it is this critique which, by developing the limit of the
moral law into the law of contradiction, resists, but also sustains, the
modern violence of revolutionary politics.

Hegel's Critique of Kant

Hegel's major critique of the Kantian Idea of freedom is to be found in
the *Phenomenology of Spirit*, 'Spirit that is certain of itself. Morality
(*Moralität*)' (Hegel, 1807: 364–409, esp. 364–82). I shall move briefly to
that critique and to the early text of Hegel, the *Natural Law* essay
(1802/3), which unfolds what is suppressed by Kant's theory of morality.
Such criticisms are for the most part taken up by Hegel's last text, the
Philosophy of Right (1821b) which I shall return to at the end of this
chapter. I wish to keep to the early text, however – which precedes
the *Phenomenology of Spirit* – in order to show in the next section
how the critique of Kant takes Hegel to the development of 'absolute
ethical life'. Both our previous aporetic deconstruction of the Kantian Idea
and our subsequent development with Derrida's *Glas* of Hegel's reading
of the law in terms of *tragic form* gain pertinence in this context. The
law of tragic form recognizes, for Hegel, the violence of civil society;
Derrida will insist however in *Glas* that this law is aporetic and not
dialectical. A dialectical development of the Kantian limit is impossible in
its possibility – this aporia forms a radical 'limit' *prior* to the philosophies of both Kant and Hegel. Hegelian recognition ends up, consequently,
as misrecognition, engendering its own fate. With the recognition of the
logic of this fate, Hegel's phenomenological development of the aporia
of modern law is seen to engender its own violence in its very desire to
re-cognize the violence of civil society. A new non-Kantian limit thus
emerges between the philosophical and the political which redeploys
the last section's distinction between democratic form and the promise of
democracy.[13]

The Kantian 'Sollen', Phenomenology and Deconstruction

Kant represents, for Hegel, 'the moral world view'. This view expresses
a fundamental contradiction which ensues, in Hegelian terms, from the
lack of mediation (*Mitte*) between the universality of moral consciousness
and the particularity of nature (whether this nature be thought in terms
of one's own sensible inclination or of the external world). For lack of
mediation, the unity of the two is 'posited' in the form of God and/or
what Kant calls the 'Highest Good' (the unity of morality and sensibility).
Kant calls God an ethical 'postulate'; we know nothing about God and

yet we must assume, ethically, his existence in order to 'fill out' in concrete terms the abstract Idea of true moral consciousness. For Hegel, this postulate is a *Sollen* (it is a prescription which posits an ethical 'must') which legislates what should be, in misrecognition of what is. In other words, the Kantian postulate is a 'symptom' (in the Freudian sense) of the lack of mediation between the infinite and the finite. The Idea of the Highest Good is thus a prescriptive postulate which only mends the existing division between moral subjectivity and material objectivity through constraint (the constraint inherent to any prescriptive). Constraint engenders the fate of what it suppresses, following a logic of 'the return of the repressed' which we saw at work when deconstructing Kant's Idea of freedom in the last section.

The *Phenomenology of Spirit* (Hegel, 1807) traces these suppressions as the development of the misrecognitions forged between what consciousness intends and what is the 'actuality' of its intentions. The truth of Kantian morality is the 'beautiful soul' which can be characterized as retreating from the real world into the self for fear of self-contradiction, who refuses, in other words, to *take* risks. No more damning a judgement of Kant could be made. The Kantian moralist ends up a hypocrite, and finally a recluse, oscillating between a 'beyond' and a 'here and now', for fear of determination in the real world. The contradiction between morality and nature is followed, for Hegel, by two further contradictions. On the one hand, moral consciousness sees nature as perverting it; and yet, bound to duty, which calls for the realization of morality, this consciousness can only posit the unity of pure and individual consciousness in a 'beyond'. This beyond must be constantly deferred because moral consciousness is made up of the *struggle* between pure and individual consciousness. The postulate of the Holy Will amounts to a misrecognized symptom of the awareness that the end of morality would be the death of the moral subject. Morality must remain moral consciousness:

> Consciousness has . . . continually to be making progress in morality. But the consummation of this progress has to be projected onto a future infinitely remote; for if it actually came about, this would do away with the moral consciousness.
>
> (Hegel, 1807: 368)

Hegel's critique of Kant would seem remarkably close here to that of deconstruction, or rather deconstruction could be seen to be much more close to Hegel than is often maintained. And yet Hegel's criticisms of Kantian hypocrisy would seem the very type of accusation that is levelled by those of Hegelian inspiration *against* deconstruction (see Rose, 1993: 72–5). There is clearly a problem here, if Derrida *also* tends to stress the appropriative, interiorizing aspect of Hegelian thought. The relation of deconstruction to Hegel needs to be clarified.

The implications of *différance* – the end of *x* (the content, for example, of the Idea of autonomy or of the Highest Good) would be the end of *x* – are indeed close to those of Hegelian dialectics. Both Derrida's and Hegel's philosophies are concerned with the impossibility of logical thought as such and of the fateful (Hegel) or contaminating (Derrida) consequences of this impossibility. Both are philosophies of the 'history' of philosophy since they acknowledge, from within conceptuality, that the concept carries within itself the fate of the failure of conceptual logic to seize the world. To think a concept necessarily means to think its fate, its inscriptions. Since this fate ensues from the resistance of the world to human form (religion, a *Weltanschauung*, a political regime), both philosophies can be considered as descriptions of the 'economies' between law, its violence, the exclusions which violence engenders and the return of what is excluded. Both philosophies should, accordingly, be thought together, their differences articulated, not placed in opposition. By considering where Hegel's critique of Kant takes Hegel, I can begin to develop these differences.

Hegel's Re-cognition of the Kantian Suppression

For Hegel, Kantian morality forms a postulate of unity which symptomatically misrecognizes the contradiction informing its understanding of non-contradictory universality. The early *Natural Law* essay pushes this argument into a revealing critique of the *socio-political* determinations of Kantian thought. I recall that the Kantian realization of duty depends on the universalization of a maxim according to the form of law of natural causality (universality). The *Natural Law* essay argues, first, that the principle is tautologous and superfluous. As one of his examples of duty, Kant maintains in the *Critique of Practical Reason* that it is immoral to keep a deposit, the owner of which has died without leaving record of it, since it cannot hold as a universal practical law. Taking the maxim as a law that every man is allowed to deny that a deposit has been made when no one can prove the contrary (according, therefore, to the principle of non-contradiction), Kant declares that 'such a law would annihilate itself, because its result would be that no one would make a deposit' (1788: 27). Like our earlier example of the promise, the maxim destroys itself when suspended as a universal law. It cannot, therefore, be the determining ground of universal legislation. Hegel retorts: to make the respect of property a universal principle of practical legislation presupposes the form of property. What is of interest is not whether something can be universalized or not – a crude game of the faculty of the understanding with its love of order and universality – but whether one can say what the necessity of the form of property is, by 'developing' this necessity.

> Where is the contradiction if there were no deposits? The non-existence of deposits would contradict other specific things, just as the possibility of deposits fits together with other necessary specific things and thereby will itself be necessary. But other ends and material grounds are not to be invoked; it is the immediate form of the concept which is to settle the rightness of adopting either one specific matter or the other. For the form, however, one of the opposed specifics is just as valid as the other; each can be conceived a quality, and this conception can be expressed as law.... If the specification of property in general be posited, then we can construct the tautological statement: property is property and nothing else. And this tautological production is the legislation of this practical reason: property, if property *is*, must be property. But if we posit the opposite thing, negation of property, then the legislation of this same practical reason produces the tautology: non-property is non-property. ... The aim is precisely to prove, however, that property must be.
>
> (Hegel, 1802/3: 77–8)

Practical reason in the form of universalization *presupposes* property, rather than legislating whether property is ethical or not. In other words, it *hides* under the form of universality the presupposition of the form of property. The point is expanded a moment later by the now recognizable argument that the logic of universalization abolishes the very thing to be universalized by universalizing it. If all have property, nothing distinguishes the particular determination of property, since if all have property, there is no need of property and, therefore, the condition of practical legislation is abolished. The form of law, the law of universality, for Hegel as for Derrida, is unethical in its very pretention to ethics. And yet there is a difference. Before suggesting the nature of this difference, let me summarize the conclusions from Hegel's argument: the concept of property as a universal hides its own particularity and violence; property as a universal is a contradiction in terms since property as a specific thing cannot be generalized.

Unlike Marx (1843a), Hegel does not believe that private property can be abolished. He does believe, however, that ethical thinking, to deserve its name, should elaborate the violence particular to the concept of property. This is why Kantian universality for Hegel is 'formal' and why Kantian ethics ends up unethical. It is false, but, more importantly, here, it is not transparent. Hence its true hypocrisy. For Hegel, the moral world must *articulate* in *visible form* the necessary injustice of the universality of form. Hegel's critique of the formality of bourgeois law is well known. I have situated it in the context of Hegel's critique of Kantian morality to show both its origins and the difference with a Derridean type deconstruction of the Idea. For Hegel, the critique of the form of law shows that within the logic of the concept of universality hide relations particular to 'civil society', and this can be developed out. The illusion of freedom can be recognized *as* illusion. As the *System of Ethical Life* (1803) develops – an argument that Marx will make much use of in 'On The Jewish Question' (1843b) and the *Grundrisse* (1858: 'Forms which precede capitalist production', 471–513) – the absolute abstraction of the individual (legal 'personality') is posited with the abstraction of possession into property. To posit something in law is to abstract from its determinations so that it can be recognized as law, transcending time and space. Formal recognition in law, the very condition of property and rights, is necessarily, at one and the same time, 'misrecognition' of social individuality and singularity, 'nonfreedom' (Hegel, 1803: 125). Under democratic law power is not articulated, but hidden. Kantian morality is, for Hegel, as the ethic of the *Bürgerliche*, the 'life of the private individual' (1802/3: 114). It both promotes in the very name of its ideals the misrecognition of injustice and disavows its own acts of violence. As the two early essays on law (*Natural Law* and *System of Ethical Life*) argue at length, to universalize the ethic of morality across the social whole is to generalize a relation specific to a sphere of *legitimate* interests, the generalization of which is *not* legitimate. In opposition to Kant, Hegel wishes, then, to acknowledge the necessary injustices of formal law by restricting it within a more transparent articulation of law and violence.

I shall now develop this understanding of *Sittlichkeit*. What is already clear from my deconstruction of the Idea of morality and the above elaboration of Hegel's critique of this Idea is that, if initially similar in their logical implications, Derrida's understanding of the *aporetic* relation between universality and singularity cannot accept precisely Hegel's wish to bring injustice into the open. His distance from Hegel at this point – a distance which brings upon his philosophy the charge of a lack of *sociopolitical* content – resides in the 'irony' that Hegel's desire for visibility creates the very opposite of what it intends: continued invisibility and misrecognition. Derrida would undoubtedly add that it is therefore in the very name of visibility and transparency that one must remain, at times, a 'hypocrite'.

Contradiction, Aporia and the Fate of Law

Sittlichkeit, the Tragico-Phantasmatic and the Aporetic

In the *System of Ethical Life* Hegel writes:

> in ethical life [*Sittlichkeit*] the individual [*das Individuum*] exists
> in an eternal way; his empirical being and doing is something
> downright universal [*ein schlechthin allgemeines*]; for it is not
> his individual aspect which acts but the universal absolute spirit
> [*der allgemeine absolute Geist*] in him. . . . In so far as the ground
> of this singularity is thought, it is purely and simply the whole
> that is thought, and the individual does not know or imagine
> anything else. The empirical consciousness which is not ethical
> [*sittlich*] consists in inserting into the unity of the universal and
> the particular [*das Einssein des Allgemeinen und Besondern*],
> where the former is the ground, some other singularity between
> them as the ground. Here in ethical life, on the other hand,
> absolute identity, which previously was natural and something
> inner has emerged into consciousness.
>
> (1803: 53/143)

The passage comes from the third section of the work, 'Ethical Life', after
the development of the 'relative identity' between universality and individuality in Kantian formal law which was considered in my last section.
The passage forms part of the introduction to the development of the
people (*Volk*). The 'idea' of the *Volk qua* the absolute identity of the
universal and the particular forms Hegel's response to the Kantian (and
Fichtean) suppression of sensibility and conflict. The absolute identity of
the *Volk* is *not*, as many anti-Hegelians have however argued, a concept
of identity, violently subsuming the singular. This would be a philosophy
of constraint or 'relative identity' in Hegelian terms, exactly what the
development of the idea of the *Volk* re-cognizes as an illusion. *Volk* and
Sittlichkeit are, accordingly, names in Hegel's work to designate the recognition of what lies hidden under the formal universality of bourgeois
law. This, in at least three ways.

First, the *Volk* is a differentiated unity in which each part (*Stand*, estate)
recognizes the integrity and necessity of the others. If this is an old Platonic
dream of political wisdom – to invent a bond (*symploke*) which links
the various parts of the *polis* – there is a decisive difference. With the
emergence of modern subjectivity, the danger to politics is precisely
the generalization of the view of one *Stand* (the bourgeoisie) across the
social whole. As the previous section elaborated, this generalization occurs,
for Hegel, with the concept of right. At the same time as enshrining in

law the freedom of the subject (juridical universality), the concept covers over the accompanying difference between the universal (law) and the particular (subjectivity). Rooted in the form of property, this universality of rights should, for Hegel, remain particular to civil society (*bürgerliche Gesellschaft*). And yet, in modern society, the universality of right has become the dominant notion of the political as such. As a result: first, the inequality between estates (or now classes) is not given political form, that is, socio-political injustices are legally hidden. This makes the violence of the law all the more violent since the law now says that its subjects are free whatever the circumstances; by recognizing them formally, the law ratifies their concrete misrecognition. The illusion (*Schein*) of polit-ical equality opens up the unrecognized distinction between political equality and economic inequality. Second, the necessary conflict arising from this inequality as well as from the differentiation of organized human activity as such, cannot be acknowledged either. Third, violence is there-fore expelled as a non-civil phenomenon from the social whole. Since, with the development of the economy in modernity, civil society has monopolized the terms in which one thinks society as a whole, what is not civil (struggle, war) is not social. Violence is misrecognized by society by being placed at the limit of the individual's domain. For Hegel, the modern form of politics has in this sense brought politics to an end. It fails to recognize that struggle is inherent to human organization, and it refuses the need to recognize socio-economic inequality in political terms. Society becomes an 'inorganic' machine of exchange between empty individuals.

Hegel's response to modern society, in the *System of Ethical Life* and through the ideas of *Volk* and *Sittlichkeit*, is, in turn, threefold (1803: 145–65). First, the State at rest (the constitution) figures the individual integrity of each estate so that no one estate can dominate the social whole (as is the case when 'civil society' (*Gesellschaft*) is confused with 'political community' (*Gemeinschaft*)). Second, the integrity of each estate is not so absolute that there is no acknowledgement from one estate of the necessity of the other estates. The state constitution develops, in other words, a bond between separate parts that binds them *as* separate from each other. This 'as' articulates the relation of mutual recognition. The articulation acquires form as the *Volk*, the absolute identity of identity and difference. Third, the State in movement (the government) concretizes the movement of recognition. The recognition of the original violence of property and commerce that constitutes the non-violent life of civil society finds form in the need for the state to go to war with other states. In other words, the government intervenes in the securities of civil society, reminding this one part of the social whole, through war, that its needs and desires are contingent, predicated on war – that is, on the necessity of the military estate, the estate which embodies, precisely, violence.

This is Hegel's exposition of a differentiated state which recognizes injustice. I shall come back to it in further detail in a moment, for the whole problem in the Hegelian exposition of recognition is that the government's suppression of civil society can 'look like' an act of domination and constraint. We need to understand how this comes about to measure up to where Hegel's critique of formal democracy takes him.

From the *Natural Law* essay (1802/3) to the *Philosophy of Right* (1821b) Hegel is always trying to *figure* difference, give form to social differentiation, as if he could remarry the political forms of medieval social life and modern subjectivity (compare Marx, 1843a: 136). This gesture sums up the profound ambivalence of Hegel's project, an ambivalence which repeats, in a different mode, the very ambivalence of bourgeois right that Hegel's gesture is concerned to redress. On the one hand, he wants to give form to that which remains invisible under the formal equality of the concept of right; on the other hand, the form which he finds suppresses in turn both the concept of right and the field to which he wishes to restrict it (civil society). In the very attempt to restrict rights to their field, in order to give form to the multiplicity of life, Hegel restricts them totally. Hegel knows this, as I shall show, but, as I shall also show, he is unable to elaborate the reasons why, always deferring the problem until the next round of *Geist*.

What this deferment implies is that the figure of articulation – represented by the *Volk* as the constitution of the state – is a *limit* which is *unfigurable* as such. Although, as far as I know, this has never been properly commented upon, one of the major concerns of Derrida's text *Glas* (1974) lies in tracking this limit throughout Hegel's philosophy, showing, from within dialectic, that Hegel's differential identities are *phantasms*. Thus the Hegelian figure of absolute identity or differentiated unity – whatever its form, absolute *Geist* (philosophy), objective *Geist* (the state) or subjective *Geist* (religion) – is always redeveloped by *Glas* as the phantasmatic repression or disavowal of a limit that resists thought or feeling as such. For Rose, I recall, 'Hegel's philosophy has no social import, if the absolute [could] not be thought' (Rose, 1981: 41–2). For Derrida, this thought is impossible in its very possibility, hence the violence of its phantasy if it takes its desire for the development of the real. In Derrida's terms this means that Hegelian recognition follows a 'logic', that there is an essential limit to this logic and that, therefore, there is an essential limit to the *visibility* of society as a whole. This limit, prior to the Kantian limit, needs to be thought according to its radical alterity, not ontologized as that between the unknowable and the knowable. Otherwise, one's understanding of the 'real' repeats, although in much more complicated form, the Kantian disavowal of time. It is in other words, and despite itself, a logic of repression. I shall come to my examples later.

Hegel's attempt to seize this limit, developing it as the differentiated and articulated unity of the *Volk* takes him to the model of tragic form. Contra Hegel's desires, the limit of which I am speaking returns in this form as the aporia of articulation, it returns as the aporia of the 'as'. Hegel's insistent desire to figure this aporia *as* a dialectical contradiction between two laws leads, always, to one law of domination and death, that of executive government or of the military. This slippage occurs because Hegel cannot figure the desired unity except in terms of one side of the limit, since *the limit itself is unpresentable*. It is from this logic of the fate of Hegel's own exposition of recognition that an aporetic notion of law emerges which assumes Hegel's desire for justice without being reducible to the fate of his own articulations, that is, ultimately, without ontologizing recognition by placing the other in a logic of contradiction. This law is precisely that of the 'aporia of law' (Derrida, 1974: 340/244). The thinking of aporia represents a non-ontological reading of law and judgement. Contradictory, double, the aporia of law translates the dialectic of tragic form into what *Glas* calls the 'stricture' of law (see especially 1974: 205–6/145–7 and 330–40/237–44). Stricture is the aporetic 'movement' which necessarily restricts the desire to present the limit back to one of the poles of the opposition which the impossible limit precedes. This limit is thus not the Kantian limit between the finite and the infinite; it is the radical impossibility of *either* accepting the delimitation of the division (Kant) *or* presenting the unity of the terms divided (Hegel).

In this context, I suggest that it is in the aporia of law that we can see, for Derrida, the truth of modernity. This 'truth', which reconfigures the aporetic relation between the limit and political form, is one of invention and decision. If this relation is not recognized, invention becomes – as is the case with Hegel's *Philosophy of Right* – an ontological 'programme' of thought and practice. These points call for elaboration.

Life According to Hegel: Tragic Form

In the *Natural Law* essay (1802/3) Hegel develops the *Volk* as absolute ethical life according to the Kantian antinomies of freedom and necessity. He recasts the opposition as one between the 'organic' and the 'inorganic'. Absolute ethical life is the living articulation between freedom from needs and the mechanical nature of needs. The military estate embodies freedom as the infinite abstraction from determination. In risking death the soldier does not simply put at risk one thing against another (the economy of exchange particular to civil society), he risks all against nothing. Death is the condition of freedom; by risking it, one recognizes one's needs as mortal and contingent, that is as unnecessary. The domain of economic exchange is thereby perceived through the military estate as a non-natural domain. On the other hand, civil society is also the realm of necessity, the realm of multiple needs, consumption, property and rights. The military estate must acknowledge this sphere as the realm of necessity upon which it also depends for its own survival. One cannot wage war in abstraction from the economy, however much it also destroys this economy. Hegel considers the relation between the two spheres of freedom and necessity to be the double relation that constitutes the people. If either sphere becomes indifferent to the other, the 'life' of the *Volk* is lost. 'Life' in the Hegelian sense is therefore the maintenance of each estate in its proper sphere, the prevention of the bad infinity of formal law from dominating the social whole, and the simultaneous recognition that civil society must be allowed to flourish within its own bounds. Absolute life is set against the domination of civil society by government in Fichte and the domination of civil society over government in contract law. Regarding the first, Hegel constantly rebukes Fichte's notion of the general will, which, formed by the government and education, destroys the necessary independence of civil society from government as well as the freedom which it grants. Regarding the second, we are already familiar with the rebuke. The generalization of these very freedoms across the social whole leads to the destruction of the state upon which these freedoms depend in the first place. This constitutes the illness of 'modern times', the law of 'comedy' (1802/3: 107, 123). The law of Right has become the law of public and international law, as a result of which there is no struggle, no opposition between domains of the social whole. 'Comedy so separates the two zones of the ethical ... that in the one conflicts are ... shadows without substance and in the other the absolute is an illusion' (108). In modern, comic life the modality of contract thinking which Hegel wishes to be specific to commercial exchange, and kept to the sphere of civil society, has become 'the principle of ethical life as a whole' (123–4). The result is the formalism of social relations which misrecognizes both the conflict *within* social society and the military force upon which right is predicated. The state becomes a bureaucratic machine rather than a living organism in struggle.

The internal differences of a living organism must find form. Hegel describes the recognition of this conflict (its form) in the following terms:

> the unity which is the indifference of objects, and which cancels [*aufhebt*] them and encompasses them within itself, and that unity which is only formal indifference or the identity of the relation between subsisting realities must themselves just be as one. ... This means that the absolute ethical order must organize itself completely as shape, since relation is the abstraction of the aspect of shape. Through becoming wholly indifferent in the

shape, the relation does not lose its nature of relation. It remains
a relation of organic to inorganic life.

(Hegel, 1802/3: 98)

The above relation finds shape in tragic form. 'The absolute relation is
set forth in tragedy' (1802/3: 108). The drama to which Hegel alludes
is not *Antigone*, for reasons which will become transparent, but the final
part of Aeschylus' *Oresteia*, the *Eumenides*. In this tragedy it is the law
of needs that is recognized as necessary to the social whole and is recognized in its violence. Tragic form enacts the re-cognition that there are
two laws informing the life of the city, the organic and the inorganic, not
just one, as in modern politics (the law of needs and rights only). Tragedy
also reveals that the recognition of these two laws is nothing but the *law*
of both these laws. This 'third' law is the 'reflection' (recognition) of the
first law in the second and of the second in the first (123); it is, in other
words, the law of dialectical contradiction. The *polis* forms the conscious
articulation of dialectical contradiction. It is the unfolding of the logic of
contradiction in objective form.

> As a result of . . . conscious separation, each estate is done justice,
> and that alone which ought to be is brought into existence (the
> reality of ethical life as absolute indifference), and at the same
> time the reality of that indifference as real relation in persistent
> opposition so that the second is overcome by the first *and this
> compulsion itself is made identical and reconciled*. This recon-
> ciliation lies in the knowledge of necessity, and in the right which
> ethical life concedes to its organic nature, and to the subter-
> ranean powers by making over and sacrificing to them one part
> of itself. For the force of the sacrifice lies in facing and objecti-
> fying the involvement with the inorganic. This involvement is
> dissolved by being faced; the inorganic is separated and recog-
> nized for what it is, is itself taken into indifference while the
> living, by placing into the inorganic what it knows to be a part
> of itself and surrendering it to death, has all at once recognized
> the right of the inorganic and cleansed itself of it.
>
> (1802/3: 104, my emphasis [R.B.])

In the *Natural Law* essay the *Aufhebung* of bourgeois right develops
the recognition, within the limits of the social whole, of the 'rights' of
each estate to their own 'laws'. This recognition forms the 'relation'
of 'separation', that is, the conscious separation from oneself of one's
other and the situating of this other as one's other. Tragedy rehearses
over time the visible payment of dues to the other *as* one's other self.
Hegel continues:

The picture of this tragedy, defined more particularly for the ethical realm, is the issue of that litigation between the Eumenides (as powers of the law in the realm of difference) and Apollo (the god of indifferenced light) over Orestes, conducted before the organized ethical order, the people of Athens. In the human mode, Athens, as the Areopagus, puts equal votes in the urn for each litigant and recognizes their co-existence; though it does not thereby compose the conflict or settle the relation between the powers or their bearing on one another. But in the divine mode, as Athene, Athens wholly restores to the people the man [Orestes] who had been involved in difference by the god [Apollo] himself; and through the separation of the powers both of which had their interest in the criminal, it brings about a reconciliation in such a way that the Eumenides would be revered by this people as Divine powers, and would now have their place in the city, so that their savage nature would enjoy (from the altar erected to them in the city below) the sight of Athene enthroned on high on the Acropolis, and thereby be pacified.

(1802/3: 105)

As *Glas* will show with regard to *Antigone* (1974: 237–9/169–71), in this tragic scene of recognition, a series of oppositions and their mediation are brought to light which determine Hegel's understanding of the political as the subsumption of two laws into the one speculative law of recognition. Light is, first, set in opposition against dark, conscious against unconscious, indifference against difference. Light then subsumes this opposition. No longer *one* of its terms or laws, it becomes the law of both. These two moves – the determination of difference as opposition and the subsumption of the two terms of the opposition through the value of one of the initial terms – are, as *Glas* shall show, forced and phantasmatic. For Derrida, re-cognition is the Hegelian phantasy that the unconscious can be mastered, that the aporia of law can come before the light of contradiction. Let me develop this point slowly by first returning to the above opposition.

The undergods are granted a specific site in the city from which they can see, and be seen by, the *polis* as a whole. The mutual recognition of light and dark is figured, in turn, in the divine intuition of Athena seated on the Acropolis. Athena figures Athens' conscious recognition of itself as a *polis*. The gods of darkness can be visibly situated within the social whole because they are nothing but the other half of this whole, its other in opposition, recognized as such. This location of the other as one's other is what Hegel calls the 'reconciliation of fate' (Hegel, 1802/3: 104). The reconciliation of fate is the containment of the two laws of the social whole within the double law of contradiction, or rather, for Hegel, the necessary development of these two laws *as* the law of opposition and contradiction:

> *Tragedy* consists in this, that ethical nature segregates its organic nature (in order not to become embroiled in it), as a fate, and places it outside itself, and by acknowledging this fate in the struggle against it, ethical nature is reconciled with the divine being as the unity of both.
>
> (1802/3: 105)

The Reconciliation of Fate

In the *Spirit of Christianity and its Fate* (1798–9), a text which precedes the *Natural Law* essay (1802/3) and the *System of Ethical Life* (1803) by four years, Hegel sets out dialectical logic in the explicit terms of the 'reconciliation of fate'. I shall refer to it before passing to Hegel's reading of *Antigone* since it explicitly works through tragic experience as the law of contradiction which reconciles two opposing laws. Hence Derrida's long and patient analysis of this early text in the first part of *Glas* (1974).

In a trespass and its punishment both the law and the trespass remain as irreconcilable opposites (Hegel, 1798–9: 224–30). Penal law is a figure of contract law for Hegel. Its essence is that it can only unify conceptually and not in reality. Its truth is the actuality of opposition. This actuality is the fate of rights. In this context we can retrospectively locate my use of the term 'fate' in Chapter 1. The term was borrowed from Hegel to designate that the failure/self-contradiction of any principle engenders (the) history (of that principle) and its 'collision' with other failures. For Hegel, by trespassing the right of another, an individual has forfeited the same right. In the sphere of rights, law is only law through its confirmation in punishment and is opposed to the individual from the start. Crime is a necessary consequence of right, and right must have satisfaction through punishment if it is to remain right. 'Right', 'might' and 'crime' are inextricably interlinked (compare Derrida on Lévi-Strauss in Chapter 1). The opposition between law and the individual is inflexible and is constantly reopened, since punishment constitutes the constant repetition of the non-identity between universal and particular. 'Law and punishment cannot be reconciled' in the sphere of rights, 'but they can be sublated if fate can be reconciled' (1798–9: 228). Hegel now proceeds to this logic of reconciliation. As we shall shortly see, tragedy delivers this logic as the law of tragedy. In the punishment of a man, the law precedes the act. In the notion of a fate the act does not follow the law, it *produces* the law. It is an act which turns life into the perpetrator's enemy. In its inverted form, death, life becomes the enemy:

Fate is here just the enemy, and man stands over against it as a power fighting against it. ... Only through the departure from that united life which is neither regulated by law nor at variance with law, only through the killing (*Töten*) of life is something alien produced. Destruction of life is not the nullification of life, but its diremption and the destruction consists in its transformation into an enemy. It is immortal, and, if slain, it appears as life's terrifying ghost, which vindicates its branches and lets loose its Eumenides. The illusion of trespass, its belief that it destroys the other's life and thinks itself enlarged thereby, is dissipated by the fact that the disembodied spirit of the injured life comes on the scene against the trespass. ... It is the deed itself [of the trespasser] which has created a law whose domination now comes on the scene; this law is the unification in the concept of the equality between the injured, apparently alien, life and the trespasser's own forfeited life. It is now for the first time that the injured life appears as a hostile power against the trespasser and maltreats him as he has maltreated the other. Hence punishment as fate is the equal reaction of the trespasser's own deed, of a power which he himself has armed, of an enemy made an enemy by himself.

(1798–9: 229)

The law produced is neither the universal of legality or morality nor the individual of crime but the recognition of the relation between the deed and its consequences. Life in its murdered form returns as the ghost to haunt the murderer; the ghost encourages the murderer to recognize that it is his own life that he has violated. For Hegel, the ghost is the other recognized as the violation of oneself. If the hostile power is the power of life made hostile, the reconciliation amounts to the recognition that the hostile other is nothing but one's other self. The path of reconciliation is not opened up for Hegel by an external law which in its necessary constraint could never bring those opposed together except through force. The law of the 'causality of fate' is nothing but the individual's suffering and his or her re-cognition after the event, *through* the experience of suffering, that they have done wrong to life. 'The extent to which, in affliction, life is felt as an opposite is also the extent of the possibility of securing it again' (1798–9: 232). Crucial to this *non-juridical* notion of law *qua* the *phenomenological development of experience* is the recognition that the other is oneself; that is, that the other can be situated and is visible. For Hegel, this relation of law forms the law of all experience. Hegel then extends the notion of fate beyond penal law and calls it 'the guilt of innocence'. All action, principled and unprincipled, is guilty since it determines the indetermination of what Hegel calls 'life':

> Where life is injured, be it ever so rightly [*rechtlich*], even if no
> dissatisfaction is felt, there fate appears, and one may therefore
> say that 'never has innocence suffered, every suffering is guilt'.
>   (1798–99: 234)

The last line is spoken by Antigone in *Antigone*. Any analysis of the
drama therefore concerns the radicality of fate and law. What predomi-
nates in Hegel's analyses of fate is the separation of life into self and
other. It is through the determination of this separation *as* an opposition
that the separation can be developed in terms of recognition or reconciliation. *Antigone* prolongs this dialectical analysis of life, and undoes it.

'Antigone', the Aporia of Law and the 'Fates' of Modernity

The reading of *Antigone* shows that Hegel's desire to articulate the organic
with the inorganic suppresses an aporia. This aporia *prevents* the development of recognition by blocking the act of separation described above
and, therefore, the recognition of the other as one's other. If this aporia
is what interests *Glas* (1974), it is because the aporia reveals that the
unity of the relation of recognition (the identity of identity and difference) is *unpresentable*. Let us be very clear here. The *limen* of the
absolute relation is not beyond presentation, another sublime unknowable. 'Kant' is not the truth of 'Hegel'. Rather the relation can only be
mispresented in being presented. Recognition is only possible *as* misrecognition. The logic of recognition restricts itself to an 'economy' of
misrecognitions. Now, it is due to this economy of the logic of recognition that the relation is *only* ever presentable as death. This, in turn,
explains why Hegel's wish to read an aporia as a contradiction transforms his attempt to reconcile the world of rights with that of violence
and death into a philosophy *of* death in which the god of indifferenced
light (Apollo or the military class) subsumes the rest of the social whole.
And, finally, this is why Hegel can only ever figure the relation between
the organic and the inorganic as an *oscillation* between the domination
of one term over the other. The mediation between the organic and the
inorganic, their *Mitte*, is unrecognizable, incomprehensible. Athena is
a phantasm.

Hegel's constant hesitations regarding the figure of the *Volk* stem from
the following awareness: light can only articulate the relation of light and
dark if it determines itself as *one* of the two terms of the relation, thereby
losing the relation *by* attempting to recognize it. The point duly complicates Hegel's attempt to sublate the Kantian limit between the infinite and
the finite. This limit 'returns' in Hegel as the slippage from the figure of
the whole to the military estate or government figuring the whole. The
'totalitarian' fate of Hegel's philosophy stems from this *necessary* slippage

from recognition to misrecognition. Much recent French philosophy is, I believe, inscribed within this fate; the merit of Derrida's *Glas* is to have taken a distance from this inscription, and thought the law of this fate through. Hence *Glas* is not just a deconstruction of Hegel's philosophy. Through this deconstruction Derrida is at the same time developing a philosophical account of the 'fates' of 'modernity'. This account returns constantly to the way in which the aporia of time is determined and suppressed and how this suppression allows for the greater violence.

Hegel's reading comes in the middle section of the first part of the *Phenomenology*'s chapter on *Spirit*, 'The true spirit. *Sittlichkeit*' and is entitled 'Ethical action. Human and divine knowledge. Guilt and fate' (1807: 266–94, esp. 279–90).[14] Hegel's analysis of Greek Tragedy is set by the time of the *Phenomenology of Spirit* in ethical immediacy; that is, prior to the separation between the substance of the community and subjectivity. Hence, Hegel's reading precedes the development of modern subjectivity (legal formality and subjective morality). Kant (and Fichte) are *aufgehoben* by the logic of Greek tragedy in the early writings, but they follow the destruction of ethical life in the later writings. Despite this later restriction of tragic form to premodern social organization, the logic of recognition informing Hegel's argument never changes, nor does his tragic understanding of law as the experience of law as double. The persistence of this 'logic' is what encourages *Glas* to generalize Hegel's reflections on *Sittlichkeit* in his reading of *Antigone* across different legal forms. For some critics this is precisely where *Glas* is too systematic, illegitimately bringing together texts from different periods, and with important redistributions of the 'same' material, as part of the same corpus. My concluding comments on the *Philosophy of Right* (1821b) could be criticized in the same vein, paying little articulated attention to the important differences between that text and the *Phenomenology of Spirit*. For Derrida – and as I have noted this chapter remains within the terms of deconstruction in order to develop the force of the 'promise' in the context of modernity – the criticism can only have local effects *as long as* the overall logic informing Hegel's understanding of the relation between time and social organization remains the same – shifts notwithstanding. This is, precisely, *Glas*'s major contention.

In immediate ethical life, Antigone's duty to bury her brother (Polyneices) conflicts with her duty to the state to leave her brother unburied since he attempted to overthrow it believing he had right to succession. These two duties, caught in a web of family and state relations that well exceed the drama of Sophocles' play, are represented initially by Hegel as two different laws: the one divine (the Penates), the other human (that of the *polis* represented by Creon). The divine law is the recognition of the singular – Polyneices is not only of the family, he cannot be substituted for another (neither husband nor son, but brother). The human law is that of the necessity of the universal; all families are subordinate to the will of the *polis* concerning public affairs. Hegel argues that at the beginning of the drama each law stands in opposition to the other in the form of the opposition between the characters of Antigone and Creon. The movement which Antigone's decision to bury her brother brings about reveals during the drama that the truth of each law is the other. The characters' suffering and experience, that is, the *time* of the conflict, brings about the law of both laws as the mediation *between* the two. Hegelian recognition is the *forming* of time in relation to the human. It is in this sense 'tragic form'. The movement of the conflict as a whole does not subsume the singular under the universal, it articulates it as a relation of identity and difference, which relation constitutes the 'time and space' of the tragedy. Thus, the precondition of tragic recognition is that each law comes to recognize the other as its other. For this to be possible – following the logic of the reconciliation of fate above – each law must assume a separated form. Even if the truth of this form is its mediation with its other, this is only possible if each comes to recognize its other as its other *in* its separation from itself. It is this separation which Hegel acknowledges as impossible in *Antigone*. Hence *Glas*'s emphasis on this moment in the Hegelian corpus.

Antigone's burial of her brother brings to light both the law of the divine and the awareness that public law is as necessary as divine law, that singularity and universality are two necessary parts of the whole. The drama 'figures' through the characters of Antigone and Creon both the guilt of innocence of each law and the appeasement of such guilt in the recognition that each law passes into its other.[15]

> The movement of the ethical powers against each other and of the individualities calling them into life and action have attained their true end only in so far as both sides suffer the same destruction. For neither power has any advantage over the other that would make it a more essential moment of the substance. The equal essentiality of both and their indifferent existence alongside each other means that they are without a self. In the *deed* they exist as beings with a self, but with a diverse self; and this contradicts the unity of the self, and constitutes their unrighteousness and necessary destruction. . . . The one character like the other is split up into a conscious and an unconscious part; and since each calls forth this opposition and its not-knowing is, through the deed, its own affair, each is responsible for the guilt which destroys it. The victory of one power and its character, and the defeat of the other, would thus be only the part and the incomplete work which irresistibly advances to the equi-

librium of the two. Only in the downfall of both sides alike is
absolute right accomplished.

(Hegel, 1807: 285)

The inseparability of human and divine law marks the recognition on the
part of each law that the other has a place in life and that ignorance of
the place of the other law or the excessive independence of one law from
the other *engenders the destruction of the ethical whole*. The tragedy of
Antigone re-marks this destruction as the recognition of the necessity
of the two laws. In the *Natural Law* essay either the dominance of public
law over civil society or that of civil society over public law spelled disaster
for ethical life. Absolute ethical life was Hegel's answer to the lack of
recognition between the law of violence and that of rights. The logic is
the same in the two texts. This logic is cast in terms of light and dark.
In both the early and later writings, Hegel's desire remains constant: it is
the 'bringing to light of the unconscious'; *Geist* is the 'teleology of
consciousness' (Derrida, 1974: 241/172). In the passing over of each law
into its other, light prevails over dark. For Hegel, this passage is phenomenological necessity, time in form. For Derrida it is an ontological
decision, necessary (one must judge), but contingent (judgements fail) –
compare *Glas* on the Hegelian ontologization of fire *qua* the suppression
of the gift of time (1974: 330–8/237–42). If visibility is one of the
terms of the opposition, its values cannot be used to conceive of the relation between the two terms. That we dispose of no term outside the
binary 'visibility/invisibility' to express what precedes and blocks the possibility of the opposition is, according to Derrida, precisely the promise
of impossibility. To think this impossibility therefore puts in question
the very limits of the Hegelian law of recognition, since its logic depends
on the *visibility* of separation and difference. Recognition ends up as
misrecognition in its very desire to recognize. Transparency is blindness.
Hegel acknowledges that the opposition between universal and singular
is not quite an opposition in the following passage, one around which
Glas understandably congregates its own analyses of 'stricture' throughout
the Hegelian corpus.

Human law in its universal existence is the community, in its
activity in general is the manhood of the community, in its real
and effective activity is the government. It is, *moves*, and *maintains* itself by consuming and absorbing into itself the separatism
of the Penates, or the separation into independent families
presided over by womankind, and by keeping them dissolved in
the fluid continuity of its own nature. But the Family is, at the
same time, in general its element, the individual consciousness
the basis of its general activity. Since the community only gets

an existence through its interference with the happiness of the Family, and by dissolving individual self-consciousness into the universal, it creates for itself in what it suppresses and what is at the same time essential to it an internal enemy – womankind in general. Womankind – the everlasting irony of the community – changes by intrigue the universal end of government into a private end. . . . The community, however, can only maintain itself by suppressing this spirit of individualism [particular to the law of the Family], and, because it is an essential moment, all the same creates it and, moreover, creates it by its repressive attitude towards it as a hostile principle.

(Hegel, 1807: 288)

For Derrida (1974: 262–3/188) the law of logic and the logic of law burst apart in the laughter of womankind. Since the opposition of singularity and universality, conscious and unconscious, light and dark includes that between man and woman in Hegel, this burst of laughter could be considered as the return of the other of ontology, something like the 'repressed truth' of the law of contradiction.[16] Now, we know from our deconstruction of the Idea in the Kantian sense and from Hegel's critique of Kantian morality that *différance* comes remarkably close to Hegelian dialectics when showing that the law of any principle (and therefore any social sphere), taken to its end, equals death. The *Natural Law* essay argued, for example, that conflict was essential to *Sittlichkeit*. As the above passage indicates, however, this also means, contra the tragic logic of *Sittlichkeit*, that the law of each sphere cannot be fully separated out and made visible without repeating this death. Social life is conflictual because its very possibility makes it impossible. For the other of ontology to be recognized, it must not be recognized. This is what an 'economy' of misrecognition implies. One must argue with Hegel against Hegel.

Before commenting further upon the above passage, let us note that Derrida finds Hegel saying the same thing in the Jena version of the struggle for recognition in the *Phenomenology of Spirit* (1807) which concerns the dialectic of two singularities rather than the pitching of singularity against universality (1974: 190–2/135–7). For a singularity to be recognized it must risk its life in combat with another. If, however, the other, the very condition of recognition, is killed, then recognition takes place at the very moment that it cannot take place, since the other's death abolishes the condition at the same time. The truth of contradiction is aporia, just as the above description of the relation between the Family and the Polis is aporetic and not contradictory. Derrida writes:

To posit oneself (*sich setzen*) as consciousness supposes exposure to death, engagement, pawning, putting in play or at pawn (*en gage*). 'When I go for his death, I expose myself to death (*setze ich mich selbst dem Tode aus*), I put in play my own proper life (*wage ich mein eignes Leben*).' This putting (in play, at pawn) must, as every investment, amortize itself and produce a profit; it works at my recognition by/through the other, at the posit(ion)ing of my living consciousness, my living freedom, my living mastery. Now death being in the program, since I must *actually* risk it, I can always lose the profit of the operation: if I die, but just as well if I live. Life cannot stay in the incessant imminence of death. So I lose every time, with every blow, with every throw (*à tous les coups*). The supreme contradiction that Hegel marks with less circumscription than he will in the *Phenomenology*.

(1974: 195/139)

He continues:

To recognize, with a light-hearted cruelty, with all the enjoyment possible, that nothing of all this is in effect viable, that all this will end in a very bad way, and that yet, on the cutting edge of this blade (*sur le fil coupant de cette lame*), more fleeting and thinner than any thing, a *limit* [my emphasis – R.B.] so taut in its inexistence that *no dialectical concept can grasp or master or state it, a desire stirs itself* [my emphasis – R.B.]. Dances, loses its name. A desire and a pleasure that have no sense. No philosopheme is attired or prepared to make its bed there. Above all not that of desire, of pleasure, or a sense in the Hegelian onto-logic. Nor, besides, is any concept. What here must be put into play without amortization is the concept that wants to seize on something. There is on this edge (*fil*), on this blade, the instant before the fall or the cut (*coupe*), *no philosophical statement possible that does not lose what it tries to retain and that does lose it precisely by retaining it*. Nothing else to say about this than what is said about it at Jena. The blow (*coup*) is the fatal contradiction of a suicide.

(ibid.)

Derrida's attention to the aporetic nature of recognition in the Jena writings confirms our path through the aporia of absolute ethical life. Death does not resolve the contradiction of recognition; it highlights the fact that: '*Aufhebung* is ... the contradiction of the contradiction and of the non-contradiction. Unity and contradiction come to the same thing' (ibid.). Thus death constitutes a necessary condition of freedom, forming a necessary passage to absolute ethical life as a unity, because it is a way of *disavowing* the impossibility of the figure of unity. In other words, if the articulation in Hegel of death as war attempts to recognize the violence which founds the 'innocence' of civil society, revealing the 'guilt' of this innocence, this articulation is at the same time a flight from thinking this violence through, by placing it *exclusively* in the sphere of death and the military estate. The law of contradiction 'acts out' (in the Freudian sense) the misrecognition of aporia. This argument runs throughout *Glas* in its attention to the impossible limit of unity.

First, absolute identity is a limit that resists conceptual seizure in the very move of the concept to grasp this limit. Second, the presentation of contradiction is impossible because the contradiction is not a contradiction. The truth of the law is not simply its other; the whole truth cannot simply be the *fate* of each law *in* the other. Rather, each law is dependent upon its other to be the law that it is in the first place; and; in being the law that it is, it *simultaneously* creates the other law. Consequently, the more the law is what it wishes to be, the less it is what it is. This law of law became apparent in our deconstruction of the Kantian Idea of freedom. Despite the fact that Hegel's critique of Kant seemed to anticipate Derrida's nervousness with the Idea in the Kantian sense, we must conclude here that the law ends up applying as much to Hegel's *Aufhebung* of the Kantian limit as it does to this limit. This is because Hegel's critique of Kantian *Kritik* remains an ontology, that is, here, a *logic* of *law*. The distinction is that between *différance* and contradiction. The latter leads to the desire for presentation (the absolute is thus another horizon, another messianist promise), the former redraws the Kantian *Grenze* as a limit which informs and derails this very desire.

In *Antigone*, for example, the more the *polis* (universal government) suppresses the singular (the family), the more it creates the singular. Hegel shows that there can be no appeasement of fate, that is, no explicit recognition between the two antagonistic laws of public and private, universal and singular, organic and inorganic. For these two laws cannot be separated out for the one to return *as* the other's ghost. The ghost that haunts the contradiction is the inability for the ghost to be recognized as such. This ghost is, for Derrida, the 'eternal irony' of the law of law. It is eternal in the sense that it *gives* time its *infinity*. I should recall here the argument of 'Before the law': the singular is the excess of any law's attempt to 'mop up' empirical sensibility. This singularity is only singular in being barred entrance to the law; for the law constitutes the fate of all institutions and all recognition in law. With regard to Hegel, this means that the law is not the movement of dialectic but the aporia of dialectic. Opposition is striction and contradiction is aporia. The unity of identity and difference *qua* the law of logic and the logic of law constitutes the misrecognition of aporia. This misrecognition haunts *Geist* empirically as the inability on Hegel's part to bring equilibrium to the relation of identity and difference. The limit is ungraspable and therefore one oscillates on either side of it – either the organic or the inorganic but never the two together *except* as contradiction. By refusing to articulate this law, Hegel suppresses aporia by developing the *unknown as* the phenomenology of *Geist*.

The Aporia of Law and the Irreducibility of Time

As *Glas* is always suggesting, this suppression of aporia is one with Hegel's determination of difference as opposition and with his determination of the limit as a relation. Each move on Hegel's part suppresses the event of time (Derrida 1974: 330–8/237–44). Hegel's philosophy of history and history of philosophy reduce history to logic; it is not a historical development of philosophical logic. This is an extraordinary, but necessary irony, the ironic fate of any political ontology. Just as Kant's principle of contradiction effaced the time of violence and the violence of time in the ethico-political domain, so Hegelian logic, the very logic *of* contradiction, ends up *also* disavowing time. The aporetic fate of Hegel's notion of the 'causality of fate' points to the persistent excess of time over Hegel's ontology of history. This excess is the very aporia of time which I located in Derrida's reading of Aristotle in 'Ousia and gramme' in Chapter 1 and which I will readdress – pursuing the implications of this chapter – in Chapter 3. This excess 'is' the 'promise'. The promise 'emerges' out of the self-restriction of all logic. Hegel wished to develop the limit in Kant as contradiction. In his rereading of Hegel's reading of *Antigone* Derrida shows that such a development is necessarily aporetic. *The aporia of dialectic 'is' the aporia of time.* At one and the same time the law is universalizing and it creates the singular which resists the universal. If Kant attempted in vain to be rid of this 'at one and the same time' according to the principle of contradiction in order to set up a universal ethics, Hegel's development of the Kantian repression of contradiction leads to the suppression of time under the logic of dialectic. The suppression leads to recognition as misrecognition. The 'truth' of this misrecognition is time, the singular.

Thus Hegel's reorganization of the contradictions and injustices hidden under the Kantian and Enlightenment understanding of freedom and political community leads in turn to their misrecognition. We can now see that this is due to two inextricably linked reasons. First, to determine difference in the form of opposition and contradiction means that the reorganization of the relation between violence and law ends up hiding violence by giving it, precisely, a site. Invisible, violence is misrecognized: visible, violence is misrecognized. One is always within an economy of violence, for the aporia of time is irreducible. Hence the Derridean distinction between the remainder and the concept is not the withdrawal of the political but the attempt to refine the way in which we reorganize the political bond so that it is *not* given a site, so that as complex a differential bond as possible can emerge. Such a refinement is democratic in a non-Kantian sense since it recognizes that the political community is only possible through struggle and exclusion and that in this sense it is always to be made and unmade. Second, the articulation of this recognition calls for a radical thinking of time since the determination of difference as opposition suppresses the recognition of the aporia of time. It is through disavowing temporality that Hegel ends up determining the logic of recognition. Thus to go through the experience of the aporia of time, letting it inform one's judgements and inventions implies recognizing – through, but beyond the Hegelian logic of recognition – that one will always be surprised, that the other will never be quite there where and when one expects. This surprise is what democratic politics is all about.

Modern Political Fate and the Suppression of the Event of Time

In the context of the above, let me conclude this chapter's principal argument by giving an example, from Hegel's last work, the *Philosophy of Right* (1821b), of the way in which Hegel's suppression of aporia has major consequences concerning the very dynamic and sites of recognition. The example is by no means innocent (hence my choice of this work to conclude), confirming the extent to which the ontologization of recognition has structured, in the last century, non-liberal responses to liberal theories of democracy. It will thereby also confirm the concluding movement of this chapter: the Derridean promise of democracy gets behind the major axis of modernity, reorganizing our relations to the contradictions of democratic law *without* ontologizing these relations.

Like the much earlier essay the *System of Ethical Life* (1803), Hegel's *Philosophy of Right* develops the idea of the state as the 'organic' self-reflection of its parts. The realm of finite need must be recognized in its contingency for the *Volk* as a whole to be rationally articulated or 'absolutely necessary'. Civil society must recognize itself and be recognized in the universal class of the 'civil servants' (§297f.). Government mediates this 'divine' intuition of the social whole by espying and controlling the *necessary* injustices which occur through the accumulation of surplus value within the sphere, or law, of civil society. Since need is accidental, infinite and self-differentiating (§185), the more complex civil society becomes, the more the division of labour intensifies the disproportion between the enjoyment of need in its own right – the civil law of property in contrast to the law of officialdom – and want or dependence. As Hegel himself notes (§§243–4), this process is infinite since the material to meet the needs of the dependent is already the property of others upon which the division of labour is predicated in the first place, and by which civil society generates its wealth. Hegel sees no answer to this paradox. As a result of this dependence, the needy, who are without rights since they are without property, do not form part of civil society. The more one attempts to regulate dependence, the more dependence grows (§245). If the state resorts to welfare, individuals never gain the self-respect and sense of independence particular to civil society in its distinction from the sphere of the family. The state is thus lost in its very attempt to regain itself. If the state attempts to employ the needy, production soars and the disproportion between luxury and poverty is intensified with the reproduction of surplus value and the lack of a proportionate number of consumers to appropriate it.

On either account the state is eclipsed *as* it attempts to recognize its parts. The more it attempts to be rational, the more it is irrational. Hegel adds in an interesting if evasive comment that 'the inner dialectic of civil society thus drives it beyond its own limits ... to seek markets beyond its own lands' (§246). Colonialism and war are dialectical developments of the 'inner dialectic' of civil society. Later, in §324 and its addition, when discussing international relations, Hegel repeats the point made in the *Natural Law* essay that the 'ethical moment' of war, in which the 'absolute' nation states become contingent in facing each other as particulars, is a consequence of the necessity of dissolving the finitude of need. He concludes the work with the well-known argument that the absolute right of the struggle between states is the tribunal of world history or 'absolute Spirit'.

Hegel calls those who necessarily drop out of the law of civil society 'the rebellious rabble' (*ein Pöbbel*) who recognize 'no law but their own' and have nothing but a 'negative outlook' on social life (§244). Hegel's comment is surprising given his awareness of the necessity of injustice and his wish, contra Kant's understanding of violence, to recognize it. And yet the whole argument of the second part of this chapter shows the reasons for Hegel's precipitate judgement – important differences between the early texts, the *Phenomenology of Spirit* (1807) and the *Philosophy of Right* (1821b) notwithstanding. For Hegel's inscription of law and time within the logic of contradiction ends up *repeating* the necessary misrecognition of the needy by both civil society and the government. This misrecognition resides in his very appellation of them as '*ein Pöbbel*'. The diaphanous law of contradiction – the conscious recognition of the 'unconscious' law of needs – forces Hegel *not* to see this stateless pocket within the state *as* an essential contingency of all states. The aporetic impossibility of rationalizing the 'empirical' infinity of need is hidden through the misrecognition of the state-less as 'a rabble'. This dialectical misrecognition is then corroborated in Hegel's later comments on colonialism and war. Hegel has argued that the recognition of the finitude of need within the whole can only be recognized as necessary within the development of the rational idea of the state. His comments show, however, that the turning of nation state to its others is not in the least rational ('re-cognizant'), but is predicated upon the fundamental irrationality of the economy, upon its essential inability to be opposed to the universal of the civil servants and the military. Colonialism is based on the unrecognized naturality of empirical need. This need engenders the 'infinity' of injustice, territorial expansion and conquest. Hegel describes the advent of war as if it happened the other way around. His desire to think of the *Volk* as unified, to think of history as logical (the law of international contradiction, the *Weltgeist*) and to think of violence as occurring *at the limits* of a state's 'own lands' leads to the misrecognition of violence. For violence is repressed precisely by being *placed* in a site. *Visibility ends up being blind.*

The *Philosophy of Right* is undoubtedly a more conservative text than Hegel's early writings since the younger Hegel could not have placed conflict outside the space of the state (compare Caygill, 1994). That it is more conservative should not deter us, however, from making the more general point that embraces all of Hegel's work, accounting for its ambivalence and hesitations concerning the figure of the *Volk*: the dynamic of recognition ends up being blind because it is unable to see beyond the law of visibility, that is, law as contradiction.

That said, to re-recognize this law as the law of aporia should deter us from ontologizing in turn what is excluded by Hegel. Ontologization is the fate of the *Pöbbel* in the hands of Marx. The rebellious rabble becomes the international proletariat opposed to capitalist imperialism. Marx is certainly right in the *Critique of Hegel's Doctrine of the State* to criticize Hegel for deriving the institutions of the social whole from a presupposed idea (1843a: 60–5, 99–100). But he gives the wrong reasons when he argues for the reversal of Hegelian idealism and for the practical and revolutionary development of the material existence of the people (1843a: 87, 118). To argue that the state's incarnation is the organic principle of the people repeats Hegel's logic, at the very moment that Marx wishes to distinguish himself from Hegel. The problem in Hegel is not the *idea* of the idea; the problem is the *logic* of this idea. This logic, the law of contradiction, is repeated in Marx's materialism, turning his thinking of 'matter' into a logical idea. Thus, like Hegel, Marx *also* reduces time to a philosophy of history. His very attempt to go beyond philosophy, plunging it into the matter of socio-technical history, remains metaphysical when he inscribes his thinking of time and practice within the Hegelian logic of contradiction.[17] The most important sign of this inscription is, paradoxically, Marx's very *ontologization* of that which Hegel's ontology represses; the Hegelian 'rabble' becomes the proletariat (compare 1843c: 245–7). But this is not paradoxical if one considers what has happened according to Derrida's thinking of aporia.

Rather than dwelling with the aporia of need, Marx effaces the aporia by positing the remainder of the difference between particularity and universality *as* the universal class of the proletariat. Marx therefore develops the aporetic 'limit' as a sublatable opposition between the bourgeoisie and the proletariat. The gesture is Hegelian, even if Marx simultaneously simplifies Hegel's idea of an absolute state by 'positing' the social universality of one class. Marx's reduction of the aporia of need prolongs and simplifies Hegel by making unrecognized violence into an ontological principle of class struggle. The modern period of revolutionary politics which justifies political violence in the name of a social subject ensues.

Derrida's thinking of aporia must be placed in the context of the preceding comments on the late Hegel and the early Marx as well as in the context of our previous comments on Kant's violent refusal of political violence. Considering law as aporia and aporia as law acknowledges the inescapability of violence, but it refuses the dialectical development of law and violence (Hegel contra Kant) just as it refuses the move to ontologize in turn the violence that is misrecognized by this development (Marx contra Hegel). Thus thinking through the aporia of law amounts to a defence of institutional inscription 'at the same time' as it defends the infinity of singular resistances to this inscription. The 'logic' of this double, contradictory responsibility is impossible. To recognize the stricture of Hegelian recognition is thus to place philosophy in an aporetic relation to modern political thought, action and institution, one which transforms the 'fates' of modernity.

We live today in a world which is increasingly violent, less and less politicized. It would be foolish not to see in this 'depoliticization' a sign of an end to political ontology, at least. It would also be foolish, however, either to bemoan the end of the modern concept of the state or to affirm its reorganization in the present supra-national status of what modernity called 'civil society', that is, today, the international economic systems. If one therefore wishes to rearticulate this depoliticization, without repeating the fates of modernity, an aporetic invention of politics is called for. It is in this sense that this chapter has argued for the radicality of Derrida's notion of the 'promise of democracy'.

One Final Hesitation

At the end of my introduction to this chapter, I noted a hesitation with Derrida's rereading of Hegel and Kant. It is appropriate to end this chapter with this hesitation, given its immediate concern with the relation between the aporia of time and material inscription (what is sometimes still called, wrongly, I believe, the 'socio-historical'). The supra-national status of the present world economy makes the sovereignty of the nation state an unsophisticated principle of organization. Throughout this chapter I have

argued that we need, nevertheless, to look at why the concept of democratic sovereignty is unmade by historical actuality. For without
philosophical articulation of the reasons, political imagination in the next
century will be limited; there will be little invention in the domain of the
political. Indeed, this domain may well collapse.

Now, the globalization of national economies is at the same time
the 'technicization' of the world. One cannot conceive of one without the
other. Marx was the first philosopher in the western tradition to begin
to articulate this process of technicization philosophically. For Marx,
techne or technics constitutes the very centre of political philosophy.
There can be no inventive political philosophy of modernity without a
prior philosophical understanding of technics: this is the very premise of
the *Grundrisse* and *Capital*. As I have just argued, however, Marx cuts
his own path of invention short and blocks an innovative thinking of the
future when he reinscribes matter and time – without the articulation of
these 'concepts' technology cannot be thought – within a logic of contradiction. This chapter has insistently made the point that, for Derrida, logic
disavows temporality. Hence Derrida's configuring of time, aporia and
the promise looks forward to, and has already begun, the work of invention, 'after' the logics of modernity, on the relations between the human
and the technical.

My hesitation immediately follows, however. By returning logic to the
aporia of time which this logic first disavows to constitute itself as such,
does not Derrida run the risk of leaving the historico-material determinations *of* time too 'undetermined', and, in so doing, of leaving these very
relations between time and matter too undeveloped for *their invention*
to take form?[18] Now, without the very development of these relations, it
could be argued that the political domain will collapse.

The reader will be sensitive to the fact that the terms of my hesitation
are of Hegelian inspiration. This whole chapter has argued that Derrida
exceeds the Hegelian critique of the Kantian law as 'unknowable'. What
I have just said implies that, whilst the aporia of time cannot fail to
resist 'organization', Derrida leaves the mediations of time 'unknowable'
by refusing to develop the history of time's inscriptions (the human's very
'experiences' of time, from that of the stone instrument to 'real time').
By doing so does he not miss the chance of transforming the 'logics' of
these inscriptions – a chance that is today a question of political responsibility? And yet, we have seen that it is through tracking the radical
irreducibility of time to any gesture of organization that Derrida can
rehearse his 'quasi-transcendental' economy of law and singularity through
which his understanding of invention is to be considered in the first place.
For Derrida, the technical is one such organization to which the aporia
of time is irreducible even though time is only ever experienced *through*
such organization. Does my final hesitation therefore now contradict both

what this whole chapter has argued and what the previous chapter argued concerning the political tenor of Derrida's understanding of the 'impossibility' of the experience of aporia?

I do not think so, although I place my hesitation here so that it may return in my conclusion, after the work on Heidegger and Levinas, with the notion of Hegelian mediation in mind. Since, for Derrida, the aporia of time is irreducible to all forms of organization, logical *or* technical, deconstruction's conceptual strategies have a powerful role to play in transforming and inventing undeveloped relations between the aporia of time, the processes of technicization and human organization. In order for this transformation and invention to be as complex as possible, the mediations of time *qua* our technical experiences of time need to be developed. This whole chapter stressed that to witness the aporia of time within logic means to *transform* this very logic. If my argument has been convincing, then to witness the aporia of time within all forms of organization is *also* to transform the very terms of these organizations. This is therefore equally true for the relation between deconstruction, technics and the technosciences.[19] Now, it is precisely here that a Hegelian-type response to deconstruction is legitimate *if* deconstruction, as has too often been the case, fails to develop the relation between aporia and transformation. In this light one could even go so far as to argue that Derrida's writing of the 'gift' of time (1974: 330–8, 237–42), when articulated exclusively from *within* philosophy, indeed risks inhibiting a dialogue between the trace as temporalization, the technical constitution of our experience of time and contemporary technoscientific reorganizations of this experience (which are radical). This risk becomes real in deconstruction when the relation between the aporia of time and technical organization is confined to a debate between philosophy and the 'technics' of the arts and not expanded to become a multidisciplinary reflection on the relations between philosophy, the arts, the human sciences *and* the technosciences. Since reflection on democracy at a *world* level will increasingly presuppose reflection on the relations between law, singularity and these sciences, the multiple strategies to be engaged with and the inventions to be made are urgent and necessarily of a political nature. This work has not yet been done. Gillian Rose's earlier criticisms of Derrida, despite their relevance here, fall short since there is no dialogue in her work either between philosophy and the technosciences. This dialogue would need, in the context of the work of this chapter, to rearticulate Derrida's deconstruction of Hegel in relation to the Kantian idea of democracy and to Marx's historical thinking of matter with and, more importantly, 'through' the technosciences. This would be the subject of another book. Let us meanwhile turn to Derrida's relations to Heidegger and Levinas before readdressing the question of democracy and technics in my conclusion.

3
Aporia of Time, Aporia of Law
Heidegger, Levinas, Derrida

'JewGreek is GreekJew. Extremes meet.'
James Joyce, *Ulysses*

Introduction

The last two chapters have shown that Derrida's thinking of aporia brings
questions of time and judgement into a singular constellation which opens
a powerful thinking of the relation between logic, institution, violence and
history. The singularity of Derrida's development of the irreducible nature
of aporia with respect to the political can now be prudently considered
by looking at the relations between deconstruction and Heidegger's and
Levinas's respective negotiations with the aporetic. An exposition of these
relations will conjoin the concerns of the first chapter with the aporia of
law and those of the second with the aporia of time.

Both Heidegger and Levinas are considered by Derrida to be major
philosophers 'after' the modern philosophical tradition, informing deeply
his intellectual engagements and strategies. Just how deeply, especially after
the repercussions of the last chapter's analysis of modernity, is, however,
my question. This chapter claims that, whilst indebted to both their genealogies of the metaphysical tradition (one in terms of time – Heidegger – the
other in terms of law – Levinas), Derrida's thinking can be identified
with neither, because his deconstruction of metaphysics is made in terms
of time *and* law. The political implications of this are important and have
often been underestimated. For Derrida, the aporia of law 'is' the aporia
of time, the aporia of time 'is' the aporia of law. What is the syntactical
weight of this 'is'? Before turning to an exposition of the stakes and argument of this chapter, I wish to develop firstly an answer to this question
through the concrete political example of Derrida's reading of the American
Declaration of Independence (Derrida, 1984: 13–32).

'And' is God: the American Declaration of Independence

Derrida argues that the problems to be found in the act of declaring the Republic of the United States of America are those of any instituting language (1984: 18). The argument suggests that these problems, if of the order of normative justification, are ultimately of a temporal nature. That is, the problem of political justification (the question of law (*droit*) and its violence) is one of time. *The aporia of law is an aporia of time.* To expound this argument, let me quote the last paragraph of the declaration:

> We, therefore, the Representatives of the United States of America, on General Congress, Assembled, appealing to the Supreme Judge of the world for the rectitude of our intentions, do, in the Name, and by the authority of the good people of these Colonies, solemnly publish and declare, That these United Colonies are absolved from all Allegiance to the British Crown, and that all political connection between them is and ought to be totally dissolved.

In his reading of this passage Derrida maintains that the independence of the United States is undecidably described *and* produced (1984: 20–1). The union of states is described as predating the signature of the declaration; at the same time, it is only produced *through* the signature. The United States is only invented as a state to be described *once* the signature has been given, after the event (*après coup*). The declaration of the republic straightforwardly represents the will of the people prior to the act of declaring, and yet this will is only first invented through this act. This disjointure of the moment of invention is of a temporal nature. The disjointure of time remarks itself in the necessary violence of the law invented: the invention of the United States must be violent since no previous law nor state can justify it. In 'Déclarations d'Indépendance' Derrida describes this temporal violence in terms of the 'undecidability of a performative and constative statement' (1984: 20). It is an argument that he has reproduced in several texts on the foundation of the law – 'The laws of reflection: Nelson Mandela in admiration' (1986b), *Mémoires for Paul de Man* (1986a), 'The Force of law: The "mystical foundation of authority"' (1992b). Many have found this reading of law too linguistic, if not literary. Since this undecidability testifies to the fact that all inventions can only be 'recognized' after the event, and that the history of their exclusions always already haunts the 'present' of the act of invention, the question is, therefore, less the relation of law to language than the relation, through judgement, of law to time. The 'textual' appropriation of Derrida's reading of law can miss the implications of this

point. Thus, whereas in Chapter 1 I stressed the need to move from language to judgement when appraising the political implications of Derrida's
work, here – after the untying of time from logic in Chapter 2 – I wish
to focus on Derrida's articulation of the necessity of judgement and invention in relation to time.

The unsurpassable violence of law (its aporia) is predicated on the *delay
of time*. An act of legislation always arrives too early and/or too late. The
violence of an act of law therefore reveals, in perhaps exemplary manner,
that time is the (self)-deferment of time to itself, or *différance*. Hence the
'fictional [*fabuleuse*] rectroactivity' of the signature (1984: 22) – its invention of that which it claims to represent – is a movement of the *future
anterior* which is the trace of the 'non-adequation of the present to itself'
(1984: 23). That the American states *will have been* united through the
signature of their representatives reveals 'at one and the same time' both
the *coup de force* of all law and the ecstatic passage of time upon
which the force of law is predicated. The trace – the passage of time –
is the 'law' of law (the law that no law can justify itself). The radical
inability to found the law 'is' the radical inability to escape the delay of
time. The future anterior of determinant law is the law of the *force*
of all law. The aporia of time and the aporia of law come together for
Derrida in the relation of delay between the passage of time and human
invention.

Derrida's reading of the Declaration of Independence neatly catches the
fact that it is the ellipsis of law *qua* time which institutions attempt to
fill in by justifying the violence of the law. It also shows that the need
to justify the law – to give it meaning, to conceal its violence and
make it effective – is only derivatively a question of ideology or of power.
It is, firstly, a question of disavowing time. The negation of the undecidability of the law – the claim, for example, that its force is a description,
re-presenting a prior union as a fact or a right – translates a *denial of
the relation between time and law*. As the above paragraph of the
Declaration of Independence betrays, the best name for this concealment
is that of 'God'. It has often been argued that the name of God closes
the infinite regress of authority; or rather, that the closure of infinite
regress names God. In the above articulation of law in relation to time,
this means that 'God' is the fantasy that everything could take place in
'the simulacrum of the instant' (1984: 25). Derrida pursues this important point with the following words:

> 'Are and ought to be'; the 'and' articulates and conjoins here the
> two discursive modalities, being and ought, the observation and
> the prescription, what is and what should be [*le fait et le droit*].
> *And* is God.
>
> (1984: 28)

The refusal to recognize the originary violence of law, the refusal to think the *socius* as necessarily divided before, through and after every act of law, derives from the desire to concentrate time into the present. God is the 'irreplaceable' name of this desire. The denial of the violence of law is nothing but the disavowal of time. Derrida's deconstruction of metaphysics is thus the articulation of time in terms of the irreducibility of law and the articulation of law in terms of the irreducibility of time.

This short excursion through one of Derrida's most profound texts brings into sharp outline the major argument of this book. For Derrida, in contrast to the metaphysical reduction of the passage of time to presence, reflection upon the political necessitates reflection upon the irreducibility of time. And this, in turn, means enduring the experience of the aporia of law (and) time. Judgements and inventions which have endured this experience have greater chance of recognizing difference according to the lesser violence.

The experience of aporia is one of time and law. The passage of time and the violence of law form two sides of the same coin. This experience is 'impossible'. Since experience is predicated upon the present, and since one cannot figure the aporia – that is, bring it into the temporalization of time without losing it – there can be no experience of aporia: or rather, aporia is, in Derrida's terms, an 'impossible experience'. *One cannot not disavow time*. If time is the delay upon itself, one cannot recognize the delay *as such*. The recognition that the aporia of time is the aporia of law does not appropriate the aporia, for such an appropriation would just lose it again, repeating, in inverse form, the above function of the name of God. This is why, for the aporia to be recognized, it must be impossible to recognize it. Recognition must be impossible, for recognition to have a chance. We saw the subtle 'logic' of this at the end of the last chapter with regard to Hegel's understanding of recognition (*Erkennen*). Chapter 1 also engaged with the paradox, concluding that this impossibility of figuring the passage of time forms, for Derrida, the very condition of decision and invention. Two major consequences follow, summing up in many ways Derrida's thinking of the political: first, the future anterior is the temporal modality of invention; second, the best invention is an impossible one. Impossible, however, in a very specific sense: an impossible invention is not a horizon. There can be no *temporal horizon* to the passage of time. The impossibility is 'now'. 'Now' marks the impossibility of concentrating time into a present; 'now' is the fact that time, to be time, is constantly 'out of joint' – it is the disjointure (*Un-Fug*) of the future anterior.[1] Given the recurrent impossibility of now, the alterity of any invention or institution is what has always to be negotiated (see 1987c: 58–60). The other of institution is in this sense the 'now' of an *absolute future*, a non-eschatological 'promise' – literally the ever-recurrent promise of the non-adequation of the present to itself.

Thus if one cannot not disavow time, one can invent in re-cognizing this disavowal. The 'now' is not only the very condition of invention; the re-cognition of its disavowal *transforms* the relations between politics and time. Political inventions, like the American Declaration of Independence, could be rewritten, perhaps, with this in mind.

The Political Stakes of Derrida's Difference from Heidegger and Levinas

The above thinking of aporia interweaves the philosophies of Heidegger and Levinas while cutting through their respective thinking of time and law at crucial junctures. Since the differences which emerge are of philosophical, cultural and political importance (certainly in the culture of contemporary French philosophy and critical theory), it is worthwhile outlining some strategic reasons for presenting my argument.

Heidegger and Levinas have consciously cast their philosophies as 'genealogies' of the metaphysical tradition, inscribing the terms and logic of this tradition onto an anterior instance. The force of their 'genealogies' lies in the attempt either to untie a certain understanding of time from its *ontologization* in the western tradition (Heidegger) or to untie alterity from time as such (Levinas). Both thinkers situate their understanding of the political with respect to this 'untying'; moreover, Levinas's philosophy is precisely elaborated against Heidegger's destruction of ontology, with its political implications in mind. Hence the singularity of Derrida's relation to metaphysics, together with its own political implications, can be dramatically foregrounded through looking at their philosophies.

In the case of Heidegger, it is important to show that his destruction of ontology in terms of time is, for Derrida, a 'failed' negotiation of the aporia of time. This negotiation leads to a politics which Derrida's thinking of aporia both comprehends and demarcates itself from. This reading allows us to talk politically about Heidegger's philosophy without reducing philosophy to politics. It simultaneously allows us to separate Derrida's work from Heidegger with respect to Heidegger's failure to think aporia aporetically. In this context, recent critical readings of the relation between Heidegger and Derrida (especially those of the 'Heidegger affair') have signally failed to see where the debate between Heidegger and Derrida lies. The failure has been unhelpful for advancing our thinking of the political.

In the case of Levinas, since Derrida's demarcation from Heidegger is in part made with the philosophy of Levinas, it is important to show in what way deconstruction also demarcates itself from Levinas's thought. This is all the more important given that Levinas has often been used in recent times to attenuate a 'Heideggerian' Derrida and to foreground the question of the law as the other of the political. Without wishing simply to reverse this tendency, I believe that forging too close a link between Levinas's thinking and that of Derrida leads to an underestimation of the political implications of deconstruction. This is not because Derrida is *more* political than Levinas. Rather, the attempt to forge an alliance between deconstruction and Levinasian ethics fails to take into account that Levinas's thinking risks being political *by not wishing to be*. It is because Derrida's thinking of the impossibility of aporia allows us to understand this reversal of intention (the reversal of the 'ethical' into the 'political') that a distinction between their respective negotiations with the radical other of thought needs to be made. As a result – if in a symmetrically opposite way to the reduction of deconstruction to Heidegger's political engagements – the association between Derrida's thinking of aporia and Levinas's thinking of alterity has also been unhelpful for advancing our thinking of the political.

When Heidegger thinks being[2] in terms of time, and time in terms of aporia, he simultaneously loses the experience of aporia by thinking time in oppositional terms, those of 'vulgar' and the 'primordial' temporalization. The opposition betrays a repetition of metaphysical logic at the very moment that Heidegger wishes to destroy logic. It allows for all Heidegger's 'subsequent' oppositions between the authentic and the inauthentic, notably those in the twenties and thirties between *das Volk* and *das Man*. These oppositions prevent Heidegger, paradoxically, from thinking the 'there' (*da*) of 'Dasein'. As we will see in passing briefly from *Being and Time* (1926) to *An Introduction to Metaphysics* (1935) the result leads to a politics of authentic 'temporality' and 'locality' pitched against inauthentic issuelessness. The passage allows Heidegger to commit the unpardonable fault of wishing, as Derrida puts it in *Of Spirit*, to 'spiritualize' Nazism, to give National Socialism a philosophical grounding (1987a: 65–6/39–40). That said, within Heidegger's treatment of aporia there remains a movement of irreducible alterity which 'deconstructs' Heidegger's own understanding of aporia. The irreducibility of this alterity allows Derrida, in turn, to work the most profound aspects of Heidegger's presentation of the aporia of time with Levinas's aporia of law.

Levinas articulates the aporia in terms of the *unpresentable* law of the other (*autrui*). The 'there' of Dasein is thus thought as an absolute past (called the 'ethical' relation to the other), a past that has never been present which precedes the articulation of being *qua* 'primordial temporalization'. Since neither the ego nor thought can make the other homogenous with the temporalization of time, the aporia is not one of time, but one of 'law'. That which I cannot appropriate, but which looks at me from an absolute past, is the law. Levinas fails, however, to think adequately the relation *between* this absolute past and the temporalization of time. This also leads to the loss of the experience of aporia

as the 'incalculable' relation between the non-appropriable law of the
other and the necessity of judgement. The loss results in what I will later
call 'a politics of ethical singularity', visible in Levinas's thinking of the
third party (*le tiers*) as well as in his comments on the 'ethical' vocation
of the State of Israel.

While Heidegger argues for the 'presentation' of aporia, Levinas, partly
in response to the political implications of this presentation, argues for
the 'unpresentable'. Neither, therefore, articulates adequately the *limit
between* the unpresentable and presentation, that is, the limit between
aporia and decision.[3] For Derrida, it is this very limit which safeguards
the 'experience' of aporia. Either subject to presentation or unpresentable, the limit is lost. This is an important point, the weight of which
we have just seen in Derrida's reading of the American Declaration of
Independence. Just as one will lose the aporia if one recognizes it, so will
one lose it if one does not recognize it. One's relation to aporia must
consequently be *itself* aporetic, if the experience of aporia is to remain
an impossible one. Otherwise one will end up as much in the piety of
the 'other' as in the piety of 'being'. Heidegger and Levinas's respective
genealogies of metaphysics in terms of (the presentation of) time and (the
unpresentable of) law end up the *same*.

In contrast to both Heidegger and Levinas, Derrida holds to the limit
by bringing together the aporia of time and of law. He thereby both
cuts across the metaphysical logic informing Heidegger's destruction of
ontology (here he uses Levinas against Heidegger) and re-relates Levinas's
reflection on the law to temporalization (here he uses Heidegger against
Levinas). Thus Heidegger's thought is related to that of Levinas and
Levinas's thought to that of Heidegger in such a way that each thought
is returned to its other to prevent it from falling out into a unilateral
determination of aporia. The result is an aporetic conception of the
political which 'avoids' the traps (conscious or unconscious) of exemplarity or locality.

Heidegger's Thinking of Aporia: A Politics of Authentic Temporality

The difference between being (*Sein*) and beings (*Seiende*) constitutes the
'ontico-ontological difference'. The being of an entity is to be found neither
in the entity nor above the entity in a universal category or genus
which would subsume the entity under it as a particular instance of itself.
The being of an entity is the articulation of the entity *as* an entity:
we will call this articulation the '"as"-structure of being'. This structure
reveals the entity before the entity's representation as an object that is
either true or false (truth as *adequatio*). Heidegger calls this letting-some-
thing-be-seen-as-something *aletheia* or unconcealment. The separation of
being from beings conceals *aletheia* under *adequatio*. This concealment

constitutes for Heidegger the history of metaphysics. Within this history, the entity 'as' an entity is covered over, becoming an object of creation, representation or invention. For Heidegger, the last avatar of metaphysical thinking is the modern technological invention of entities. The calculative thinking which informs this process of invention issues from the modern rational reduction of the world to 'nature' (from Descartes onwards). With this reduction, both the world and the being which articulates the world 'as' a world – Dasein – are at risk. There is no world, for Heidegger, without the 'as', and there is no 'there' of Dasein unless the 'as' is artic-ulated. This risk lies behind the major concern of *Being and Time*'s (1926) destruction (*Destruktion*) of ontology in the 1920s, and informs Heidegger's notorious phrase in the 1930s in *An Introduction to Meta-physics* that 'the inner truth and greatness of the movement [of National Socialism is] the encounter between global technology and modern man' (1935: 152/199). Heidegger's unpardonable political engagements can only be understood with respect to the most vital core of his philosophy. And the question of both is that of the temporalization of time.

Derrida argued as early as the late 1960s in 'Ousia and gramme' (1968) that Heidegger's destruction of ontology within the horizon of time was informed by an oppositional logic which returned Heidegger to metaphysics at the moment that he wished to 'destroy' it (1972: 31–78/29–68, esp. 73–8/63–7). I will first elaborate the above 'as'-structure of being in respect of this destruction of classical ontology, showing how and why Heidegger formulates it as an opposition between two temporalizations of time. This will take me to an analysis of the existential of 'being-towards-death' in *Being and Time* together with the adjacent theme of *Unheimlichkeit* (respectively, §46–§53 and §40, §56–§60, §68c). I shall then show how, conducted within an oppositional logic, this destruction leads to a political thinking of authentic tempo-rality, one which simultaneously appropriates the aporia of time, misrecognizes the very thing which it is trying to think – the 'there' – and allows Heidegger to 'figure' primordial temporality as an aporia of place (the *polis* in the commentary on *Antigone* in *An Introduction to Metaphysics* (1935: 112–26/146–65)). Derrida's respective position con-cerning aporia will emerge through the political 'fate' of Heidegger's thinking. The conclusion will confirm that Derrida's insistent focus on alterity within Heidegger's oppositional logic 'inverts' the presentation of the aporia of time into an aporetic relation with the law.

The 'As'-Structure of Being in Relation to (a Logic of) Time

For Heidegger, to ask the question of 'being' prior to its determination and oblivion in the epochs of metaphysics is to reopen the 'as' (as an 'as'), to articulate it explicitly. If the articulation of an entity as an entity depends upon Dasein, the relation between the two is to be thought in the form of the transcendence of time: that is, time's throwing-out of itself beyond itself (the 'passage' of time). Without this 'ecstasis' of time there would be no consciousness and, subsequently, no 'as'. Ecstasis is concealed when the transcendence of consciousness is projected *beyond* time as a category of being. In classical ontology, the transcendent is thought in the shape of an 'eternal' or 'highest being' either embracing or reposing outside the finitude of time and space. This concept of transcendence harbours a contradiction. The concept of 'eternity', as eternal presence, is predetermined by a particular temporalization of time, the present. In other words, eternal presence is nothing but the very disavowal of time, whilst being structured by it. Moreover, it is structured by a particular *modification* (or, temporalization) of time, the generalization of the present. Heidegger calls this understanding of time – that of the succession of 'nows' (*Jetzte*) – the 'vulgar' concept of time. According to *Being and Time* (1926), this specific temporalization of time constitutes metaphysical thought as such. To destroy (*abbauen*) metaphysics is, consequently, to consider the *logos* with respect to time. For Heidegger this means two things: first, the need to rethink ontology according to the ontological projection beyond time of the vulgar concept of time; second, the need to root the vulgar concept of time upon a more 'primordial' (*ursprünglich*) notion of temporality which the former conceals (§65). The 'destruction' of metaphysics comprises these two gestures (compare Heidegger, 1929).

If, for Heidegger, traditional organizations of the concept of transcendence repeat time in thinking transcendence in the form of the present, the repetition is in fact a denial of 'true', primordial temporalization. The vulgar concept of time covers over an ecstatic temporalization of time which lets time as the 'now'-sequence spring forth in the first place. As the very possibility of the three modifications of time – past, present and future – primordial temporalization forms time through the inextricable and mutually constitutive relation between the temporal ecstases (a play of retention and protention).

> The future, the character of having been, and the present, show the phenomenal characteristics of the 'towards oneself', the 'back-to', and the 'letting-oneself-be-encountered-by'. The phenomena of the 'towards . . .', the 'to . .', and the 'alongside . . .', make temporality manifest as the [ecstasis] pure and simple. *Temporality is the primordial 'outside of itself' in and for itself.* We therefore call the phenomena of the future, the character of the having been, and the present, the 'ecstases' of temporality. Temporality is not prior to this an entity which first emerges from *itself*; its essence is a process of temporalizing in the unity of the ecstases. What is characteristic of the 'time' which

is accessible to the ordinary understanding, consists ... in the fact that it is a pure sequence of 'nows', without beginning and without end, in which the ecstatical character of primordial [*ursprünglich*] temporality has been levelled off. But this very levelling off ... is grounded in the possibility of a definite kind of temporalizing, in conformity with which temporality temporalizes as inauthentic [*uneigentlich*] the authentic [*eigentlich*] 'time' we have just mentioned.

(Heidegger, 1926: 329/377)

We will come back to the oppositional logic informing this passage in a moment. In the levelling-off of the ecstatic understanding of time, time 'falls back' (§67c) into a succession of past, present and future which is predicated on the consideration of each temporality as a 'now'. The vulgar concept of time is engendered by the 'reckoning' with time particular to Dasein's calculation of time through measuring-instruments (§81).

Time [which is manifest in clock-using, horology] is that which is *counted* and which shows itself when one follows the travelling pointer, counting and making present (*Gegenwärtigen*) in such a way that this making-present temporalizes itself in an ecstatical unity with the retaining and awaiting which are horizonally open according to the 'earlier' and the 'later'.

(1926: 421/472)

According to Heidegger, this temporalization of time (the 'everyday' experience of time) is 'nothing else than the existential-ontological interpretation of Aristotle's definition of time' (ibid.). We here return to our analysis in Chapter 1 of Derrida's understanding of aporia as an impossible experience. To untie the necessary relation between aporia and judgement, I considered it important to think aporia with regard to Aristotle's treatment of time as 'aporetic' in *Physics*, IV (see Chapter 1, pp. 31–3). It was noted that, unlike Heidegger, although in his footsteps, Derrida did not resolve Aristotle's understanding of time as aporia by making an opposition between vulgar and primordial temporality. It is now appropriate to develop this difference in order to see in detail in what consists Heidegger's specific resolution of Aristotle's aporetic of time and in order to demarcate from it Derrida's own understanding of the aporia of time.

To recall: for Aristotle, time is aporetic; it both is and is not. If it is considered in terms of its divisibility, it is to be considered in terms of *now*. And yet, the very *now* of time which gives it its being also robs it of any being, since *now* is always already past or future. The thinking of time is therefore an 'aporetic'. Time provokes a course of thought which 'ends up' as the aporia (without passage) of thought (*Physics*, IV, 218a). For Heidegger, this ontological 'counting' of time is a prejudgement on the nature of time, one to which all discussions of the concept of time since Aristotle have clung. Only by temporalizing time in this way (the 'now-time'), can one think time as both what is and what is not.

The Aristotelian aporetic of time is thus reorganized by Heidegger according to the logic of a 'fall' from 'authentic' to 'inauthentic' time and reconfigured in terms of its condition, 'primordial temporalization'. For Heidegger, Aristotle's aporetic is constituted in the metaphysical conceal-ment of the originary ecstasis of time.

This passage from one temporalization to another only works, however, if the ecstases are articulated as a *unity*, a unity which is *lost* in the 'making-present' of time. As Heidegger put it above, 'time's essence is a process of temporalizing in the unity of the ecstases' (op. cit., p. 106). This unity – the very essence of time – is provided by the ecstasis of the future. For Heidegger:

> Primordial and authentic temporality temporalizes itself in terms of the authentic future and in such a way that having been futurally, it first of all awakens the present. *The primary phenomenon of primordial and authentic temporality is the future.*
>
> (1926: 329/378)

The authentic future which unifies the ecstases is death. That is to say, temporality is revealed through Dasein's experience of death, which, as authentic, is 'anticipatory resoluteness'. Death experienced authentically is the temporalization of time out of the authentic future (1926: 335/384). The calculation of time levels this experience off. In other words, ecstasis is re-cognized in the experience of being-towards-death. Being-towards-death is the very possibility of primordial temporality. If, therefore, this existential does not work *within its own terms*, the unity of primordial temporalization and, consequently, the very opposition between vulgar and primordial time are inevitably placed in question. Before moving to an analysis of the existential of death let me generalize the argument up to this point.

Some General Points Concerning Heidegger

First, the 'as'-structure of being must be considered within the horizon of authentic temporalization. To open up the 'as' of entities from under metaphysical concealment (ontological 'or' technical) means reflecting upon the 'as' according to primordial temporality. Such reflection (the questioning of being) develops the ecstatic unity of past, present and future, since this unity constitutes in the first place transcendence. Consequently, opening up the 'as'-structure of beings and articulating the unity of primordial temporality form one and the same gesture. For the early Heidegger this articulation is the *ecstatic structure of Dasein itself*. Heidegger's presentation of the existential 'being-towards-death' (§47-53) confirms that the above 'unity' of time is nothing else than the self-projection of Dasein from the future. For Heidegger, in other words, being-towards-death confirms that the unified ecstasis of authentic time is structured from the future as Dasein's self-affection.

I have already said that Heidegger understands modern technology as the completion of metaphysics because he interprets its reduction of the 'world' to 'nature' as a vulgar temporalization of time. For the world to be re-presented to a subject as an object (*Gegen-stand*), the world must be 'reckoned-with' in terms of the 'now-time'. An object is only possible as something 'present'. I should now add that the rooting of the Aristotelian aporetic of time upon primordial temporality allows Heidegger to interpret the modern technicization of the world in terms of vulgar time and *oppose* to it an 'authentic experience of death'. Heidegger's earlier comment on the 'truth' of National Socialism concerning 'modern man and global technology' is to be understood in this context. National Socialism constitutes the possibility of collective 'authentic' temporalization, set in Promethean resistance to the disjoin-ture of vulgar time: it is *das Volk* which gathers itself out of *das Man*. As I said earlier, Heidegger's political engagements are to be situated at the most vital core of his philosophy. This is the scandal that has to be confronted.

Finally, Heidegger argues that all discussions of time within the meta-physical tradition cling to the definition of time that constitutes Aristotle's aporetic of time. His interpretation of Aristotle with respect to an oppo-sition between vulgar and primordial time is consequently a destruction of metaphysics as such. This opposition, pitching the primordial against the vulgar, is *not itself temporally organized*: or rather, it is itself a disavowal of time. Thus, the very terms in which Heidegger destroys metaphysics within the horizon of time are not themselves reflected upon (as inscribed) within time. That the manner in which Heidegger destroys logic is itself informed by logic has several major consequences.

Opposing one temporalization of time to another, Heidegger neces-sarily thinks the relation between temporalizations in terms which his very destruction of ontology is meant to account for. The consideration of the passage of one time to another as a 'fall' is an eminently *metaphysical* way of speaking of the phenomenon of time. Thus, at the very moment of reading ontology as the disavowal of time, Heidegger continues to disavow time.

The contradiction means that Heidegger's determination of the Aristotelian aporetic of time in the form of primordial temporalization *loses* the aporia of time *qua* the 'passage'/'delay' of time. Or rather, Heidegger's loss of the aporia manifests itself as the opposition between the 'unity' of ecstatic time and the disjointure of vulgar time. For Derrida, Heidegger's opposition between two concepts of time prolongs the disavowal of time because it temporalizes the aporia of time. Still thinking metaphysically, Heidegger does not negotiate with .aporia aporetically. Derrida's own understanding of aporia and tradition follows from this demarcation.

The above opposition informs all Heidegger's oppositions between the 'authentic' and the 'inauthentic', the 'proper' and the 'improper'. The latter are nothing but continuations, modifications, and revisions of the opposition between two conceptions of time.

Despite Heidegger's persistent, symptomatic claims to 'phenomeno-logical neutrality', these oppositions are normative. As *logical organiza-tions* of time, they prescribe how time *ought* to be thought. They cannot, therefore, be justified in the terms of a temporal destruction of onto-logical logic. In other words, at this level of untying time from logic, a logical gesture informing this untying is necessarily prescriptive. It organizes the 'delay' of time in terms of a 'rooted' relation to the world, with the ensuing political choices. Heidegger's Nazism should, in other words, be articulated at this level.

This tension between the destruction of logic and the logical terms of this destruction haunts every page of *Being and Time*. Despite axiomatic changes concerning both the temporalization of time and the relation of Dasein to temporalization, this tension *also* haunts Heidegger's later work – from the 'The Anaximander fragment' (1946) to the conference 'Time and being' (1962).

Finally, the tension betrays the fact that Heidegger is not a thinker of the 'there' (*da*) of time.

The last observation is not one which Derrida has explicitly elaborated (he would undoubtedly avoid the sharpness of the formulation). That said, his readings of Heidegger – from 'Ousia and gramme' (1968) to *Aporias: Dying – awaiting (one another) at the 'limits of truth'* (1994a), *Specters of Marx* (1993) and *Politics of Friendship* (1994b) – always work to 'trouble' the Heideggerian movement of 'unity' and to reveal within it a constitutive movement of 'disjointure'. As a result, following the terms of my argument above, Derrida rearticulates the Heideggerian opposition between two concepts of time as a further metaphysical interpretation of the self-deferment of time to itself (the *différance* of time). In this reartic-ulation of Heidegger's opposition, the attributes projected upon the 'now' of the 'now-time' (basically, dissipation and fracture) are *tied back* to the description of what I called in my introduction the 'now' of impossibility. This 'now' is the originary 'gap' in the continuity of time that allows for time in the first place, but equally troubles any attempt to 'unify' it. In other words, the Heideggerian dissipation of the 'present' is rethought by Derrida as the disunity which precedes the metaphysical opposition between the 'unity' of primordial temporality and the 'fracture' of vulgar time. The description of the 'present' as the vulgar time of dissipation is thus seen as a *retrospective projection* on Heidegger's part which issues from his *denial* of originary disunity. (This is, of course, a classic move of deconstruction.)

This originary disunity is not a new temporalization of time to be 'opposed' to Heidegger's oppositions. For Derrida, it is the excess of time that constitutes time – again, the *différance* of time. This excess is irreducible, it is what *Specters of Marx* calls the 'undeconstructible condition of any deconstruction' (1993: 56/28). Derrida's aporetic complication of the Heideggerian 'there' is nothing else than what Derrida calls 'the promise to come'. Consequently, by revealing the logic informing Heidegger's understanding of the 'there', I am rearticulating exactly *where* Heidegger could be interested in Nazism *with* Derrida's understanding of the 'promise of democracy' developed in the last chapter. There is no question of salvaging Heidegger in this negotiation. With regard to this promise, and from within Heidegger's misrecognitions, Derrida is arguing that an aporetic understanding of time and place precedes Heidegger's opposition between the unity of time and place and the metaphysical (especially modern and technological) dissipation of this unity. In the above text *Aporias* the example for this strategy of interpretation is that of the experience of death. With these points in mind, we can now turn to the existential 'being-towards-death' to see in what way it both structures the unity of ecstatic time and simultaneously displaces this unity.

'Being-Towards-Death': the Aporia of Time as Dasein's Self-Projection

It is because Dasein anticipates its death that its temporal structure flows back from the future. The anticipation of death (the future as horizon) pulls the present out of the present and re-presents it from the perspective of the future which it anticipates. The horizon of the future thus organizes Dasein's relation to its present and its past: time is both ecstatic (its temporal modalities are ecstasies tending forward and back in inextricable relation to each other) and unified. For this to be the case, Dasein's death must be recognized as a limit *for* Dasein, a limit from which it temporalizes the present from the future. In *Aporias* (1994a), Derrida argues that the precondition of this is that the limit of death *as* death is figured as Dasein's *own* possibility. Through this figuring of the limit, the aporia of death is lost by being presented. In the context of our argument on primordial temporality, we should stress the stakes of this observation by Derrida: the presentation of the aporia of death re-presents Heidegger's determination of the delay of time as an opposition between primordial and vulgar temporality. In other words, the presentation of the limit of death as Dasein's own limit is the *condition* of the (futural) 'unity' of the temporal ecstases for Dasein.

Since death is absolutely singular, both the logic of re-presentation and the temporality on which this logic is predicated (the vulgar present) fail to meet death. No one can replace or 're-present' another in his or her death. 'The possibility [of death is] one's ownmost, non-relational and not to be outstripped' (Heidegger, 1926: 251/294). No one, however, can experience his or her own death either. It would seem that death, as a radical ellipsis of time, is actually both what is most one's own and least one's own. For Heidegger, the accent is put, however, on the 'propriety' of death. The impossibility of death is the '*possibility* of its impossibility' (1926: 262/306, my emphasis). To relate to death as something that is absolutely impossible for Dasein is to anticipate death as a possibility (and neither as something actual nor as 'something' radically absent). With the impossibility of death appearing as such, death constitutes a horizon from which Dasein possibilizes its existence. Anticipating death as possibility, Dasein thereby 'understands itself as anticipation' (1926: 263/307). Heidegger turns the impossible impasse of death (its aporia) into a possibility. Death possibilizes Dasein as a self-projection (*as* possibility). The 'as'-structure of being *qua* primordial temporality is released through freedom for death: 'Being-towards-death, as anticipation of possibility, is what first *makes* this possibility *possible*, and sets it free as possibility (1926: 262/307). The self-projection unifies the temporal modalities that articulate Dasein as a *unity* of time coming from the future. Being-towards-death thus structures Dasein as self-temporalization from the future. Presenting the limit of death to itself, Dasein temporalizes itself out of the future. The presentation of the limit of death (the possibility of impossibility, or impossibility 'as such') is nothing less than the presentation of the aporia of time as Dasein's self-affection *qua* primordial temporality. Dasein takes up the 'delay' of time as possibility. Time becomes a possibility.

In this presentation of the limit, the 'there' of 'thrownness' is *taken over* as a futural possibility of the self, as 'the potentiality for its *own* being' (1926: 264/308, my emphasis). The anxiety of being-towards-death holds open the certainty of death but holds it open as the 'as' of the *possibility* of death, that is, a certain but indefinite possibility for Dasein. Dasein's coming 'face to face with the thrownness of its there is at the same time its potentiality for being' (266/311). The face to face with, and taking up of one's own death, recasts the 'there' of 'thrownness', which precedes Dasein, as the 'basis' for its own nullity. Through its relation to its own death, Dasein does not absorb this basis into its own 'power' (285/331) but assumes it as its own possibility for which it is responsible.

> Nullity does not signify anything like not being-present-at-hand or not-subsisting; what one has in view here is rather a 'not' which is constitutive for this *being* of Dasein – its thrownness. The character of this 'not' as a 'not' may be defined existentially: in being its *self*, Dasein is, *as* a self, the entity that has been thrown. It has been *released* from its *basis*, *not through* itself but *to* itself, so as to be *as this basis*. Dasein is not itself the basis of its being, inasmuch as this basis first arises from its own projection; rather, as being-its-self, it is the *being* of its basis.
> (Heidegger, 1926: 284–5/330)

Dasein is the self of self-projection, which self-projection is the unity of past, present and future structured through the anticipation of death.

> Taking over thrownness signifies *being* Dasein authentically *as it already was*. Taking over thrownness is only possible in such a way that the futural Dasein can *be* its ownmost 'as-it-already-was' – its been (*Gewesen*). ... As authentically futural, Dasein *is* authentically as 'having been'. Anticipation of one's uttermost and ownmost possibility is coming back understandingly to one's ownmost 'been'. Only in so far as it is futural can Dasein *be* authentically as having been. The character of 'having been' arises, in a certain way, from the future.
> (1926: 326/373)

Now, if the 'there' is not taken over and made the 'basis of one's own nullity', then the 'nothing' of the 'there' remains the prerogative of *das Man* (the 'they'). Heidegger's opposition between two concepts of time becomes one between two modalities of 'not being at home'. Authentic 'being-towards-death' is authentic *Unheimlichkeit*. The recognition of death returns Dasein from *das Man* to being-in-the-world. It gives it back its 'not' as authentic 'being-guilty' (*Schuldigsein*) (§57–58). *Das Man* is, on the contrary, the disjointure of Dasein. Represented by others, unable to assume its own future, dwelling from 'now' to 'now', translating the 'not' into a *lack* from which it can be redeemed in an eschatological future which it 'awaits' (§67), *das Man* lives vulgar time. Unable to face death, *das Man* constitutes itself through the refusal to temporalize itself out of the future (1926: 335/384). *Das Man* is indeed nothing but this refusal. The refusal holds the 'there' back. The being-there of Dasein is consequently lost. I will call this dwelling nowhere the 'bad nothing' of inauthentic '*Unheimlichkeit*'.

Authentic and Inauthentic '*Unheimlichkeit*': the Political Determination of the Aporia of Place

Whilst *Being and Time* predominantly elaborates the existential of *Unheimlichkeit* as the authentic taking up of 'nullity', inauthentic *Unheimlichkeit* should be considered as the 'homelessness' (or, 'issuelessness' as *An Introduction to Metaphysics* (1935) puts it) of *das Man* lurching – in distinction to the self-affection of resolute Dasein gathering itself through its temporalization of time from the future – from one 'now' (*Jetzt*) to the next. Led in fear of death, anticipating the future as a future present, inauthentic *Unheimlichkeit* is unable to take over the past as 'its future possibilities'. It is unable to make the past, through futural temporalizing, 'its' past. Heidegger's analysis of 'being-towards-death' according to two temporalizations of time is reconfigured here as an opposition between two understandings of *place* and two understandings of the *past* as *heritage*. On the one hand, *das Man* is uprooted, temporally and spatially disoriented because it does not anticipate death. Its uprootedness consists in lurching from present to present – what, for *das Man*, is precisely 'home'. On the other hand, Dasein reposes in the weight of the 'there' having 'rooted' itself in possibility, in its resolute anticipation of the future – what, for Dasein, is precisely 'true' homelessness. Abiding in the 'present' of vulgar time, *Das Man*'s home is homeless; reposing in the weight of the 'there' from future self-projection, Dasein's homelessness is home. Heidegger's articulation of the Aristotelian aporetic of time as primordial temporality is, through the appearing as such of the aporia of death, *the aporia of place*, place as aporia – authentic *Unheimlichkeit*. Before I put the logic of the existential of 'being-towards-death' into question, let me follow this translation of the aporia of time into an aporia of place by looking briefly at the commentary of the second major chorus of *Antigone* (ll. 332–72) in *An Introduction to Metaphysics* (1935: 112–26/146–65).

In this text the aporia of place is understood as the *polis*. Following the above paradoxical articulation of 'true' homelessness, the *polis* is not the space of a 'city or city-state' in the traditional sense of the political (1935: 116/152). Any reflection upon the political according to the criterion of homogeneity is one according to the temporality of 'vulgar time'. The political space is theorized as a homogeneous present which projects onto the outside of its walls the absence which prevents it from being 'presently present'. Such a conception of the political only thinks difference by recognizing it at the limits of its space. In contrast to this 'Kantian' conception of political space, the Heideggerian *polis*, articulated in terms of primordial temporality, is a site of difference in which the issuelessness of authentic *Unheimlichkeit* is 'figured'. This figure is the 'as such' of the aporia of place – wherein the problem, however. Both *contra* Hegel's 'dialectical' reading of law in *Antigone* and yet still in the wake of Hegel's aesthetics of presentation (I recall the last chapter's comments on Athena), the *polis* is the *presentation* of aporia 'as' aporia. Despite going beyond traditional inscriptions of the political in terms of a homogeneous site, Heidegger here develops, as Philippe Lacoue-Labarthe puts it, 'a politics of finitude' (1986). In our terms, the presentation of the aporia of space *as* an aporia issues in a political determination of locality.

Heidegger's interest centres on the following two separate stanzas from the chorus of *Antigone* (his translation in parentheses):

> There is much that is strange (*Vielfältig das Unheimliche*),
> but nothing that surpasses man in strangeness
> (*Unheimlicheres*) . . .
>
> . . . Everywhere journeying, inexperienced and without
> issue (*ohne Ausweg*), he [man] comes to nothingness.
> Through no flight can he resist
> the one assault of death,
> even if he has succeeded in cleverly evading
> painful sickness.
> (Heidegger, 1935: 112–13/146–7)

The Greek term translated by *Unheimlich* is *deinon*. For Heidegger *deinon* renders the Greek understanding of being as 'the overpowering power of *phusis*'. In an earlier section of *An Introduction to Metaphysics* this power of *phusis* forms the particular interpretation of the *polemos* in Heraclitus' fragment 'War (*polemos*) is the governor of all things' (1935: 113–14/146–65). Prior to either war or peace in an anthropological sense, the *polemos* articulates the being of the world as *phusis* (its constant setting-apart). *Polemos*, wrongly anthropologized when translated as 'war', is a term for originary difference (compare Derrida, 1994b: 403–19/203–16). This overpowering violence of difference, if preceding man, is borne by him. Man is the most strange (*Unheimlicheres*), that is, the most violent (*deinataton*), because, in carrying over this violence, he departs from 'familiar paths and limits' and shatters himself against the worlding of the world in order to 'gather' and 'bring it to manifestness' (1935: 115–16/150–1). The question of *Unheimlichkeit* in this commentary is that of *how to walk*.

If the basic trait of the human is to be thrown out of familiar paths, this trait, called authentic *Unheimlichkeit* in *Being and Time*, is here figured as the *polis*. The 'da' of Dasein is a locality in which its issue-lessness is figured 'as' issuelessness. Just as the ecstases of time are joined (*gefügt*) by the future of being-towards-death, so the paths meet in the *polis*. The impasse of path becomes the path of impasse:

> *Pantoporos aporos ep'ouden erchetai.* Everywhere journeying, inexperienced and without issue, he comes to nothingness. The essential words are *pantaporos aporos*. The word *poros* means: passage through ..., transition to ... path; he ventures into all realms of the essent, of the overpowering power, and in so doing he is flung out of all paths. Herein is disclosed the entire strange-ness of this strangest of all creatures ... he becomes the strangest of all beings because, without issue on all paths, he is cast out of every relation to the familiar and befallen by ruin and catastrophe. ... But there is a point at which all these paths meet, the *polis*. The *polis* is the historical place, the there *in* which, *out of* which and *as* which historical Dasein is.
>
> (Heidegger, 1935: 116–17/152)

Authentic issuelessness is demarcated from the inauthentic 'etcetera' of paths that go nowhere:

> Man, as he journeys everywhere, is not without issue in the external sense that he comes up against outward barriers and cannot go on. In one way or another he can always go further into the etcetera. He is without issue because he is always thrown back on the paths, caught in the beaten track, and thus caught he encompasses the circle of his world, entangles himself in appearance, and so excludes himself from Being. ... The violence that originally created the paths engenders its own *mischief* of versatility [*Vielwendigkeit*], which is intrinsically *issueless*, so much so that it bars itself from reflection about the appearance in which it moves.
>
> (1935: 121/158)

'Mischief' is the translation of the German *Unfug*. The passage pitches one issuelessness against another: the first, that of an explicit relation to the finitude of being predicated on the taking over of the *polemos* of the world (the good nullity of Dasein in *Being and Time*, the meeting of the paths in the *polis*); the second, the exclusion of being through the bad issuelessness of the present and appearance. The relation is thought of in terms of a fall from jointure (*Fug*) to disjointure (*Unfug*). In *Being and Time* this relation is thought in terms of the 'fall' of one temporality to another within which are situated two modalities of 'being-towards-death'. Here, the fall is one from place to placelessness within which are situated two kinds of 'being-without-a-path':

> Man can never master the overpowering. ... Every violent curbing of the powerful is either victory or defeat. Both, each in its different way, fling him out of home, and thus, each in its different way, unfold the dangerousness of achieved or lost being. Both, in different ways are menaced by disaster. [Consequently] in venturing to master [b]eing, he must risk the assault of the non essent ..., the *violent one* must risk dispersion, in-stability, disorder, mischief (*Un-Fug*). The higher the summit of historical being-there, the deeper will be the abyss, the more abrupt the fall into the unhistorical, which merely thrashes around in issueless and placeless confusion [*in der ausweglosen und zugleich stätte-losen Wirrnis*].
>
> (1935: 123/161)

Heidegger's attempt here to rearticulate political space in terms of temporality founders on the fact that this space continues to be considered as an opposition between the authentic and the inauthentic. As a result, Heidegger repeats a metaphysics of locality which projects disjointure outside of itself. From here Heidegger can give a philosophical grounding to National Socialism through 'rooting' the latter on the existential of authentic *Unheimlichkeit*. What I wish to stress in this context is that the above opposition covers over a more radical thinking of the 'there' by casting this 'there' in the terms of an opposition between the authentic place of issuelessness and the inauthentic issuelessness of placelessness.[4]

Now, this opposition has always already informed Heidegger's interpretation in *Being and Time* (1926) that *das Man* covers over from the beginning the 'thereness' of the 'there'. This is why in Heidegger's analysis of the existential 'being-towards-death' Dasein is interpreted as having to *extricate itself* from a *das Man* which precedes it. The 'as'-structure of nullity, of death, of the being of entities is, for this reason only, conceived as a willful *struggle* – one made in the name of futural ecstasis and the 'good' *Unheimlichkeit* of assumed nullity – against *das Man* of vulgar time and inauthentic *Unheimlichkeit*. This struggle is reinterpreted in *An Introduction to Metaphysics* (1935) as the constant struggle to 'bring being into manifestness' *against* the 'risk' of issuelessness. The struggle constitutes a retrospective phantasy consequent upon Heidegger's opposition of two temporalizations of time. The phantasy reorganizes in the logical form of two kinds of experience of 'homelessness' a 'there' which precedes Dasein and which it cannot make into its own self-temporalization. The uncovering of this 'there' from behind Heidegger's writing of it

shows the very opposition between these two kinds of homelessness
to be anthropocentric, prescriptive and illegitimate. In this sense the
opposition constitutes itself through disavowing the 'there'. Heidegger's
presentation of the aporia of death, his articulation of the aporia of
time as primordial temporality, and, finally, his rearticulation of primordial temporality as the *Fug* of the *polis* constitute the refusal to think
the *différance* of time *as* the originary delocalizing movement of time
(and) space.

The 'Da of Dasein', the 'As'-Structure of Death – Heidegger's Disavowal

Rather than articulating the 'taking over' of the 'there' with a view to
Dasein's self-projection, it should be considered more in terms of a non-
appropriable relation between Dasein and 'the other' which makes up the
'there' into which Dasein is thrown. Thrownness, in other words, should
be reinterpreted as a radical alterity which Dasein can never appropriate
to itself. This is at least Derrida's rethinking of the 'there'. Thus, in his
reading of 'being-towards-death' in *Aporias* (1994a) Derrida shifts the
accent of Heidegger's analysis from the possibility of impossibility of death
(death *as* death) to the impossibility of the appearing of the 'as such' of
death. He writes:

> There are several ways of thinking the possibility of impossibility
> as aporia. . . . What difference is there between the possibility
> of appearing as such of the possibility of an impossibility and
> the impossibility of appearing as such of the same impossibility?
> . . . To Heidegger, it is the impossibility of the 'as such', that,
> as such, would be possible to Dasein and not to any form of
> entity and living thing. But if the impossibility of the 'as such'
> is indeed the impossibility of the 'as such', it is also what cannot
> appear as such. Indeed, this relation to the disappearing as such
> of the 'as such' – the 'as such' that Heidegger makes the distinc-
> tive mark and the specific ability of Dasein – is the characteristic
> common both to the inauthentic and to the inauthentic forms of
> the existence of Dasein, common to all experiences of dying
> (properly dying, perishing and demising).
>
> (Derrida, 1994a: 75)

For Derrida, this is not just a point of logic. If the aporia of death cannot
be figured, that is, if no relation to death can appear as such, if there is
no 'as' to death, then Dasein's relation to death is always mediated through
an other. The 'as' of death always appears *through* an other's death, *for*
another.

> If death is indeed the possibility of the impossible and therefore the possibility of appearing as such of the impossibility of appearing as such, either, then, man, or man as Dasein, never has a relation to death as such, but only to perishing, to demising, and to the death of the other. . . . The death of the other thus becomes . . . 'first', always first.
>
> (ibid.)

Rather than confirming the futural possibilities of the self, the anticipation of death reveals that the other is always there before Dasein, and, more importantly, that the other structures Dasein's sense of self in the first place. This reintroduces *Mitsein* back into Heidegger's analysis of the *singularization* of Dasein in the anticipation of its own death (compare Jean-Luc Nancy, 1986). It testifies to the impossibility of Dasein appropriating the 'there', and to the fact that Dasein's possibilization can only be thought through *with respect to the other*. The recognition of the limit of death is always through another and is, therefore, at the same time the recognition of the other. So articulated, being-in-the-world is *prior* to the division between Dasein and *das Man*. The 'there' reappears from under Heidegger's oppositional logic as irreducible to *either* temporalizations of time, and, therefore, *either Unheimlichkeit*. The opposition between the primordial and vulgar temporalizations of time is radically displaced through the tying of the ecstases of primordial temporality to the *radical alterity* of the 'there'. The 'there' is neither authentic nor inauthentic; it distends the unity of time by disrupting incessantly the process of Dasein's self-projection. All Heidegger's oppositions consequent upon this temporal opposition are to be reinterpreted accordingly.

To interpret the 'there' as *das Man* out of which Dasein must extricate itself is an explicit move to keep time *within* Dasein's domain. It is to allow the temporalization of time to be exclusively thought in the form of Dasein's *self*-projection. Hence the 'throwness' of Dasein is interpreted, through anticipatory resoluteness, as Dasein's past. In this sense, the very opposition between two kinds of *Unheimlichkeit* (authentic taking over of the 'not' and the dissipated 'not' of dwelling from present to present) covers over the fact that 'primordial temporality' disavows (I would stress here the Freudian sense) the 'there'. By always already thinking the 'there' in terms of *das Man*, Heidegger protects Dasein from disappropriation. As a result of this disavowal, the relation between Dasein and the 'there' is figured as a constant struggle against a phantasmatic *das Man*. This phantasm draws upon itself the attribute of dissipation and disappropriation. Constrained by the force of Heidegger's metaphysical logic, *das Man* can do nothing else but dwell nowhere, passing from now to now. The term 'dissipation' is thus a metaphysical phantasy working in opposition to an equally phantasmatic heroic Dasein which serves to cover over an originary movement of 'homelessness' that can be neither thought nor fixed within oppositional logic. As I noted a moment ago, Heidegger's political engagements of the 1930s – his attempt to give Nazism a philosophical grounding from within the university – can therefore be considered as a *consequence* of the metaphysical logic informing Heidegger's understanding of the 'there'. It is this metaphysics which informs his analysis of modernity in the 1930s against which he pitches the political will of the German *Volk* to tear itself from the decline of being in global technology. The preceding reveals that such a projection constitutes what Derrida calls in *Of Spirit* (1987a) Heidegger's 'spiritualization' of Nazism (1987a: 43–73/23–46). Heidegger considers National Socialism in the light of his destruction of metaphysics whose horizon is primordial temporality. As Derrida puts it, Heidegger's gesture 'capitalizes on the worst, that is on both evils at once: the sanctioning of nazism, and the gesture that is still metaphysical' (1987a: 66/40).

The Call prior to the Temporalization of Time

To conclude this section on Heidegger, it is worth turning to an argument that follows the elaboration of the existential of 'being-towards-death' in *Being and Time* (1926), that concerning the attestation (*Bezeugung*) of authentic resoluteness (§54–§60). Heidegger's analysis of authentic resoluteness has often been interpreted as providing the key to the philosopher's voluntarism in the 1930s: it should consequently be read within the schema of 'disavowal' that I have proposed up to now. Something else, however, is also going on; something which Derrida has consistently thematized since the early 1980s in terms of 'law'. Let us recall, firstly, Heidegger's argument.

Primordial temporalization as the taking up of possibility must be *attested*. For how else, given the opposition between two modalities of time, can one cross from one *Unheimlichkeit* to the other? As we saw in Chapter 2 when dealing with the limit of an opposition, this classic metaphysical question structures all oppositional logic. In Heidegger the attestation comes through the 'call of conscience'. The call of conscience is a demand to Dasein to 'possibilize' from the future. The who to whom the call of conscience is made is Dasein gone astray in *das Man*. Dasein is brought back to 'itself' (1926: 268/313), from its alienated self lost in the *das Man*, by 'choosing to make the choice' of a 'potentiality-for-being' (273/318). With the focus on 'destroying' metaphysics in terms of time and articulating time as Dasein's self-affection, it is important for Heidegger to retain the call *within* the temporalizing structure of Dasein.

The call precedes all understandings of the voice of conscience as moral laws or rules. Ethics, à la Kant for example, presents the law as universal, that is beyond temporal and spatial inscription. For Heidegger, this presupposes a vulgar concept of time since, ultimately, ethics considers the law with respect to the 'eternal' (that is, an eternal present). The accompanying moral understanding of human imperfection as a 'lack' repeats this ethical denial of finitude: the present of humanity is related to a future present which may redeem it on the condition that humanity behaves in *relation* to this future present. In this sense, ethics – whether it be thought from the side of humanity or from the side of the law – is a transcription of vulgar time's fear of death. Ethics is to be understood temporally. Moral conscience is read by Heidegger as an *effect* of the call of conscience. The call reinscribes the voice of conscience back onto the groundless nullity of Dasein. Moral conscience, interpreted temporally, is the 'there' of Dasein. The call says nothing (273/317). It calls Dasein back onto its groundlessness *as* groundlessness and, in so doing, it calls it 'forth into its ownmost possibilities' (ibid.). The caller is thus nothing but the 'bare that it is' (278/322) of facticity, the recognition of 'being-in-the world' and the articulation of *Unheimlichkeit as Unheimlichkeit* (276–7/ 320–1). In other words, the caller of the call is Dasein itself. Heidegger notes that the call comes 'from me beyond me' (275/319). The call from Dasein to Dasein back to its own most 'being-guilty' is what Dasein *wills* in wanting to have a conscience (271/316). The call interpreted as Dasein's calling to itself from beyond itself is 'anticipatory resoluteness'. In the 1930s the call becomes the call to Germany to capture back, from the future, the 'questioning spirit' of 'primordial Greek knowledge' (1933: 473).

From the brief elaboration of this rich and complicated analysis of 'attestation' let me make several points and conclude.

First, Heidegger anthropomorphizes the 'there' in terms of Dasein by making the caller a part of Dasein itself. The originary split between, on the one hand, the 'there' preceding either primordial temporality or vulgar time and, on the other, Dasein is thereby *covered over* by a *philosophy of the will*. The will to conscience denies the passage of time; it is the 'presentation' of the aporia of time *qua* Dasein's self-affection. Both the *Rektoratsrede* of 1933 and the subsequent shift to the theme of *Gelassenheit* (1951/2, 1959) could be read and interpreted in this light.

Second, by conflating Dasein's temporalization and time, Heidegger effaces the future anterior of any act of anticipation. The effacement is predicated on the opposition between an authentic will which hears the call and an inauthentic will which hears it without hearing it.

Third, this opposition cannot be justified with regard to Dasein. One way to begin to consider it is in terms of an instance *within* and yet *outside* Dasein, a radical alterity that is nowhere else than in Dasein and yet is not Dasein – that is, an alterity prior to *either* the temporalization of Dasein *or* to its disappropriation. Thus one way to account, in the first place, for Heidegger's opposition between two modalities of time, between two ways of 'being-towards-death', between, finally, two ways of 'home-lessness', resides in conceptualizing an alterity that precedes Heidegger's destruction of metaphysics, that is which *precedes* the temporalization of time. This instance is the 'delay' of time, time's aporia.

In recent work (1994b: 347ff./164ff.), following a cryptic remark by Heidegger earlier in *Being and Time*, Derrida thinks of this alterity as 'the voice of the friend' whom 'every Dasein carries with it' (§34). I cannot go into the modality of this voice here. Suffice it to conclude that this voice articulates the 'there' of the other in 'being-towards-death' and names an 'absolute past' which makes possible Heidegger's oppositional understanding of time in the first place as well as all the oppositions which follow from this understanding. Prior to the temporalization of time, this voice is absolutely originary: the heterogeneity of its precedence over primordial temporalization makes it the law of all laws, what, we recall, *Specters of Marx* (1993) named the 'undeconstructible justice . . . the unde-constructible condition of all deconstruction' (1993: op. cit.). The aporia of time inverts into the aporia of law. The other of time is law.

Let us now turn to Levinas.

Levinas's Thinking of Aporia and the Fate of the Ethical

Levinas's Other: Derrida's Dual Relation to Levinas

We have just seen that within Heidegger's analysis of the presentation of time there insists a radical alterity which exceeds the ecstases of Dasein as temporal self-affection. Levinas's ethical thought constitutes an attempt to open up and pursue this alterity within ontology: hence its importance to Derrida. Levinas thereby places both western metaphysics and Heideggerian ontology in the sphere of 'the same' and ties them back to the aporetic relation to the other (what he calls 'a relation of non-relation').[5] Arguing that Heidegger pursues the concerns of the very tradition which he wishes to 'destroy' by casting his destruction in terms of the *self-appropriation* of Dasein, and, later, the *gathering* of being, Levinas reduces the ontico-ontological difference to the 'neutral' (1961: 12–18/42–8, 94–100/122–7, 142–9/168–74). From out of this gesture of reduction an alterity 'appears' which is other to all phenomenal appearance. This other is the 'first' of ethics upon which all ontology is predicated. Whilst this reduction is, as we shall see, theoretically problematic, the power of Levinas's move resides in the conviction that Heideggerian ontology continues to conflate logic and time. We have seen how Derrida articulates this conflation in the previous section. Levinas's articulation is similar yet different. The modality of the similarity and the difference will be the issue of this section since it will allow me to show how the difference between Levinas and deconstruction concerns the 'there' of time and is, again, one of a 'political' order.

For Levinas, the above conflation denies the 'ethical' relation to the other, an alterity which precedes the temporal ecstases of past, present and future. Heidegger's understanding of Dasein in terms of the futural horizon prolongs the metaphysical tradition of freedom as the 'autonomy' of the ego (see, especially, Levinas, 1976). Being, or primordial temporality, therefore forgets 'responsibility' for the other which precedes the temporalization of the ego. The temporalization of time *qua* primordial temporality does not, consequently, 'destroy' the ontological denial of time; it repeats it all the more subtly. For Levinas, 'Dasein' is responsible for the other, not because the other is Dasein's 'possibility', but because Dasein cannot appropriate it. Dasein is therefore *not* Dasein (being-there). Rather, and crucially, the 'there' of 'Dasein' is the *other* who looks at *me* before I can look at it. The 'there' is the relation to the other; Dasein is the '*I*' whose being (*Sein*) is its non-substitutable exposure to the other. The 'da' of 'Da(-sein)' becomes the other; the 'Sein' of '(Da-)sein' becomes the 'I'. The 'there' is the ethical.

Heterogeneous to time *qua* the temporalization and synthesis of time, the alterity of the other is thus an unsurpassable and 'impracticable' law. Levinas understands the word 'law' in a very particular sense: law in the 'ethical' sense is not a determined law (legal, juridical or moral) within time or beyond time *qua* the eternal (the ethical in an ontological sense); law is that which exceeds time 'in' time. That which the 'I' *cannot* recuperate (radical impossibility of being-there) is that towards which the 'I' is *responsible*. In other words, that which exceeds the *temporalization* of time (in the Heideggerian sense), or the excess of time (double genitive), or the time of the other – is in this sense, and in this sense only, the 'law'. The alterity of the other is the unpresentable 'aporia of law' in contrast, and in resistance to Heidegger's presentation of the aporia of time as primordial temporality.

This ethical way of looking at the conflation of time and logic in Heidegger is, however, ambivalent in Levinas: Derrida's relation to Levinas is structured around this ambivalence. Despite the use of a radical notion of alterity 'against' Heidegger, Derrida's insistence on the alterity which unmakes Heidegger's destruction of metaphysics forges in turn a *dual* relation to Levinas's own thinking of alterity.

On the one hand, it uses Levinas against Heidegger to confirm this movement of alterity; and to reflect upon that which is radically other to the temporalization of time according to a radical understanding of law. Thus one of Derrida's major 'philosophical' gestures which we saw in Chapter 1 with his essay 'Before the law' – namely, to show the radical inability of giving a history of transcendence, that is, precisely, of temporalizing the 'there' – is thought of in terms of law. The last para-graph of the first section of this chapter (p. 104) made in fact the same point. The aporia of genealogy (the inability to recount or account for the origin of transcendence which allows for the very gesture of genealogy in the first place) is considered by Derrida according to the aporia of law. Levinas, with Blanchot undoubtedly, has been crucial to this way of under-standing the excess of temporalization.[6]

On the other hand if, as we saw at the end of the last section, Derrida marks the fact that this movement of alterity is already 'there' in Heidegger, the mark is made so as not to *oppose* to Heidegger another tradition of thought which would repeat the errors of his own thinking of exemplarity and locality. It is, precisely, to keep the 'there' as complex as possible, as a 'play' of time and law, one which refuses the exemplary localization of thought. Levinas falls into the above trap of oppositional thinking when he demarcates the Jewish thinking and practice of the law from the Greek thinking and practice of being, and when, as a conse-quence of this logical demarcation, he calls the 'authentically human' the 'being-Jewish in every man' (1988: 192). In this demarcation, Levinas runs the risk of exemplifying and localizing the aporia of law – in which case, as we saw with Heidegger, the aporia is no longer a radical impasse. It is because of this risk that Derrida's wish, in a text as early as 'Violence and metaphysics: Essay on the thought of Emmanuel Levinas' (1967a: 117–228/79–153), to tie Levinas's philosophy back to a tradition of ontology is still relevant. In this text Derrida convincingly argues that the other presupposes being to 'be' another. For the other to appear as 'other', for me to 'relate' to the other in a relation of 'non-relation', the cate-gories of being are presupposed. Our reading of the Heideggerian 'as'-structure of being will have attuned us to this criticism. We have also seen that, for Heidegger, this structure is nothing but the ecstasis of time. Faithful to the general movement of 'Violence and metaphysics', I shall develop why Levinas's understanding of the other as the excess of time still lends itself to criticism working from within the ecstatic structure of time. The relation between the irreducibility of the other to time and the inverse irreducibility of the categories of being to 'speak of' the former irreducibility will arise from this development. I will then be able to show, in turn, why the danger of 'precedence' (the Other over others, Jewish alterity over others, and finally human alterity over other forms of alterity) continues to haunt Levinas's thinking of the other despite the fact that the later Levinas in *Otherwise than Being* (1974) forcefully incorporates Derrida's criticisms (see here Critchley, 1992: 145–87).

The question which I now wish to follow in relating Derrida and Levinas to the aporia of law is whether the ethical relation is therefore as *aporetic* as Levinas would wish. This was the question which we have already asked of Heidegger's negotiation with aporia. Thus in apparent opposition to Heidegger's philosophy of presentation Levinas goes too far in the other direction, losing the aporia of the law by surrendering a differentiated articulation *between* the other and the same, between ethical relation and temporalization, ending up like Heidegger with a non-aporetic 'invention' of aporia. The effect of this loss is the loss in turn of the *incalculable* nature of the relation between the other and its others (the community at large). I wish to consider here the relation between *autrui* and *le tiers* (the third party) and show the way in which a logical hierarchy returns *through* Levinas's very desire to place radical alterity outside logic. The second effect (as with Heidegger) is that of a politics of locality at the very moment that Levinas is thinking, contra Heidegger's understanding of authentic *Unheimlichkeit*, the other as a 'non-place'. This politics is one of ethical singularity. We shall therefore see that Levinas's very resistance to Heidegger's conflation of logic and time leads him at the same time to a political logic of aporia.

The first part of my argument distinguishes Levinas's thought from that of Heidegger by considering the thinking of the ethical relation as a thinking in ethical resistance to the Heideggerian 'da' of Dasein. It elaborates the ethical relation in terms of the Idea of the infinite, of teaching, of the lapse of time, of responsibility and finally of the impossible 'experience' of death. This last articulation of the ethical relation draws together the way in which Levinas's thinking of the other is one which punctures Dasein's self-affection *qua* the alterity of time. Following the above comments, I stress how this alterity of time is, for Levinas, 'ethical'. I then suggest what the particular modality of the above problems with Levinas's thinking of the other is. This takes me to the second part of my argument concerning the loss of aporia.[7]

The Other as Absolute Past

In the context of our exposition of Heidegger's disavowal of the 'there', the other is most coherently articulated in *Totality and Infinity* (Levinas, 1961) as an 'absolute' past, a past which exceeds the temporal ecstases of past, present and future. We will begin here, returning later to the less coherent articulations of the other in this text. The articulation of the other as an absolute past moves from Levinas's rewriting of the Cartesian 'idea of the infinite' in the *Meditations* (1641) (a classic contribution to the emergence of the modern autonomous subject) to a temporal analysis of teaching. *Totality and Infinity* thereby returns the modern subject to its ethical condition.

For the Descartes of the *Meditations*, the idea of God is the name of the infinity which surpasses me. In the third *Meditation* ('Of God, that he exists') only the idea of God is considered to be irreducible to the conceptual, imaginative powers of the Cogito and, therefore, something of which the Cogito cannot be a cause. The ideas of men, animals and angels can be provided by a mixture of other ideas of corporeal things and of God. The ideas of corporeal things can be formed by the idea which the Cogito has of itself or can be the fruit of the imaginations of its imperfection. The Cogito who is a finite substance can have no idea, however, of an infinite substance unless it has been placed in the *Sum* by a substance which is infinite. This is Levinas's ethical translation of the Cartesian fact that finitude presupposes the infinite:

> The transcendence of the Infinite with respect to the I which is separated from it and which thinks it, measures (so to speak) its very infinitude. The distance that separates *ideatum* and idea here constitutes the content of the *ideatum* itself. Infinity is characteristic of a transcendent being as transcendent; the infinite is the absolutely other. The transcendent is the sole *ideatum* of which there can only be an idea in us; it is infinitely removed from its idea, that is exterior, because it is infinite. To think the infinite, the transcendent, the Stranger is hence not to think an object.
>
> (Levinas, 1961: 20/49)

This inscription is a 'past' 'cause' which has never entered into the synthetic time of cause and effect and, therefore, of temporalization. As the later text 'God and philosophy' succinctly puts it:

> The idea of the infinite is an idea carrying a signifyingness ('signifiant d'une signifiance') prior to presence, to any presence, prior to any origin in conscience, an-archic and so only accessible in its trace; carrying the meaning of a meaning older than its exhibition, not exhausting itself in this exhibition . . ., breaking with the coincidence between being and appearing.
>
> (1975: 107)

For Levinas, contra Heidegger, classical concepts of transcendence (of the eternally present in Heideggerian terms) re-mark the ethical relation to the other which is a trace of the radical absence of God. This absolute past is an ethical reinscription of western understandings of transcendence: as 'ethical', it is 'infinite'. Thus Levinas's rereading of the metaphysical tradition with respect to the 'ethical' excess of time (double genitive) constitutes an ethical contestation of the reach of Heidegger's destruction of metaphysics according to time. Levinas's reading of teaching confirms both this reinscription of transcendence onto the other who always comes first and the fact that this other is thought in 'infinite', ethical terms.

That the other is there before me is nothing other than the pedagogical situation. Ethical transcendence is met every day as the transmission of knowledge from the 'I' to the 'you'. However every day, the relation is the expression of the infinite in the finite (another formulation of the above 'idea' of the infinite). It is pertinent at this juncture to recall the classic text on education, Plato's *Meno*, in which the antecedence of knowledge prior to the 'I' forms an aporia of thought. Socrates articulates the aporia in the following terms:

> It is impossible for a man to discover either what he knows or what he does not know. He could not seek what he knows, for since he knows it there is no need of the inquiry, nor what he does not know, for in that case he does not even know what he is to look for.
>
> (*Meno*, 80e)

Socrates takes this aporia up only to resolve it with the myth of reminiscence. The teaching of the ideal by Socrates to another (in the context, that of the ideal geometric forms to Meno's slave) is nothing but the reminiscence by the slave of an anterior life. The myth of reminiscence thereby unties the *aporia* of memory by inaugurating the oppositions, which become metaphysical, between infinite and finite, transcendental and empirical, soul and body, *logos* and *techne*, form and matter. Instituting them, the myth covers over the non-originary nature of thought which Socrates, and the metaphysical tradition which he inaugurates, 'forget' by articulating the aporia of thought in terms of reminiscence. Indeed, one should argue that the myth of reminiscence is nothing but the forgetting of the aporia *as* the logic of opposition.

Although Levinas does not make reference to *Meno*, he often speaks of the Socratic maieutic. Its ironic structure is conceived of as an ethical dilemma. That is to say, Levinas's understanding of teaching rearticulates the Socratic aporia of thought as the ethical relation to the other which is disavowed in the oppositional thought of ontology, including that informing Heidegger's temporalizations. The temporalization of time disavows the other. The other which precedes me is my teacher: the law of the other is that I must learn 'my' past which is given to me through another. In distinction to Dasein, the past is not, then, *my* past but the gift of the other to me: this is why the other is a law and why Levinas thinks the alterity of the 'there' through a reinscription of *religious* terms, terms which remain humanist. For the other is *another human*, trace of the radical absence of God. (One can see the whole ambiguity of Levinas's thought here: beyond the concept of the human as a subject, ethical alterity remains, nevertheless, exclusively human.) In *Totality and Infinity* this other is the *maître*:

Teaching does not simply transmit an abstract and general content already common to me and the other. It does not merely assume an after all subsidiary function of being midwife to a mind already pregnant with its fruit. Speech [*la parole*] first founds community by giving, by presenting the phenomenon as given; and it gives by thematizing. The proposition relates the phenomenon to the existent, to exteriority, to the infinity of the other uncontained by my thought.... Teaching as the work of language, as an action exercised by the Master on me, is not a mysterious information, but the appeal [*appel*] addressed to my attention.... The eminently sovereign attention in me is what essentially responds to an appeal. Attention is attention to something because it is attention to someone. The exteriority of its point of departure is essential to it: it is the very tension of the I. School, without which no thought is explicit conditions science.

(1961: 71–2/98–9)

Levinas continues:

The transitivity of teaching, and not the interiority of reminiscence, manifests being; the locus of truth is society. The *moral* relation with the Master [sic] who judges me subtends the freedom of my adherence to the true.... Our relations are never reversible. This supremacy posits him in himself, outside of my knowing, and it is by relation to this absolute that the *given* takes on meaning. ... My freedom is challenged by a master who can invest it.

(1961: 74–5/100)

These are dense and important passages from which much could be drawn concerning recent 'French' thinking on alterity and to which I will return in my general conclusion. Let me, here, highlight the following.

The aporia of thought is nothing but the aporia of heritage or tradition. Contra Heidegger, the 'figure' of *aporia* is interpreted in ethical, not temporal terms, or rather, as we shall see in a moment, time is thought ethically – that is, in terms which interpret the interruption of self-affection *in respect of* the alterity of another human being. Inheritance is the transmission of the given *from* teacher *to* student.

What is important for Levinas in this act of transmission is not the *what* or the *how* of transmission, nor indeed the *where* or the *when*, but the *who* of transmission. The *who* is 'first' and the *what* or the *how* are always already interpreted as the given (*le donné*) coming 'after' the *who*, *within* the ontological, phenomenological or theoretical gesture.

The who is the *maître*, thematizer of the given (*le donné*). In other words, the given is first a gift (*un don*) exceeding the consciousness of the receiver and only then an object opposed to a supposed subject. The given is subordinated to human alterity. This is what, for Levinas, the tradition has forgotten – it has forgotten the 'infinitude' of its own facticity. The other, condition of the given, is therefore *separate* from what it gives. Hence my earlier stress on the religious terms in which this reflection upon alterity is couched.

Heidegger's understanding of 'thrownness' is reinscribed as a past which affects the 'ego' as a master to whom the 'I' is 'irreversibly' passive, however 'free' the 'I' then becomes. This means in turn that the Levinasian *maître* radically cuts across the Heideggerian articulation of the 'there' as an opposition between authentic and inauthentic *Unheimlichkeit*. The *maître* is precisely what Heidegger's opposition between primordial temporality and vulgar time disavows in order to constitute itself as such.

This means, finally, that the *maître* will haunt *any* subsequent 'self-appropriation'.

The Other as the Ethical Recurrence of Time

This haunting – or 'spectrality' to use Derrida's term (1993) – is always thought by Levinas as both the radical affectivity of the ego (the absolute past of the *maître*) and the very diachrony of time. The radical affectivity of the ego *qua* the absolute past of the other re-marks itself as the recurrence of time. The diachrony of time is both the fact that the other comes before me and the constant 'interruption' of the self's temporal experience. Thus, whereas for the Heidegger of *Being and Time* (1926) and *Kant and the Problem of Metaphysics* (1929), time is considered exclusively in terms of the 'temporalization' of time, for Levinas time is the suffering of its passing, the 'not yet' of the imminence of death. Time is that which exceeds its temporalization: the excess of time (double genitive). This excess of time is transcribed in ethical terms. The suffering of the delay of time, which the I has always already 'experienced' as the radical passivity to the absolute past of the other, delivers me over, *at the same time*, and *all the time*, to the other (as others). In other words – and this is the haunting of the *maître* – the absolute past *qua* recurrence of time *produces itself* in my responsibility *for* others. In delay upon the other, receptive to the other who gives to me, I am at the same time always already exposed to the other. The *maître* from whom I learn is 'also' the neighbour to whom I give. The delay of time, which is marked in the fact that there is teaching, re-marks itself in my unconditioned responsibility to others. Time is not only irrecoverable; being irrecoverable, time is ethics.

The blow of the affection [of the neighbour] makes an impact, traumatically, in a past more profound than all that I can reassemble by memory, by historiography, all that I can dominate by the a priori – in a time before the beginning. (Note: The passivity of affection is more passive than the radical receptivity Heidegger speaks of in connection with Kant [in *Kant and the Problem of Metaphysics*, 1929] where the transcendental imagination offers the subject an alcove of nothingness so as to precede the given and assume it.) The neighbour strikes me before striking me; as though I had heard before he spoke. This anachronism attests to a temporality different from that which scans consciousness. It takes apart *the recuperable time* of history and memory in which representation continues. For if, in every experience, the making of a fact precedes the present of experience, the memory, the history, or extratemporality of the a priori recuperates the divergence and creates a correlation between this past and the present. In proximity is heard a command come as though from an immemorial past, which was never present, began in no freedom. This *way* of the neighbour is a face.

(Levinas, 1974: 140–1/88)

The 'impossible' experience of radical passivity produces itself both as the recurrence of time and as my 'infinite' responsibility for others. Indeed, for Levinas, and the point comes out more clearly and more coherently in *Otherwise than Being* than in *Totality and Infinity*, radical passivity, the recurrence of time and responsibility for others are the same 'experience'. These experiences are consequently all impossible. Temporal delay is ethical debt. We will come back to this important point in a moment. First, let us note how Levinas elaborates responsibility as a radical impossibility. Not surprisingly, the elaboration is to be found in Levinas's rewriting of the Heideggerian existential of 'being-towards-death'.

The 'Impossible' Limit of Death, Levinas's Hesitation and its 'Fate'

In *Totality and Infinity* (1961: 200–60/232–86) and the short article 'Deficiency without care in the new sense' (1976: 77–89) Levinas focuses on the problem of the *limit* of death which we looked at earlier with Derrida's *Aporias* (1994b). For Levinas, Heidegger appropriates the limit rather than returning it to *the other* of time. The existential of 'being-towards-death' is consequently a 'being-able' (*pouvoir-être*), not the impossibility of all power. The limit experience of the human always provides for Heidegger the occasion to relocate the human in this world. Hence Heidegger's treatment of death in terms of 'nullity': the future of

Dasein is either Dasein's future, or nothing (Levinas, 1976: 82–3). The other is forgotten in primordial temporalization. The Heideggerian concept of the world is the ego in this sense. For Levinas, on the other hand, the 'impossibility' of death for the ego confirms that the experience of finitude is one of radical passivity (1974: 166/129). That the 'I' cannot experience its 'own' death means, firstly, that death is an imminence *without* horizon, and secondly, that time is that which exceeds my death, that time is the generation which precedes and follows me (1961: 260/282–3, and Levinas's development on 'fecundity' at the end of the book). The recognition of death is not the 'taking-over' *of* time, for Levinas, but the confirmation of the human's submission *to* time. The impossibility of death recalls the distinction between the temporalization *of* time (Heideggerian 'memory') and the *passing* of time (the excess of 'memory'). Death is not a limit or horizon which, re-cognized, allows the ego to assume the 'there'; it is something that never arrives in the ego's time, a 'not-yet' which confirms the priority of time over the ego, marking, accordingly, the precedence of the other over the ego (1961: 208–13/232–6). The impossibility of death confirms the impossibility of ethical experience:

> My death comes from an instant upon which I can in no way exercise my power. I do not run up against an obstacle which at least I touch in that collision, which, in surmounting or in enduring it, I integrate into my life, suspending its alterity. Death is a menace that approaches me as a mystery, its secrecy determines it – it approaches without being able to be assumed, such that the time that separates me from my death dwindles and dwindles without end, involves a sort of last interval which my consciousness cannot traverse, and where a leap will somehow be produced from death to me ... the I in its projection towards the future is overturned by a movement of imminence, pure menace which comes to me from an absolute alterity. ... But immanence is at the same time menace and postponement. It pushes on, and it leaves time. To be temporal is still to be for death, and still to have time, to be against death. ... It is a relation with an instant whose exceptional character is due not to the fact that it is at the threshold of nothingness or of a rebirth, but to the fact that, in life, it is the impossibility of every possibility, the stroke of a total passivity alongside of which the passivity of the sensibility, which moves into activity, is but a distant imitation. ... On the way to death, but a death ever future, exposed to death, but not *immediately*, [the I] has time to be for the Other, and thus to recover meaning despite death.
>
> (1961: 211–13/234–6)

By refusing death as a limit, Levinas, in a move symmetrically opposite to that of Heidegger, argues that death *im*possibilizes existence. In confirming the alterity of time and the alterity of time as the alterity of the other, death confirms the ecstasis of time (time's throwing out of 'itself' from 'itself') as the ethical relation, that is, as the 'impossible' alterity of the other. Now this point is crucial for two sets of reasons: we need here to go carefully, but we must also be incisive.

To turn to the initial set: firstly, if death constitutes an impossible alterity, then death is not for me *nor*, however, is it for the other either. For the alterity of death rather than signalling the other signals the *alterity* of the other, the other, if one wishes, as the recurrence of time. Death not only means that the ego is in constant self-alteration (the initial point contra Heidegger's existential of death), but also that the other is only 'other' in the constant re-marking of the alterity of the other. Thus, the alterity of the other is not *the other*, but its alterity, its 'self'-alteration. This alterity not only exceeds the ego, it *also* exceeds the other. It is in this sense, precisely, that there 'is' no other, that the other is time; and that time is 'equally' the recurrent alterity of others. As I said in Chapter 1, and the whole force of the point can be disentangled, I believe, from Derrida's relation to Levinas, 'time is ... the *différance* of the singular' (p. 43).

Second, if no experience of the absolute past and no experience of death mean no experience of 'responsibility', it is because all three testify to the *delay* of time. Each experience issues from the passage of time, for which the human is always too late. This is a thesis of considerable consequence. Derrida's comments in the introduction to this chapter on the American Declaration of Independence as well as his whole thinking of the 'incalculability' of responsibility in 'Before the law' (1985), 'The Force of law: The "mystical foundation of authority"' (1992b), *Specters of Marx* (1993) and many other texts are indebted to this thesis and have made much of it. It implies that no one can call him or herself responsible if he or she takes time seriously: or, inversely, taking time seriously draws to an end any horizonal understanding of ethics. For since the logic of any horizon (compare the work of Chapter 1) is interrupted from the beginning by the self-contradictory nature of this very logic, and since this self-contradictory nature can be traced to the return of the disavowal of (the aporia of) time, then time undermines from the beginning the coherence of an ethical programme. As the section on Lévi-Strauss in Chapter 1 and the section on Kantian ethics in Chapter 2, if not the whole of Chapter 2, showed us, the fate of positing the ethical is to become unethical. To be ethical means not being ethical, not knowing the ethical, not even consistently using the term *all the time*. The disjointure of time is justice *qua* the excess of any norm or rule. This is the reason why, working Levinas with Heidegger, Derrida will write:

> The necessary disjointure, the detotalizing condition of justice, is ... that of the present – and by the same token the very condition of the present and of the presence of the present. This is where deconstruction would always begin to take place as the thinking of the gift and of undeconstructible justice, the undeconstructible condition of any deconstruction, to be sure, but a condition that is itself *in deconstruction* and remains, and must remain (that is the injunction) in the disjointure of the *Un-Fug*. ... Otherwise justice risks being reduced once again to juridical-moral rules, norms or representations, within an inevitable totalizing horizon.
>
> (1993: 56/28)

The delay upon time that makes up the finitude of the human gives rise to the indefinite 'infinity' of responsibility. The ethical is the surprise of the other, what Derrida calls in the same work and elsewhere, the *arrivant* (1993, 1994a, 1994b).

The point concerning the impossibility of death is important for a second set of reasons. It also highlights where Levinas hesitates in his analysis of alterity and where, therefore, one can distinguish Derrida's thinking of alterity and responsibility from that of Levinas. Levinas's hesitation has a long and complicated history which includes an *Auseindersetzung* with Derrida which I do not have space to enter into in detail. I refer the reader to Simon Critchley's careful exposition of the misunderstandings, disagreements and differences in his *The Ethics of Deconstruction* (1992: Chapters 3 and 4).[8] Suffice it to schematize this history in the following pages in the context of my argument.

Levinas's thinking of alterity in *Totality and Infinity* (1961) as well as in essays prior to, or contemporary with this work, is riven by an explicit ambiguity regarding the 'place' of alterity in the relation between the other and the same.

On the one hand, when Levinas speaks of the other, he *means* the alterity of the other. This is the thinking of alterity that we have remained faithful to up until now. In this formulation Levinas's capitalization of the other as either *l'Autre* or *Autrui* marks the absolute past, the recurrence of time as the delivery of the ego over to others (in French *autrui*). Thus, rather schematically, Levinas's distinctions are something like the following. *Autrui* or *Autre* is the alterity of time *qua* the infinite responsibility of the ego to *autrui*. Phenomenal human beings to whom the I is responsible *ad infinitum* are called *autrui* (lower case). *Autrui* (upper case) is the *face* of alterity 'in' phenomenal human beings, such that I am always responsible *to* others. In other terms, *Autrui* is the 'ad infinitum' of *autrui*; and *l'Autre* is the alterity particular to the face, the transcendent infinite in the finite (what Levinas also designates *l'Autre* as against *le Même*).

On the other hand, and in the same breath, both *Autre* and *Autrui* also constitute in Levinas's writings figures *of* alterity. No longer the alterity of the figure against which the ego meets its own limits, they become alterity itself. This is especially the case in *Totality and Infinity* where the ego is considered in terms of an economy of enjoyment out of which it comes to 'meet' *l'Autre* (see in particular 1961: 115–60/ 143–86, esp. 122–3/148–9). This logic of a meeting between other and ego is in direct contradiction with the first formulation of the other as an absolute past. For the 'I' can only 'meet' someone in the *present*.

I would argue that it is due to this contradiction in Levinas's formulation of alterity (on the one hand the alterity of figure or, on the other, the figure of alterity) that Derrida's text 'Violence and metaphysics' takes a great deal of care pointing out that Levinas's thematization of the other 'as' other presupposes the 'as'-structure of Heideggerian ontology (1967a: 125–37/84–92). In this text Derrida convincingly argues that the other presupposes being to 'be' another and that Levinas unsuccessfully sets up a distinction between ethics and ontology. Thus, a philosophy of (ethical or any kind of) difference must install itself in the categories of the philosophical tradition to destroy this tradition, theorizing its complicity with that which it wishes to give a genealogy of. It must reside in an 'economy of violence', practising from within this economy the 'lesser violence' (1967a: 136, n. 1/313, n. 21). To welcome the other *as* other, *as Autrui*, the other must come into form. *Autrui* is never quite *Autrui*, that is, radically other, the alterity of form, in being thematized *as Autrui*. Language presupposes being. Thus, the 'as'-structure of being is the very condition of the appearance of the other 'as' other and therefore the very possibility of Levinas thematizing *Autrui* as non-thematizable. Levinas is consequently not thinking being in terms of the 'as'-structure of an entity's being (he is confusing ontology and thematics); nor is he thematizing his own necessary entanglement in ontology in order to give voice to that which precedes it *qua* a relation which allows the other and the same to be thought as 'a relation of non-relation'. In other words, Levinas's theory of alterity does not think the 'economy of violence' in which any other is caught if it is to be recognized *as* other. For the other to be other it must already be less than other: one cannot 'welcome the other as other' (ibid.). In consequence, alterity can only be the loss of the other in its self-presentation, that is, the 'trace' of the other. This trace signals the collapse of any temporal horizon, that of being or of the other. Much of Derrida's 'Violence and Metaphysics' is taken up with this twofold problem, from which arises the thinking of the lesser violence in an economy of violence.

We can see, however, from the above contradiction that Levinas opens himself up to this kind of criticism precisely because he seems unsure where to focus the alterity of the other: in the *alterity* of the other, or in the alterity of the *other*? I would suggest here that Derrida's criticisms partly ensue from this hesitation or confusion on Levinas's part, and that it is the hesitation or confusion that is of particular interest. For the difference between these two modalities of alterity – the alterity of figure and the figure of alterity – is analogous to and as important, philosophically *and* politically (as I shall develop), as the difference of the 'as such' which structured Derrida's reading of the Heideggerian aporia of death.

To recall – Derrida noted that for Heidegger, 'it is the impossibility of the "as such" [of death], that, as such, would be possible to Dasein and not to any form of entity and living thing. But if the impossibility of the "as such" is indeed the impossibility of the "as such", it is also what cannot appear as such' (1994a: 75). He continued: 'The death of the other thus becomes ... "first", always first' (ibid.). In this context we earlier opposed Levinas to Heidegger's understanding of death as primordial temporality. Now, however, we have the same problem with Levinas's understanding. He writes, for example, in *Totality and Infinity* that 'Death, source of all myths, is *present* only in the Other, and only in him does it summon me urgently to my final essence, to my responsibility' (1961: 154/179, my emphasis – R.B.). In sharp contrast to my earlier elaboration of the radical alterity of death, the alterity of the other is here figured *as such*. As a result, the 'I', rather than seeking self-resolution through the futural horizon of its death, is appropriated by the other. The 'I'␣'s essence resides in the relation to the other's death. Death is present only in the 'Other'. The radical alterity of death is inscribed as 'the Other'. The 'as such' of the alterity of the other – the Other – here returns in Levinas's symmetrical opposition to Heidegger's 'as-structure' of being.

For some, this may appear a minor point. The implications are, however, large: hence my attention in this chapter to Heidegger and Levinas's respective perspectives on death as well as my developing these perspectives in a reflection upon the political. In his desire to demarcate the other from being, Levinas's opposition to ontology uncannily repeats ontological criteria. For, placed outside being, the other becomes another being, turning back into its other at the moment it distinguishes itself from it. Levinasian ethics cannot control this inversion without acknowledging that it is not the other or being that matters, but the 'impossible' limit between the two. As a result of Levinas not theorizing the impossibility of this limit, nor prioritizing in his reflections on alterity the status of this impossibility, just as Dasein's self-projection from the future filled in the 'there', so now 'the other' covers over the 'there'. The point is theorizable, however, in terms of aporia. The ethical, by being demarcated too much from the ontological, ends up itself ontological *because the limit is not developed*. With the limit between the other and the same unarticulated, the other ends up as the 'same'. Levinas has lost the aporia of the other by determining it 'as' the aporia of law, rather than thinking this aporia in aporetic relation to (the form of) temporalization. To do so means thinking the relation between radical alterity and being as irreducible, but *unlocatable*. The alterity of the other is nowhere else than in being, but it is not reducible to being either, the alterity of the other exceeds the forms of temporality but it is not outside these forms – 'existing' somewhere else – either, etc. If the above sounds Hegelian, and to an extent my point is, let us nevertheless recall from Chapter 2 that Hegel locates the limit also when he reduces the alterity of time to the logic of contradiction. So we cannot simply mobilize Hegel against the inconsistencies of Levinas. There is no selection here between thinkers: our interest is the 'there'.

Now, it would appear that, if Levinas stressed the absolute pastness of the other, the above objections could be answered. The later *Otherwise than Being or Beyond Essence* (1974) would seem to remove, for example, the lack of articulation between other and same by stressing that the other is *related to the trace of an absolute past*. The other does not *figure* the absolute past, it is related to it as its 'trace'. The other is thus not itself a radical alterity but the trace of a radical alterity, the 'trace of a trace'. The 'as such' of the other is both the violent inscription of radical alterity in the world and, at the same time, due to this violence, the *infinite deferment* of this radical alterity. We are in the familiar territory of what throughout this book I have called the 'fate' of inscription. This latter trace is most often called 'God' or 'illeity' by Levinas (see particularly 1975: 93–127/1989: 166–98). Radically absent, God is the one name 'not entering into a grammatical category' (1974: 206/162).

If my previous treatment of the *maître* as both absolute past and as the recurrence of the neighbour has sought to underline that this latter conception of alterity is already in *Totality and Infinity*, it is not to suggest that we should ignore Levinas's hesitation between the above two formulations of alterity. On the contrary, both the distinction and the contradiction remain central to the way in which Levinas 'determines' the excess of time. It is in the particular nature of this determination that Levinas ends up being political despite himself. I can here return to my argument.

We have seen that in the more profound understanding of alterity – one which gets behind the Heideggerian 'as'-structure of primordial temporalization – the excess of the very determination of the other *as* other is nothing else than the *impossibility* of welcoming the other as other. This notion of alterity is one that 'Violence and Metaphysics' considers as becoming constantly figured in *Totality and Infinity*, confirming the major thesis of this book that 'time is violence' (Derrida, 1967a: 195/133), that the movement of temporalization always returns the absolute alterity of the other to the same. Radical alterity is thus nothing but the 'guilt' of always having determined the other as 'another', of having sacrificed another for it or it for another. The impossibility of radical alterity re-marks itself as the absolute future of the other or the excess of time. Radical alterity inscribes itself in time as the failure of the relation between the other and the same. For there are always *more* than two. This failure 'forms' the trace of absolute otherness. Thus the aporia of law is not the other but the *oscillation* 'between' the other and determination, which oscillation is the 'always more than two'. The aporia of law 'is' the passage of time, with the other always appearing in the same and not being respected except in and as the same. This 'between' re-marks the recur-rence of time, the infinity of responsibility. It forms the 'and' within the originary complex of 'aporia *and* decision' discussed in Chapter 1. Therefore, as soon as the other figures this 'and', the relation is fixed. As we saw above concerning the presence of the other's death, the ethical inverts into the unethical in Levinas's sense that the other becomes, against itself, 'ontological'. This is why, as Derrida stresses, responsibility lies in the impossibility of responsibility: one cannot be exclusively responsible to the other without losing the alterity of the other *as* others. It is because there is no Other that there are others. This is in part what Levinas means by 'illeity'. However, his inconsistent use of *autrui, Autrui, l'autre, l'Autre, absolument autre* and *un autre*, together with his concomitant tendency to confuse the alterity of time and that of the other, blur the point. The lack of clarity risks reversing the responsibility of the ego (moral autonomy) into the responsibility of the other (an ethics of the figure of the Other). The rest of this section will show the stages of the reversal.

The 'Third Party' and the Limit

From our earlier analysis of the ego, the other and time we saw that the relation between the ego and the other is a relation which exceeds the order of understanding and calculation. Calculation arrives with *le tiers* (the third party) whose arrival introduces the problem of justice and deter-mined law. It is with this arrival that conceptuality and ontology are made possible and calculation begins.

> The act of consciousness is motivated by the presence of a third party alongside of the neighbour approached. A third party is also approached; and the relationship between the neighbour and the third party cannot be indifferent to me when I approach. There must be a justice among incomparable ones. There must then be a comparison among incomparables and a synopsis, a togetherness and contemporaneousness, there must be themati-zation, thought, history and inscription.
>
> (Levinas, 1974: 20/16)

Since my relation to the other is an absolute past, it is necessarily only with *le tiers* that conscious relations of equity are posed, that is, that what is incomparable is compared. Given that comparison of the incomparable will necessarily fail, the incomparable will always recur as the 'infinity' of calculation. Since, moreover, this relation is an absolute past, the arrival of *le tiers* is *not* an empirical event. Not only are 'we' always already with others, in memory, in time, etc., but *le tiers* 'looks at me in the eyes of the Other' (Levinas, 1961: 187–8/213). Levinas explicitly states the plurality of the relation in the following terms:

> The third party is other than the neighbour, but also another neighbour, and also a neighbour of the other, and not simply his fellow. What then are the other and the third party for one another? What have they done to one another? Which passes for the other? The other stands in a relationship with the third party, for whom I cannot entirely answer, even if I alone answer, before any question, for my neighbour.
>
> (1974: 200/157)

That the other becomes determined is, then, expressly against Levinas's own intentions, revealing an aporetic 'logic' stronger than Levinas's logic of the other. This aporetic logic problematizes Levinas's ethical opposition to Heidegger's conflation of logic and time and reveals where Derrida's respective negotiation with aporia can allow us to develop this 'fate' of Levinas's thinking of the other. Such an approach prolongs the insights of Derrida's 'Violence and metaphysics'.

Following Levinas's own terms, the third party is already there as the other and yet the third is also distinct from the other. As a result, responsibility is 'troubled' by the entry of the third party. Let me quote Levinas again before questioning his argument:

> The description of proximity as a haliography of the one-for-the-other subtends society, which begins with the entry of the third man. In it my response prior to any problem, that is, my responsibility, poses problems, if one is not to abandon oneself to violence. It then calls for comparison, measure, knowing, laws, institutions – justice. But it is important for the very equity of justice that it contain the signification that had dictated it.
>
> (1974: 116/p. 193, ch. 3, n. 33)

Out of representation is produced the order of justice moderating or measuring the substitution of me for the other, and giving the self over to calculus. Justice requires contemporaneousness of representation. It is thus that the neighbour becomes visible, and looked at, presents himself, and there is also justice for me. The saying is fixed in a said, is written, becomes a book, law and science.

(1974: 202/159)

Calculation, conscience, the question of justice all emerge when the third has arrived, although the third has *always already* arrived. The third is from the first there, and yet it is third, coming 'after' a singular relation between the ego and the other. This double arrival of the third confirms Levinas's difficulty in thinking the limit between, on the one hand, the unpresentable other and, on the other, the visibility of relations *between* the other, the ego and the third; that is, the limit between the law of the other and the movement of temporalization. For if the other is necessarily forgotten in the comparing of singularities in the space of representation, if this forgetting allows for the infinity of the other as radically other, then the concept of responsibility translates the impossible limit between responsibility as substitution (radical passivity) and the ego, consciousness and comparison. Responsibility is in other words the negotiation between the two. It is therefore risky to make a definitive distinction (be it formal or pedagogical) between the other and *le tiers*. The distinction could both fix this limit as the other and place the other in distinction to others. The fixing of this limit makes the *unjustifiable* nature of my responsibility to one other as against another other justifiable. An essentialism of the other ensues when radical alterity is determined in this manner.

This is the reason why it is important to draw a distinction between *Autrui* and *autrui*. That Levinas is content at times to write the other as the trace of the other and, at other times, to figure the other as alterity, that he is content to even speak of a 'third' betrays both an incoherence and a particular refusal to measure up to the complicity of his categories with the tradition. My responsibility to the other is that I can never be responsible to the other, that the third has precisely always already arrived. It is in this sense that responsibility is an infinite, impossible experience, that there is no concept as such of responsibility. I am always on the *limit* between the other and the third, in the aporia of law (and) time.

Let me quote in this context a passage from Derrida's 'Donner la mort' (1992a: 11–108). The passage forms part of a sustained commentary on Kierkegaard's interpretation in *Fear and Trembling* (1843) of the 'sacrifice' of Isaac by Abraham :

What binds me, in my singularity, to the absolute singularity of the other throws me immediately into the space or the risk of absolute sacrifice. There are also others, in infinite number, the innumerable generality of others, to whom the same responsibility should bind me, a general and universal responsibility (what Kierkegaard calls the ethical order). I cannot respond to the call, to the demand, obligation, nor even to the love of another, without sacrificing to him the other other, other others [*sans lui sacrifier l'autre autre, les autres autres*]. Every other is quite other [*Tout autre est tout autre*]. The simple concepts of alterity and singularity are constitutive of the concept of duty as much as that of responsibility. They lend, a priori, the concepts of responsibility, decision and duty to paradox, scandal and aporia. The paradox, the scandal or the aporia are nothing themselves but the sacrifice.

(1992a: 66)

Alterity cannot be figured. The unpresentable order of alterity re-marks itself as the fact that this alterity is the occasion for sacrificing others for it. This sacrifice is *unjustifiable*. These themes redeploy my exposition of singularity in Chapter 1. Derrida writes:

How will you justify the fact that you find yourself here, speaking French, rather than speaking any other language. And yet we are also doing our duty by behaving in this way. There is no language, reason, generality or mediation to justify this ultimate responsibility which leads us to the absolute sacrifice.

(1992a: 71)

If this seems Levinasian, there is a slight, but important change of accent. Derrida's 'economy of sacrifice' precedes the distinction between other and third party, conjoining the disjointure of 'there' with temporalization. As a result, firstly, there is no possibility nor risk of figuring the other as 'logically' prior. When Levinas argues that the name God is 'a proper and unique noun not entering into any grammatical category' (1974: 206/162), when he argues that language necessarily 'betrays' this uniqueness, the radical alterity of God is fixed. It is fixed *as* 'God'. Although Levinas's God is not the God of ontotheology – the God, for example, of the American Declaration of Independence which fills in the excess of time – it is still God. Still God, it also fills in the excess of time, not, of course, by concentrating the trace of time within the present, but by thinking this trace within a specific understanding of alterity – the other is always already *a human being*, one related to a specific understanding of divinity. In radically singularizing the name of God, Levinas fixes the aporia of law *beyond* contamination, ultimately unrelated to time. God remains a human God, and the there remains a human anarchy.

The contradiction renders Levinas's thought pious; or rather, Levinas's piety restricts his thinking of alterity to an ethical transcription of a radical absence which is best articulated in terms of the Judaic understanding of God. What comes first, however, is not God, followed by the contamination of his name which philosophy must reduce, but the suspension of the aporia of time in law and the suspension of the aporia of law in time. Religious discourse ensues from this suspension, and, whilst to be understood in terms of it, it cannot be made *equivalent* to it. Religion may well indeed give us privileged access to this suspension; it cannot, however, in whatever form, stand in for it: otherwise the 'there' is lost. That Levinas makes them here equivalent by refusing to suspend the name of God means, first, that his understanding of 'betrayal' reinstalls an oppositional logic there where, beyond time and space, there can be no logic in Levinas's own terms and, second, that his understanding of alterity remains exclusively 'ethical' and humanist. The 'there' is thereby disavowed and the other humanized. It is ultimately in this humanization of the other of time, consequent upon the disavowal of the radical inhumanity of the there that the other is justified. The risk of justifying the other becomes a reality when Levinas figures the humanity of the other in the form of the Jew, thereby ready to justify ethically both the State of Israel and his own 'sacrifice' to this state. Let me conclude this chapter on this difficult terrain.

The Politics of Ethical Singularity: The End of the Singular

I wrote at the beginning of this section that Derrida's concern in 'Violence and metaphysics' to re-relate the other to Heideggerian ontology was made in the concern to keep the 'there' as complex as possible. I noted also that simplification of this complexity could lead to the exemplary localization of thought. Levinas's move to inscribe the history of western thought back onto the 'first' of the 'ethical relation' is at the same time a move to prioritize Jewish thinking on alterity over the essentially Greek nature of the western *logos*. In this move, the alterity of the other becomes figured as the other of the Jew. The fixing of the ethical is then confirmed in the gesture which gives Israel an *ethical vocation*, that, precisely, of the anarchic other. The irony of Levinas's gesture here could not be more acute; we need to be clear about it. I will refer to comments of the 1970s on Israel in 'Zionisms' (1971, 1979, 1980: 209–34/1971: 267–88) in *L'Au-delà du Verset* (1982a) and *A l'Heure des nations* (1988) and an interview after the Chatila and Sabra camp massacres during the Israeli occupation of Lebanon in 1982 (1982b).

For Levinas, as for several contemporary thinkers, the Holocaust reveals, on an empirico-historical level, the 'truth' of the western desire to forget or appropriate the radical obligation to alterity to which the Jewish tradition of thought remains faithful. As a result of this fidelity to radical alterity (to the non-place of the law) Jews have been the object, throughout the history of western civilization, but most savagely between

1942 and 1945, of persecution, murder and genocide. The western desire
for autonomy resists listening to its radical *other* and attempts to expel
it or assume it as a 'moment' within a 'recuperative' logic of (re-)appro-
priation. The Holocaust marks, consequently, the 'political fatality' of
western philosophy, its nostalgic desire for an origin, the unity of the one,
the gathering of a place (Levinas, 1982a: 223). For Levinas, National
Socialism takes this closure to 'sociality' to its limit (ibid.).

In the essay 'Zionisms', Levinas does not wish to give an exemplary
value to the sufferings of Jews in the Holocaust. He is the first to be
aware of the paradox of universalization: the more one generalizes a
particular suffering, the more one loses its singularity. And yet, the Jews'
sufferings are given a universal value when Levinas in another text, 'On
Jewish philosophy' in *A l'Heure des nations* (1988), determines this same
fidelity as 'authentically human' and when he suggests, inversely, that the
'authentically human' is nothing else than 'the being-Jewish in every
man [*l'être-juif dans tout homme*]' (1988: 192). Levinas's move must first
be understood within the historical context that would make this kind of
gesture strategically appropriate. After the Shoah, and contra the western
exemplarity of Heidegger's logic of *authenticity* which forgets the 'there'
as 'other', Levinas recalls us to the other *of* the 'there'. And yet, arguing
this is not enough. I say this not because I wish to move against Levinas's
memory of the Shoah; but because remembering the Shoah in essentialist
terms attenuates the very memory of it. Here again Levinas repeats
Heidegger's logic of authenticity in his very move against it. The call to
our human 'essence' is at the same time the re-call to a specific other ('the
being-Jewish in every human'). The alterity of the other is determined
ontologically and particularized empirico-historically. That this other is
the figure of 'alterity' and not of 'identity' changes little at this level.
As we have seen throughout this chapter, a figure gathers, gives form,
reduces difference. Just as one cannot present the aporia of time or figure
the aporia of place, one cannot figure the alterity of time. Levinas thus
reontologizes the ethical by associating it with a proper name and giving
this name exemplary status. One exemplarity (the Greek and the German)
is exchanged for another (the Jew) despite or beyond the difference in
their exemplarities. Levinas becomes political by remaining too ethical.
This fate arises from the humanization of the 'there'.

Both the universality of the Jewish fidelity to the Other and the universality of their suffering as an *example* to humanity are not rationalist
universalisms. For Levinas this is the point; for us, it is also the point –
a non-universalist universality is still universalist, despite itself. In his essay
on Zionism Levinas forcefully argues that the particularity of Zionism
actually lies in its refusal of particularistic tendencies, those that inform
the ideology of the nation state (1982a: 226). Exploiting Talmudic
teaching on the 'absolute future' of the messianic age, he continues

that Zionism concerns 'the promise of a future of the other' and not 'the promised land' (1982a: 213, 217–18). The state of Israel figures a state beyond the state, it figures 'a world which is coming' (*un monde qui vient*) (ibid.). Separating this world from any form of messianist eschatology, Levinas concludes that the state of Israel announces 'a new form of politics', one that 'promises' a non-teleological idea of peace which exceeds 'purely political thought' (1982a: 217, 227–8).

Levinas's wording of this 'promise' of the other will recall Derrida's understanding of the future as the 'promise' of the 'democracy to come', a promise which emerged in the first section with regard to the rearticulation of the 'da' of Dasein. For some, these two promises may appear the same. This second section has, however, worked to show that Levinas and Derrida's negotiations with aporia are different. The political reality of the difference between the figure of the 'as such' of alterity and the alterity of the figure of this 'as such' makes its mark at this very point.

Levinas's desire to separate Zionism from any particularistic tendency forms, in the very same move, an attempt to give an ethical guarantee to the political existence of a modern state. The aporetic logic which reverses Levinas's understanding of the other into an engagement with the political cannot be controlled for the very reason that the law is here unrelated to time. The paradox of inversion runs free because the aporia of law has not been held aporetically, that is, suspended in time. As a result *the limit* between the ethical and the political is crossed and a politics is justified. A particular state (a particular place in time and space) is ethically justified as the place which promises the non-place. The other as radically other to all places has more of a home in a particular state because it is different to any other state. The ethical singularity of Israel marks the end of the ethical and ethical thinking. Ethics is an 'impossible' experience in this sense. Thus the full force of Derrida's thinking of aporia and the indeterminacy of the promise can be measured in the context of the *political fate* of Levinasian ethics, a discourse, of course, to which Derrida's understanding of the promise is also markedly indebted.

Levinas's comments in an interview after the Chatila and Sabra camp massacres during the Israeli occupation of Lebanon in 1982 demonstrate the above end. In the interview Levinas distances himself from the violence of the occupation but states that the defensive politics of the state of Israel has an 'ethical' necessity:

> It's an old ethical idea which commands us precisely to defend our neighbours. My people and my kin are still my neighbours. When you defend the Jewish people, you defend your neighbour.
> (1982b: 292)

The interviewer rejoins that according to Levinas's own thinking of the ethical the other of the Jew must be the Palestinian. Levinas responds that there is 'also' an 'ethical limit' to this defence of one's neighbour. This means that there is 'also' responsibility to the Palestinian victims. I said a moment ago that, although *le tiers* was not an empirical event in Levinas, it was inscribed in a logical order that always risked turning the infinity of alterity, the impossibility of responsibility, into a specific relation which excluded the *third* from responsibility. Levinas's comment on the relation between Jew and Palestinian exemplifies this risk. The unjustifiable sacrifice of one other against an other has become a justifiable defence of the 'Other' of the Jewish neighbour against the homeless Palestinian. The non-place of alterity has become the place of Israel's borders. And this, because radical alterity is 'being-Jewish *in every man*' (my emphasis). The irony of Levinas's philosophy is cruel.

In his ethical justification of the politics of Israel, Levinas reproduces the same 'logic' as Heidegger's attempt to ground National Socialism on fundamental ontology. Grounding the movement within a philosophy of finitude, Heidegger justified its politics. The German *Volk* had a spiritual-historical mission to recapture the greatness of the Greek beginning – the *polemos* of being. When Levinas states, conversely, that the defence of the Israeli state is 'ethically necessary', he turns the very 'anarchy' of the other opposed to Heidegger's 'paganism' into another place harbouring a spiritual mission. The 'promise' of the future of the other is forgotten in Levinas's very desire for the state of Israel to remember and figure its promise of non-locality, to be 'a state beyond a state'. This memory is also a political project of 'spirit'. Levinas's anarchy, like Heidegger's *Volk*, disavows the 'there' in this spirit's name.

> Self-affirmation is immediately responsibility for all. Political and already non-political. Zionism, after the realism of its political formulations at the beginning, reveals itself finally to be equal to substantial Judaism, as a great ambition of Spirit.
>
> (Levinas, 1982a: 224)

Conclusion

Where is the worse? That is perhaps the question *of spirit*?
J. Derrida, *Of Spirit: Heidegger and the Question*

The *what* invents the *who* just as much as it is invented by it.
B. Stiegler, *La technique et le temps, 1:*
La faute d'Epiméthée

In a long parenthesis to be found in *Specters of Marx* Derrida writes:

Even beyond the regulative idea in its classic form, the idea, if
that is still what it is, of democracy to come, its 'idea' as event
of a pledged injunction that orders one to summon the very thing
that will never present itself in the form of full presence, is the
opening of this gap between an infinite promise (always untenable
at least for the reason that it calls for the infinite respect of
singularity *and* infinite alterity of the other as much as for the
respect of the countable, calculable, subjectal equality between
anonymous singularities) and the determined, necessary, but also
necessarily inadequate forms of what has to be measured against
this promise. To this extent, the effectivity or actuality of the
democratic promise, like that of the communist promise, will
always keep within it, and it must do so, this absolutely undetermined messianic hope at its heart, this eschatological relation to the to-come [*l'à-venir*] of an event *and* of a singularity,
of an alterity that cannot be anticipated. Awaiting without
horizon of the wait, awaiting what one does not expect yet or
any longer, hospitality without reserve, welcoming salutation
accorded in advance to the absolute surprise of the *arrivant* from
whom or from which one will not ask anything in return and

who or which will be asked to commit to the domestic contracts
of any welcoming power (family, State, nation, territory, native
soil or blood, language, culture in general, even humanity),
just opening which renounces any right to property, any right
in general, messianic opening to what is coming, that is, to the
event that cannot be awaited *as such*, or recognized in advance
therefore, to the event as the foreigner itself, to her or to him
for whom one must leave an empty place, always in memory of
the hope – and this is the very place of spectrality.

(1993: 111–12/65)

The passage resumes in the most concise manner the methodological
orientation of deconstruction and its consequent relation to the fields of
ethics and politics. The deconstruction of the empirico-transcendental
difference releases time and singularity from logical determination. This
book has attempted to explain the 'method' of this release as well as the
latter's ethico-political implications. In a sense it has done nothing but
interpret this passage. The following should, then, be clear. When Derrida
places his thinking under the term 'democracy', it is not with regard
to a specific political regime, although it is not opposed to it either. It is
with regard to an absolute future that informs all political organizations,
but which is heard most, despite their legal form, within democratic
organizations of power. This absolute future is the promise that the 'we'
of the community (family, nation, world, even, as Derrida says in the
above passage, humanity) – *qua* the 'we''s radical lack of identity – will
have returned from the beginning to haunt any determination of the
community. The previous chapters have articulated this spectral 'we' in
terms of the 'fate' of inscription, the aporia of time and law and the transformation of the logics of disavowal. 'We' re-marks the excess of time
over 'human' organization. The only community of 'we' that is possible
is the impossibility of 'we', and this impossibility makes possible. This is
the 'promise of democracy'.

   The essential lack of identity to all human organization is more and
more 'apparent' in contemporary relations between humanity and the
world. Internationalization and the increasing 'spectralization' of human
identity which accompanies it are, for example, the political 'givens' of
today and tomorrow. Whether one thrives off them (the international
Mafia), muddles through them (present democratic organizations), opposes
them (today's forms of nationalism, racism and fundamentalist politics)
or attempts to articulate them (the task of present and future political
invention), we all live *within* this process of spectralization. Spectralization
is not just a monopoly of the richer industrialized countries. Any country,
any locality determines its understanding of time, place and community
in relation to this process of 'global' spectralization. This process originates

with that of hominization so it would be wrong to see present spectral-ization as heralding an unprecedented era. That said, it is taking place today at a historically unprecedented speed, one which will become all the more acute, at the level of human reception and negotiation of the 'inhuman', with the exponentially accelerating developments in machine intelligence and in the biotechnical recombination of 'non-human' and 'human' DNA.

With regard to this picture of 'spectralization' two comments are called for. First, and as Derrida argues throughout *Specters of Marx*, the latter process is unthinkable without the technicization of the world and of the human. Indeed, the 'spectral' is nothing less than a way of describing effects of technicization. Given that this process is originary, it is to be understood both philosophically and historically. Thus, if 'spectralization' is transforming the co-ordinates of political reality today, the fact calls for a radical thinking of the relation of technics, one within political reflec-tion and forming an integral part of political philosophy as such. For, as I maintained at the end of Chapter 2, innovative political reflection depends upon an understanding of the dynamic of technical processes. Since these processes always already involve human organization, such a dynamic is also that of the human, although it is, precisely, not reducible to the human; and just as the dynamic of the human *also* involves from the start the technical, just as it is equally not reducible to the technical.[1] Marx is obviously crucial in this reflection, but a Marx – following our brief reading of him with regard to Hegel – without the ontological framing (the logic of contradiction) which often removes the very thing that he wishes to think – the relation between the human and 'matter', or, more simply, technics. It is this 'framing' which allows for the philo-sophical prioritization of the human over the technical and contributes to a violent politics of 'human emancipation'. Within such a perspective, or its opposite (the prioritization of the technical over the human), one is not considering either the human or technics according to the constitu-tive relation '*between*' the human and the non-human. Today such lack of consideration is politically blind and irresponsible.[2]

Second, at stake in this process of spectralization lies the *human expe-rience* of *time*. Most immediately, it is clear that with the digitalization of memory support-systems, our experience of time is being rapidly fore-shortened, creating, among other things, the problem which I mentioned in the Introduction – the tension between the international nature of the electronic and digital gaze and the corporal realities that make up much of human life. Less immediately, but more profoundly, it is also clear that future technical intervention on the genetic 'ingredients' of the human will accelerate processes of evolution at such a speed (if this remains the right term) that present conceptions of history, inheritance, memory and the body will need to be dramatically reorganized, if the 'selection' of what is 'human', and what is not, is not to become the monopoly of an organ-ization between the technosciences and capital. Just as these techniques together with developments in machine intelligence will soon wish to suppress human 'failure(s)' (precisely our submission to time), so the real time of the teletechnologies risks reducing the *différance* of time, or the aporia of time, to an experience of time that *forgets* time.

In this context of increasing spectralization *qua* the reduction of our experience of the aporia of time, what purchase has the above 'spectrality' of the 'promise'? Put more succinctly, in the context of deconstruction's approach to the contemporary world, how are we to think the relation between Derrida's formulation of the promise and technics? What in other words is the relation between the impossible experience of the aporia of time and present and future foreshortening of the human experience of time? The question is big. It is not within the parameters of this book to attempt to give an answer. Since, however, the terms of the ques-tion have arisen from within my particular elaboration of Derrida's philosophy, and since the stakes of the question are political (and urgent), I will conclude the book with several reflections on this point. They may be taken in the spirit in which they were written – as invitation to greater debate.

From a Derridean perspective, there is an answer to the above question. It was touched upon at the end of Chapter 2, and it informs the mobili-zation of Heidegger and Levinas's thinking of time and justice at the beginning of *Specters of Marx* (1993), one which the last chapter devel-oped in the context of their respective political fates. For Derrida, the untying of the aporia of time from its disavowal in logic is at the same time the untying of the aporia of time from the *technical organiza-tion* of time. If the aporia of time is irreducible to logic and is the very source of deconstruction, it is *also* irreducible to technics. The logical disavowal of time and the technical organization of time are both considered by Derrida as procedures of calculation and organization which the incalculability of the *passage* of time exceeds. This excess is the 'justice' of the promise, the irreducible source of deconstruction which I referred to at several strategic moments in the last chapter. The excess constitutes, therefore, the very condition of deconstruction's interventions in the fields of technics. For, just as it allows Derrida to intervene in and transform the logics which disavow the aporia of time (Chapter 3, uninterested in the 'post'-modern, showed how far these logics extend beyond 'modernity'), so this excess, according to Derrida's very thinking of aporia as the condition of deconstruction, calls for intervention and transformation concerning the technosciences. Conse-quently, whilst I said in the Introduction to this book that I would be considering Derrida's specific way of 'marking the excess of the *politico-*

philosophical organization of temporality' (p. xvi), I can now add, in the context of technical spectralization, that this also calls for marking the excess of technics.

This does not mean that technics and logics are synonymous for Derrida. On the contrary, Derrida has been foremost in arguing that metaphysical logic is itself the disavowal of technics. *Of Grammatology* (1967b) (in particular the work on Rousseau), 'Plato's pharmacy' (1972a) and texts like 'Freud and the scene of writing' (1967a) all underline the *'originary technicity'* of the human: the identity of the human resides in the differantial relation between the human and its 'supplements' (especially 1967b: 347 ff./244 ff.). They also trace the manner in which metaphysical logic constitutes itself *through* the expulsion of technics from human identity; how it is this very expulsion that allows for the thinking of the *arche* and *telos* of 'Man'; and, therefore, how all the conceptual limits which 'man [draws and by which he] calls himself man' are phantasms emerging from, and in turn organizing, the separation of the human from the non-human (1967b: 348/245). In this context, Derrida's elaboration of 'arche-writing' through the Saussurean theory of the sign, which we followed closely in Chapter 1 with respect to 'inscription', could be here reread as a profound, innovative engagement with the originary technicity of the human. The deconstruction of philosophy is in this sense nothing else than the re-siting of the technical within the human. The technical is constitutive of the process of hominization. Thus, the concept of 'Man' as distinct from the technical – a concept which is accompanied by the subordination of technics to the category of 'means' (to Man's end) – is to be understood and reflected upon as a stage in this process of organization.

With regard to the *aporia* of time, Derrida places less stress, however, on the irreducibility of technics to logic (the move of the above texts which thereby transform the terms of metaphysics) than on the irreducibility of the aporia of time to technics. This seems to me a crucial intellectual move in Derrida's more recent writings, one which marries with his understanding of 'impossibility' that we read in Chapter 1. Here Derrida will tend to elaborate *both* logic and technics in terms of a notion of contingent determination and calculation (see 'Invention de l'autre', 1987c). The reason is that both constitute finite 'organizations' of time. Thus, for Derrida, despite real time's reduction of the human experience of the passage of time, the passage of time – what I called in the previous chapter the 'delay' of time – *cannot be technicized*, it cannot be absolutely reduced; and this is what makes any organization contingent. Just as a human invention like law cannot reduce the delay of time, so technical invention (which in the coming years may be less and less organized by what we understand now as the 'human') cannot reduce, or 'figure' the aporia of time. Chapter 3's concern with the figuring of the 'there' could be reread here as well. Whereas the chapter was concerned to show the political dangers of this figure *qua* the human saturation of the 'there', here one could now articulate how the affirmation of the technical over the human forgets the aporia of time *qua* the 'relation' between the human and the nonhuman. The *différance* of time is the absolute future of technical determination, the 'messianic' promise that trembles in every technical invention, delivering the latter over to contingency, a contingency that marks, precisely, the finitude of all organizations, thereby giving human organization its chance (compare Derrida, 1993: 268/169). Thus what the previous chapters all elaborated in terms of the 'fate' of a conceptual gesture applies equally to technics. Technical invention has always already gone wrong, become 'other'. There is no technical apocalypse of the human. Often informing the above-mentioned scenario of genetic selection and machine intelligence, this apocalyptic idea repeats, for deconstruction, the Platonic fiction that time can be transcended; that is, it ends up repeating the Platonic disavowal of time, returning squarely to metaphysical logic at the very moment that it believes itself to be leaving it. Pure technics is pure metaphysics. Subordinated to the passage of time, technics is, however, finite and the future contingent. For deconstruction, therefore, philosophy's reflection on the technical recalls its processes to the finitude which makes them possible in the first place. This move repeats in the domain of the technosciences Derrida's early deconstruction of the human sciences, which Chapter 1 elaborated in relation to Saussurean linguistics.

Now, whether one agrees or disagrees with the general orientation of Derrida's thinking here, I believe that three points should be made in this context. First, the issue of time and of the human experience of time is now an eminently political issue and concerns, ultimately, whether politics has a future as a specific *human* organization of time or not. Again, one can agree or disagree with Derrida's way of addressing this issue; what is clear, above and beyond the specific arguments of this book, is that his philosophy is necessarily political *because* it is a thinking of time, and, therefore, detractors of deconstruction on the absence of the political in Derrida's work are either just not reading or are just not thinking, or, more likely, are themselves working with an explicit or hidden metaphysical understanding of the political which makes them quickly impatient with Derrida's investigations. Second, if one does disagree with this general orientation, then it is incumbent upon the critic to give an analysis of time which shows that Derrida's understanding of *the irreducibility of the aporia of time* is untenable. Third, accepting this irreducibility as well as all that it implies regarding contingency, I believe – and here my hesitation returns from Chapter 2 – that Derrida is nevertheless avoiding something in the above type of analysis of technical finitude. This avoidance has consequences for the range of invention that is called for, *if* there is to be an effective dialogue between philosophy, the human and social sciences, and the technosciences. In other words, it concerns the future of politics.

In Chapter 3 Heidegger's opposition between primordial temporality and vulgar time was seen to amount to a disavowal of the 'there' which repeated the metaphysical disavowal of time. I also showed how *within* Heidegger's oppositions Derrida espies an alterity irreducible to the oppositions of *Being and Time* (1926). I then developed this alterity through looking at Levinas's thinking of the other in terms of the excess of time as well as his simultaneous saturation of it in terms of human alterity (one that ultimately encouraged him to make a highly problematic identification of this very alterity). My purpose in the previous chapter was to show the full force of Derrida's aporetic thinking in relation to both these thinkers. What should now be stressed, however, is that this way of untying the 'there' from out of Heidegger and Levinas's philosophies reduces the terms in which the 'there' is thought, however much it also complicates them. For, as we shall see, it plays down an articulation of the 'there' as the 'and' between the 'promise' and technics.

As Bernard Stiegler has shown in his important *La technique et le temps, 1: La faute d'Epiméthée* (1994: Part 2), what Heidegger disavows in *Being and Time* is the *technical* constitution of temporality. There can be no access to the past, no anticipation of the future *without* technical objects. Developing the Derridean thought of orginary technicity as well as insights in recent paleontology, Stiegler convincingly shows that technical objects constitute the very process of Dasein's experiencing of time, that is, of remembering and anticipating. Without memory support systems – from a tool to a digitalized archive – there would be no experience of the past and nothing from which to 'select' in order to invent the future. Thus, the Heideggerian ecstasis of time which we saw to be the condition of the 'as'-structure of being in Chapter 3 requires technics. Without technics there would be consequently no relation between man and being in the first place. Since, as we have seen, Heidegger tends to oppose being to technics, and since his political choices, as well as his subsequent understanding of *Gelassenheit*, ensue from this opposition, one may measure the force and the reach of Stiegler's reading.[3]

Following this reading, then, Heidegger's phantasmatic opposition in *Being and Time* between primordial temporality and vulgar time is a metaphysical disavowal of the *originary technicity* of the 'there' (Stiegler, 1994: 211–43). Heidegger's desire to set Dasein's self-affection against a phantasmatic projection of rootlessness in the modern technological world would constitute not simply a disavowal of time, but a disavowal of the *technical* constitution of time, and, therefore, of the originary relation between the human and the nonhuman. It would be Heidegger's metaphysical desire to be rid of originary technicity which makes Heidegger anthropomorphize the 'there' *qua* Dasein's self-affection, thereby untying Dasein from technicity and projecting this technicity of the 'there' onto a phantasmatic instance whom this Dasein has to combat (*das Man*). The *telos* of Dasein *qua* authentic *Unheimlichkeit* is predicated on the disavowal of technics which uproots Dasein in the first place: this uprooting is phantasmatically displaced to the figure of the 'inauthenticity' of *das Man*. Since this covering over of originary technicity engenders, then, the opposition between the authentic *Unheimlichkeit* of the *Volk* and the inauthentic issuelessness of *das Man*, one could argue forcefully, from out of Stiegler's analyses, that *it is primarily the denial of originary technicity that informs Heidegger's engagements with Nazism.*[4]

Now, just as in the previous chapter I showed how Derrida found the resources within Heidegger to articulate an alterity which exceeded primordial temporalization, so it is possible, Stiegler argues, to find in *Being and Time* the sources necessary to think the constitutive alterity of the technical for Dasein (Stiegler, 1994: 245–59). The Heideggerian destruction of metaphysics in terms of time throws the individual into the 'already-there' of the world as *Mitdasein*. *Being and Time* shows that this world is in fact factical, always already made up of entities that are 'ready-to-hand' (*Zuhandensein*). Completely underestimated by Heidegger in his desire to understand the 'there' in terms of Dasein's self-affection, the 'ready-to-hand' actually forms the originary relation between the human and the nonhuman prior to all metaphysical oppositions between the human and the technical (including that of *Being and Time*). It also articulates the 'facticity' and 'nullity' of Dasein in terms of originary pros-theticity. In other words, for Stiegler, the 'there' to which Dasein is 'called back' should be articulated in terms of the originary relation between the human and the technical (1994: 262–70).

We should recall from Chapter 3 that it is precisely here in his reading of *Schuldigsein* and the call of conscience that Derrida articulates the alterity of Dasein in terms of an instance which whilst both 'inside' and 'outside' Dasein is precisely not technical, but is the 'voice of the friend whom every Dasein carries with it' (Heidegger, 1926: §34). In his recent *Politiques de l'amitié* – in an interpretative commentary on Aristotle's understanding of the friend – Derrida suggests that this radical notion of friendship (prior to any anthropological instance) is *also* 'irreducible' to technics (see 1994b: 223ff.).[5] This 'voice' precedes all (forms of) organization and is, I believe, best located for Derrida in genealogies of religion, that is in the very condition of religious thinking and religious organization.

This said, and following the movement of Chapter 3, does Derrida's thinking of the 'there' in terms of the promise disavow in turn the orig-inary relation between the human and the nonhuman? Is this what he himself avoids thinking in his analysis, for example, of Heidegger's politics in terms of 'spiritualization'? In other words, with attention to the radical alterity of time, do Derrida's earlier analyses of originary technicity become eclipsed? If not – *and the above questions are indeed misplaced* – then *how* does one develop the relations between the promise and originary technicity, knowing simultaneously *that they are the 'same'*? This, of course, is the question of the relations between contemporary philosophizing and the technosciences. It is perhaps the most political question to put to Derrida's philosophy today.

To see in sharp focus Derrida's 'avoidance' of the articulation of these relations, it is here opportune to return to his text *Of Spirit: Heidegger and the Question* (1987a). Its analysis of Heidegger's political engagements is itself cast in terms of what Heidegger 'avoids'. Derrida argues that Heidegger's wish to demarcate his thinking of time from 'metaphysical subjectity' (1987a: 61/37) turns against him all the more roundly in his very wish to avoid this logic. Heidegger cannot avoid the double or ghost of *Geist* despite, indeed by, wishing to excise it from the logic of subjectity which informs the 'concept' of *Geist* in the metaphysical tradition. Hence his understanding of ecstasis of time in terms of spirit is haunted by its metaphysical double. In trying to root Nazism upon a post-metaphysical analysis of time, Heidegger makes the worst error and justifies Nazism by giving racism a metaphysics. If I made constant indirect reference to Heidegger's engagements and to *Of Spirit* in the last chapter, what I did not stress, concerned to show that Levinas was not innocent of this logic either, is the fact that, for Derrida, Heidegger's philosophization of Nazism betrays in the most acute and naive form the irreducibility of the 'logic' of contamination. Speaking of Heidegger's spiritualization of racism, Derrida writes:

> What is the price of this strategy? Why does it fatally turn back against its 'subject' – if one can use this word, as one must, in fact? Because one cannot demarcate oneself from biologism, from naturalism, from racism in its genetic form, one cannot be *opposed* to them except by reinscribing spirit in an oppositional determination, by once again making it a unilaterality of subjectity, even if in its voluntarist form. The constraint of the program remains very strong, it reigns over the majority of discourses which, today and for a long time to come, state their opposition to racism, to totalitarianism, to nazism, to fascism, etc., and do this in the name of spirit, even of the freedom of the spirit, in the name of an axiomatic – for example, that of democracy or 'human rights' – which directly or not comes back to this metaphysics of *subjectity*. All the pitfalls of the strategy of establishing demarcations belong to this program, whatever place one

occupies in it. The only choice is the choice between the terrifying contaminations it assigns. Even if all forms of complicity
are not equivalent, they are *irreducible*.

(1987a: 65–6/39–40)

We should now be familiar with this gesture, especially after Chapter 3.
If a deconstruction of politics is made impossible because of this irreducibility, I have argued that, for Derrida, this very impossibility is the
aporia of time. I have suggested, furthermore, especially through my
reading of Levinas, that the irreducible aporia of time is re-marked in the
human organization of time as the irreducibility of the 'law of contamination'. Thus the non-organizable experience of the aporia of time should
be endured for the possibility of lesser violence. Derrida's thinking of
aporia locates the avoidance of this logic in Heidegger and constitutes the
terms in which his engagements with Nazism are to be thought.

Now, in the context of the above argument on originary technicity and
the need to develop the organization of time in terms of technics, this
very use of aporia can, I believe, appear too philosophical. The impossible
aporia of logic *qua* the aporia of time can appear too determined by the
very logics which Derrida is deconstructing. As a result Derrida's argument
concerning the irreducibility of subjectal logic *looks like* eliding the
mediations between the human and the nonhuman and underestimating the
speed with which the human is losing its experience *of* time. The 'promise'
ends up, therefore, *appearing* too formal, freezing Derrida's deconstructions
of the tradition into a finite, but open set of 'quasi-transcendental' logics
which turn the relation between the human and the technical into a
'logic' of supplementarity without history (the technical determinations of
temporalization).[6] Quasi-transcendental analysis remains the other of the
logics which it deconstructs, thereby remaining itself logical. Derrida's
mobilization of the aporia of time, as irreducible to the logical and the
technical, is a logic! It refuses to lose itself in matter, in technics! *Of Spirit*
looks, again, like a good case in point of this 'fate'.

Once Derrida has negotiated the writings of the thirties, he reads
Heidegger in terms of the promise, which, *unarticulated in relation to the
technical constitution of time*, leads him to close the text in an unmedi-
ated, imaginary exchange between Heidegger and Christian theologians.
The debate concerns the 'ontological' status of the promise in Heidegger's
reflections on Trakl's poetry (Heidegger, 1953). Is the promise prior
to Christian notions of spirit or is it the same thing as that which the
Christian concepts of 'promise' promise? After my Chapter 1, the incon-
clusive nature of the debate at the end of the book should not be
misunderstood. Just as, there, the trace was understood as neither in
history nor outside it, so, here, the promise both *precedes* the tradition
and can only be thought *through* the tradition. The event of the promise

only takes place in that which it makes possible. A genealogy of what is irreducible to the world can only go *through* the world. Thus, the religious terms in which Derrida closes this text concerning the promise confirm that the earlier political fate of Heidegger's avoidance of the ghost of 'spirit' ensue from his inability to negotiate with the aporetic status of all 'genealogy'.

What Derrida has avoided in this analysis is an articulation between the technical nature of Heidegger's political engagements and the promise. And this despite the fact that Derrida would be the first to argue that the promise is not an instance separable from technicity – that is, it is nothing but the contingency of technicization (the argument that brings in the aporia of time). Due to this lack of articulation, however, the promise can indeed 'look' formal. In other words, and the case of Heidegger is paradigmatic of the problem, in the absence of an articulation between originary technicity and the irreducibility of the promise to both logic and technics, and despite the fact that neither can be separated from the other, Derrida's thinking of time can appear formalist. In the context of increasing technicization, the point is politically telling.

My last comment highlights the problem. What is the 'ontological' order of the promise and of originary technicity? In the first chapter I emphasized that the promise was nothing else than the deconstruction of the tradition. For I was eager to place Derrida's more recent comments on the promise in relation to the early work of deconstruction so that the complex, mediating and mediated nature of the promise could be developed. Here, in the context of the theme of the originary technicity of man, my argument proves to be slightly misplaced, since there is indeed a shift which Derrida has not expounded. In *Of Grammatology* the trace was said to 'connect within the same possibility . . . the structure of the relationship to the other, the movement of temporalization, and language as writing' (1967b: 69/47). In 'Violence and metaphysics' Derrida argued forcefully that 'time is violence' (1967a: 195/133). In 'The violence of the letter: from Lévi-Strauss to Rousseau' Derrida maintained that 'arche-writing' was 'the origin of morality as of immorality. The nonethical opening of ethics. A violent opening' (1967b: 201–2/140). This opening is rewritten as the 'promise' in *Specters of Marx* (1993: 56/28).

And yet, if time is from the first technically organized, if access to the experience of time is only possible through technics, then the 'promise' must be *more originary* than 'originary technicity'. Even if they are inseparable – and what else is the law of contamination but this inextricability? – they are not on the same 'ontological' level. There are, consequently, 'two' instances of 'radical alterity' here which need articulation and whose relation demands to be developed: the radical alterity of the promise and the radical alterity of the other prior to the ego of which one modality (and increasingly so in the coming years) is the technical other. While inseparable, both these instances cannot be originary, without making the concept 'originary' nonsensical. Derrida avoids the articulation of this relation in *Of Spirit: Heidegger and the Question* (1987a): first, because his reading of Heidegger's 'spiritualization' of Nazism – despite recurrent reference to the question of technics – is one ultimately made with regard to the inextricable relation between the promise and religion, and not, also, with regard to Heidegger's disavowal of originary technicity. This evasion comes to the fore when, secondly, Derrida talks of the promise as 'pre-archi-originary' (1987a: 183/112) – a term whose somewhat awkward formulation signals an 'ontological' priority over the trace as originary technicity, but betrays in its very formulation a lack of articulation between the two. It would thus seem opportune at this point to immerse philosophy in the technosciences for the promise to appear *through* the relation between the human and the nonhuman. Derrida's justified mobilization of religious concepts to think the 'nonhuman' other of logic and technics needs, in other words, to be related to the 'nonhumanity' of matter. For it is *through* the development of this relation that the future 'space' of human organization, within accelerating processes of technicization, is to be invented.

Let me conclude with a loose speculation, imagining for one moment two possible futures of Derrida's philosophy.

The first would be what one may call within classical concepts of the political a 'left-wing' 'Derrideanism'. It would foreground Derrida's analyses of originary technicity, 'avoiding' the risk of freezing quasi-transcendental logic by developing the trace in terms of the mediations between human and the technical (the very process of hominization). In order to think future 'spectralization' and establish a dialogue between philosophy, the human sciences, the arts and the technosciences, this future of Derrida's philosophy would return to the earlier texts of Derrida which read metaphysical logic in terms of the disavowal of *techne*.

The second could be called, similarly, a 'right-wing' 'Derrideanism'. It would pursue Derrida's untying of the aporia of time from both logic and technics, maintaining that even if there is only access to time through technics, what must be thought, articulated and witnessed is the passage of time. To do so, this Derrideanism would mobilize religious discourse and prioritize, for example, the radically 'passive' nature of the arts, following up on more recent work of Derrida on the absolute originarity of the promise and of his reorganization of religious discourse to think and describe it.

In this imaginary dialogue where do we stand at the end of this book? There is, of course, *no answer* and *no choice*. As each stage of this book has argued, the aporia of time, if developed through that which it engenders, calls for the *transformation* of that which it makes possible. Since, within the very terms of deconstruction, technics is predicated on what Chapter 3 called the 'passage' of time, then deconstruction itself demands a non-hegemonic series of inventions of the 'between' between philosophy, the human sciences and the technosciences. If this book has shown how much is at stake in reflection in this move – finally, the very possibility and future of the political – as well as how important Derrida's deconstructions are for this reflection, then the book will have succeeded in its purpose. For it will have enjoined the reader to go back to Derrida's works with the fate of the political in mind.

Notes

Introduction

1. The following makes a twofold distinction between 'politics' and the 'political'. I understand the term 'politics' as designating the domain or practice of human behaviour which normativizes the relations between a subject and its others (other human subjects, nature, technics, or the divine). I understand the term the 'political' as the instance that gathers or founds such practice *as* a practice. The 'political' is, in Platonic vein, the trait that allows us to describe/recognize a gesture of thought or action *as* political. In this apparently commonsensical definition of both politics and the political, religion also constitutes a politics – in the sense that I consider religion, as a specific determination of what is and is not of the domain of the political, to be itself of the domain and practice of politics. I am therefore using the terms politics and political in a larger sense than a pragmatic definition would allow, one only possible, in fact, after the thought of Hegel. One of Derrida's major points will be that reflection on the political as a trait is impossible for essential reasons which the same reflection may re-mark.

2. 'Disavows' in the Freudian sense, that is in the sense of a refusal to perceive a fact which impinges from the outside. Freud's example in his use of the term is the denial of a woman's absence of a penis (see Freud (1923), 'The Infantile Genital Organisation', esp. p. 310, n. 1). The term is, however, appropriate for the way in which the tradition of philosophy has 'denied' finitude. The concept will be used frequently in my argument.

1 From Language to Law, an Opening onto Judgement

1. These terms are defined later in the chapter.

2. For a highly lucid and convincing analysis of this gesture, see G. Bennington, 1991.

3. G. Bennington was also one of the first in the Anglo-Saxon world to place major emphasis on the political implications of the deconstruction of

horizonal thinking. See his 'Deconstruction and the philosophers (the very idea)' (1987). While having several reservations concerning its determination of the *telos* of philosophy, I am greatly indebted to this text.

4. To avoid confusion, I will henceforth refer to Derrida's essay on Kafka's tale by the English title 'Before the law' and to Kafka's tale by the original German title 'Vor dem Gesetz'.

5. The literariness of literature distinguishes itself therein from empirical examples of literature. As we will see later concerning non-literary accounts of the law, Derrida's interest in literature concerns a relation to law that can be found in other forms of writing apart from that of literature. Literature distinguishes itself, however, by specifically re-marking the aporetic relation to the law and by re-marking it in a singular fashion, and this is what constitutes its 'literariness'. This distinction between empirical literature and the literariness of literature is crucial to the following account of aporia and judgement.

2 The Political Limit of Logic and the Promise of Democracy

1. This judgement – shared in varying degrees by Deleuze, Foucault, Lacoue-Labarthe, Levinas, Lyotard, the later Kristeva and, although to a much lesser extent, Nancy – is informed by a resistance to the *ontologization* of politics. It is in the context of this resistance that Hegel's thought has become the embodiment of metaphysical logic. Marked as being *the* thinking of appropriation and *the* conceptual determination of loss and contingency, Hegel's philosophy is considered the major philosophical forerunner of twentieth-century political terror (in its Fascist or Communist variants). The following combats this reading whilst remaining *within* the terms of deconstruction – terms which, as we shall see, comprehend the necessity of Hegel's thinking whilst re-inscribing his ontological gestures within a more general account of the relation between thought and time.

2. 'Re-cognition' in the sense of learning again what one 'understood' to 'know' but now 're-cognizes' as an illusion (*Schein*). Recognition in Hegel is the experience of knowledge *through* time. As we shall see later, it constitutes a 'tragic' understanding of experience: hence Hegel's constant mobilization of Aristotelian categories of the tragic (notably, 'fate', irony' and 'recognition') to articulate the relations between thinking and sensibility. The relation between re-cognition and time will be crucial in demarcating Derrida's philosophy of time from Hegel's philosophy of history. Henceforth, to avoid the reader's lassitude, 're-cognition' will generally be written without a hyphen except in extreme cases, although the above meaning should always be born in mind.

3. The attentive reader will be aware that the following account of Hegel through *Glas* (1974) also prepares for a detailed examination of the theses of *Specters of Marx* and of the Marxian corpus, specifically the book's distinction, in the immediate context of Marx and Engel's debacle with Stirner

in *The German Ideology* (1845–7) and Marx's later theory of fetishism, between ontology and 'hauntology' [*hantologie*] (1994a: 31/10). For the political purposes of this chapter the reader should perhaps recall most from *Specters of Marx* that ontology '*locates* the dead' (ibid., my emphasis – R.B.).

4. I have argued this in detail in 'Les frontières du sublime: La déconstruction et la tradition moderne' in J. Derrida et al. (1994a) *Le Passage des Frontières*.

5. On the terms of this debate, and for references, see Amy Gutmann (1985) 'Communitarian critics of liberalism'.

6. Lyotard's anti-Hegelianism should be seen in the context of his Kantian refusal to determine the law.

7. This argument is complex and needs much more lengthy exposition than space can allow me here. Suffice it to say, in the most general terms, that if Kant wishes to distinguish transcendental logic from general logic at this point (the tying of a priori concepts to the temporal and spatial conditions of sensibility), he also repeats the metaphysical disavowal of time that the *Critique of Pure Reason* (1781) simultaneously combats by placing the faculty of reason outside time. Since this faculty allows, in the first place, for the very possibility of both 'transcendental' and 'speculative' logic (in the Kantian sense), the first *Critique*'s attempt to relate metaphysical concepts to time is informed by an atemporal analysis of reason. Kant's safeguarding of the principle of contradiction and his desire that it determine the 'form' of ethical orientation (universality) ensues, ultimately, from the metaphysical decision at the very beginning of Kant's philosophy to prolong the anthropocentric phantasm that reason lies outside time. As we shall see in Chapter 3, Heidegger's subsequent re-relating of reason to the finitude of the transcendental imagination (Heidegger, 1929) is crucial with respect to the overall intentions of Kant's project (a philosophy of finitude). It is also informed, however, by a metaphysical logic which undercuts the radicality of the interpretation (the re-inscription of reason within time), prolonging the phantasm that man forms the world. It is in the light of these negotiations between thought, time and the world that my Chapter 2 shows the political implications of Derrida's thinking of aporia in relation to the so-called 'logics' of Kant and Hegel, and my Chapter 3 in relation to the 'logics' of Heidegger and Levinas. A reading of the *Critique of Judgement* (1790) with respect to time, the transcendental imagination, invention and form would prolong the direction of these comments.

8. The following account of Hegel is greatly indebted to Rose's work, differences notwithstanding.

9. The quasi-concept of *stricture* is developed on pp. 87–92.

10. I recall throughout this reading of Kant my arguments on the institution of linguistics in the first part of Chapter 1.

11. I will recall this important thesis when I address the thought of Levinas in Chapter 3.

12. G. Bennington has been the most incisive defender of deconstruction regarding these ethico-political paradoxes. See his *Sententiousness and the Novel* (1985: 137–71) and *Legislations* (1994: esp. 240–73).

13. Beyond the argument of this chapter's introduction, to what extent the following respects Hegel's distinction between the dialectical and the speculative, or is suspicious of the possibility of this distinction, would be the subject of another book concerning the nature of the aporetic in Derrida and Hegel's philosophies of time and law. On the above distinction, see G. Rose's major article 'From speculative to dialectical thinking – Hegel and Adorno' (1993: 53–64). Suffice it to say here that Derrida's thinking of aporia in terms of time allows the dialectical and the speculative to be brought together. Derrida thereby stresses, for example, the fact that the 'speculative proposition in the Hegelian sense of the word ... states the dialectical identity of identity and nonidentity' (1974: 33/24), that Hegel determines difference as opposition (329/236) and considers Heidegger's understanding of the 'gift' of time as more radical than speculative development which suppresses, phantasmatically, the remainder of time (319–39/228–44). The following develops the political dimension of this approach to Hegel.

14. To keep to the coherence of the German term, I am translating *Schicksal* by the term 'fate' (not 'destiny', as in A. Miller's translation) following the earlier writings.

15. It is worth recalling at this point that in Aristotle's *Poetics* 'character' (*ethos*) is the colouring of a dramatic situation.

16. Here the importance of my earlier comment concerning Derrida's 'sophistication of Kant's thought' (Derrida, 1985: 210/128) in Chapter 1 – that 'time is the *différance* of the singular' (p. 43) – becomes manifest.

17. This short reading of Marx does minimal justice, undoubtedly, to the complexity of Marx's thinking on matter, especially his understanding of the historical development between the technical and the human (Marx's so-called 'historical materialism'). My point is not made, however, with the aim of closing down the text of Marx, but of opening it up to the future in recognition of where its predominant logic turns the relation between the human and the technical into a *politics* of human redemption. It is in Marx's ontologization of matter that the history of matter is organized all too violently around the human. Here, to put it crudely, but succinctly, Marx inherits Hegel's phantasm of Athena: hence the violent fate of Marx's political philosophy. Without articulating the reasons for this fate, the more interesting Marx will not emerge. Compare here, of course, Derrida's *Specters of Marx* (1993).

18. I refer the reader to Bernard Stiegler's major work on the relation between matter and time: *La technique et le temps, 1: La faute d'Epiméthée* (1994, trs. Richard Beardsworth and George Collins, Meridian Series, Stanford University Press, forthcoming), in which Stiegler argues forcefully that time is constituted through technical mediation. The temporalization of time thus changes with a change in the technical process that forms it. I will turn to his argument in the Conclusion.

19. Following Stiegler (1994) I understand by this term the amalgamation of the 'natural' sciences and technics at the beginning of the modern age. For Stiegler it is this amalgamation that determines the specificity of modernity.

3 Aporia of Time, Aporia of Law

1. On the 'out of joint'-ness of time, see *Specters of Marx* (1993: esp. 45–57/ 23–9). In the course of a reading of spectrality in terms of time, Derrida works Heidegger's opposition between the order (*Fug*) of 'Presencing' (*Anwesenheit*) and the disorder (*Un-fug*) of the vulgar present (*Gegenwart*) – to be found in *Der Spruch des Anaximander* (Heidegger, 1946) – with Levinas's ethical concept of 'anarchy'. This chapter could be considered as an oblique development of these pages.

2. Taking exception to the capitalization of *Sein* in the English translation, I will here always translate 'Sein' as 'being' with a lower-case 'b'. The substantivation which accompanies capitalization may work in Heidegger's German (given that all nouns are capitalized). In English, however, it creates the linguistic illusion, contrary to the very destruction of ontology in terms of time, that being is a subject (like God). That I wish to resist the 'piety' evident in the English translation is of course an interpretative strategy. For there is much in Heidegger's thinking that is itself pious and invites piety – including his very thinking of being in terms of primordial temporality. To deconstruct this piety whilst continuing to capitalize Heidegger's term 'Sein' is, in the context, unfortunate.

3. With more space, and in the context of our readings of the 'limit 'in Chapter 2, this would be the occasion to rearticulate Hegel's speculative philosophy with the 'post'-metaphysical, and not subsume it under the term 'modernity'.

4. The distinction between two kinds of issuelessness – between the 'site' of issuelessness and the 'placelessness' of issuelessness – comes to a head in the commentary on Antigone as a clash between *phusis* and *techne* (Heidegger, 1935: 122–6/160–5). I have commented on this distinction in my article 'From a genealogy of matter to a politics of memory: Stiegler's thinking of technics' (1995). Whilst central to the analysis of the 'there' as I am elaborating it here, to develop the distinction fully in terms of aporia would demand a partial reorganization of Derrida's negotiation with aporia. Since this reorganization can be most effective if one first takes on the complexity of Derrida's own negotiation with aporia, and since this book is for the most part concerned with elaborating this complexity, I again reserve engagement with the problem until the end of the book.

5. Following my wish not to capitalize the Heideggerian concept of being, it is appropriate not to capitalize either Levinas's concept of the other (*Autre* or *Autrui*). There is an immediate difficulty here, however, which is not to be met in German given its standard capitalization of substantives. That is, Levinas himself capitalizes the terms, although his capitalization is, as I shall argue, not entirely consistent. For reasons of coherence, and to attenuate the risk of piety which threatens any act of capitalization, I will,

nevertheless, write it henceforth with a small letter. My preference is a question of strategy and context.

6. In this context the implications of Chapter 1 can best be thought through with regard to Derrida's relations to Heidegger and Levinas.

7. It should be emphasized that, whilst faithful to 'Violence of metaphysics', the following reading of Levinas forms an interpretative commentary of the relation between Derrida's thinking and Levinas's.

8. My argument takes issue, however, with Critchley's general claim that Levinasian ethics serves as the 'political' supplement to Derrida's negotiation with aporia.

Conclusion

1. The 'relation' between the human and the technical is therefore one of simultaneous inclusion and exclusion.

2. There is much to discuss here, just as there is large disagreement about how to proceed. Suffice it to repeat, in the context of my argument and after the matter of the last two chapters (specifically concerning Marx, the last two sections of Chapter 2), that the profundity of Marx's understanding of technical processes is cut short by his wish to *politicize* the relation between the human and the technical according to an ontological logic which freezes the categories of his 'otherwise' historical understanding of technical-human evolution and heritage. This logic – whether in Marx or in the inheritors of his materialism – allows for modern, if not often 'post-modern', understandings of the technical and the political in the first place. Despite the apparent 'socio-historical' colour to these understandings, they are metaphysical through and through and must be deconstructed for a radical understanding of technics and technicization to emerge. In what ways one 'deconstructs' these understandings today, is, however, one of the subjects of this conclusion, concerned as it is with the specific dynamic of technical processes in relation to the aporia of time. As we shall see, who 'freezes' what, when and how is perhaps the whole question. Indeed, it may be the question of the human as such.

3. As the informed reader will be aware, my reading of Heidegger is combative, giving the impression, perhaps, that I misunderstand the role of technics in Heidegger's thinking of the history of being. However ambivalent and complicated Heidegger's thinking of technics is, an axiomatic distinction between *phusis* and *techne* and 'thinking' and *techne* remains in place, however, from the beginning to the end of his work. As Chapter 3 should have made clear, my combative stance is adopted with respect to the political consequences of this distinction.

4. For such a reading see my 'From a genealogy of matter to a politics of memory: Stiegler's thinking of technics' (Beardsworth, 1995).

5. For the point to be convincing, the passage which I refer to in *Politiques de l'amitié* would need much more detailed consideration in relation to the

overall reasoning of the book. I believe, nevertheless, that my argument is sound.

6. This was my argument in 'From a genealogy of matter to a politics of memory: Stiegler's thinking of technics' (1995).

Bibliography

Arendt, H. (1961) *Eight Exercises in Political Thought: Between Past and Future*, New York: Viking Press.

Aristotle (1984a) *Poetics*, in J. Barnes (ed.) *The Complete Works of Aristotle*, Princeton: Princeton University Press.

—— (1984b) *Physics*, in J. Barnes (ed.) *The Complete Works of Aristotle*, Princeton: Princeton University Press.

Beardsworth, R. (1994a) 'Les frontières du sublime: La déconstruction et la tradition moderne', in J. Derrida et al., *Le Passage des frontières*, Colloque de Cerisy, Paris: Galilée.

—— (1994b) 'Nietzsche and the machine: Interview with Jacques Derrida', *Journal of Nietzsche Studies* 7: 7–64.

—— (1995) 'From a genealogy of matter to a politics of memory: Stiegler's thinking of technics', *Tekhnema: Journal of Philosophy and Technology* 2: 85–115.

Bennington, G. (1985) *Sententiousness and the Novel: Laying down the Law in Eighteenth Century Fiction*, Cambridge: Cambridge University Press.

—— (1987) 'Deconstruction and the philosophers (the very idea)', *Oxford Literary Review* 10: 73–130.

—— (1991) 'Derridabase', in Geoffrey Bennington and Jacques Derrida, *Jacques Derrida*, Paris: Le Seuil. Eng. trans. Geoffrey Bennington, *Jacques Derrida*, Chicago: University of Chicago Press, 1993.

—— (1994) *Legislations: The Politics of Deconstruction*, London: Verso.

Bernasconi, R. (1985) 'The trace of Levinas in Derrida', in R. Bernasconi and D. Wood (eds) *Derrida and Différance*, Coventry: Parousia Press.

—— (1986) 'Levinas and Derrida: The question of the closure of metaphysics', in R. A. Cohen (ed.) *Face to Face with Levinas*, Albany: State University of New York Press.

—— (1987) 'Deconstruction and the possibility of ethics', in J. Sallis (ed.) *Deconstruction and Philosophy*, Chicago: University of Chicago Press.

Bernstein, J. (1992) *The Fate of Art: Aesthetic Alienation from Kant to Derrida and Adorno*, Cambridge: Polity Press.

Caygill, H. (1989) *Art of Judgment*, Oxford: Blackwell.

—— (1994) *Hegel and the Speculative Community*, University of East Anglia: UEA Papers in Philosophy, New Series 3.

Critchley, S. (1992) *The Ethics of Deconstruction*, Oxford: Blackwell.

Culler, J. (1983) *On Deconstruction: Theory and Criticism after Structuralism*, London and New York: Routledge & Kegan Paul.

de Man, P. (1971) *Blindness and Insight*, 2nd edn 1993, London: Routledge.

—— (1979) *Allegories of Reading: Figural Language in Rousseau, Nietzsche, Rilke and Proust*, New Haven: Yale University Press.

Derrida, J. (1962) *Edmund Husserl's 'L'origine de la géométrie'*, Paris: Presses Universitaires de France. Eng. trans. John P. Leavey, Jr, *Husserl's 'Origin of Geometry': An Introduction*, Lincoln: University of Nebraska Press, 1989.

—— (1967a) *L'écriture et la différence*, Paris: Seuil. Eng. trans. Alan Bass, *Writing and Difference*, London: Routledge & Kegan Paul, 1978.

—— (1967b) *De la grammatologie*, Paris: Minuit. Eng. trans. Gayatri Spivak, *Of Grammatology*, Baltimore: Johns Hopkins University Press, 1976.

—— (1967c) *La voix et le phénomène: Introduction au problème du signe dans la phénoménologie de Husserl*, Paris: Presses Universitaires de France. Eng. trans. David B. Allison, *Speech and Phenomena*, Evanston: Northwestern University Press, 1973.

—— (1968) 'Ousia et gramme: note sur une note de *Sein und Zeit*', in J. Derrida, *Marges de la philosophie*, Paris: Minuit, 1972. Eng. trans. Alan Bass, *Margins of Philosophy*, Chicago: University of Chicago Press, 1982.

—— (1972a) *La dissémination*, Paris: Seuil. Eng. trans. Barbara Johnson, *Dissemination*, Chicago: University of Chicago Press, 1981.

—— (1972b) *Marges de la philosophie*, Paris: Minuit. Eng. trans. Alan Bass, *Margins of Philosophy*, Chicago: University of Chicago Press.

—— (1974) *Glas*, 2 vols, Paris: Denoël/Gonthier, 1981. Eng. trans. John P. Leavey, Jr, and Richard Rand, *Glas*, Lincoln: University of Nebraska Press, 1986.

—— (1977) 'Limited Inc.', in *Limited Inc.*, Eng. trans. Samuel Weber, 2nd edn, Evanston: Northwestern University Press, 1990.

—— (1980) 'En ce moment même dans cet ouvrage me voici', in J. Derrida, *Psyché: Inventions de l'autre*, Paris: Galilée, 1987. Eng. trans. Ruben Berezdivin, 'At this very moment in this work here I am', in Robert Bernasconi and Simon Critchley (eds) *Rereading Levinas*, Bloomington: Indiana University Press, 1991.

—— (1981) *D'un ton apocalyptique adopté naguère en philosophie*, Paris: Galilée, 1983. Eng. trans. John. P. Leavey, Jr, 'Of an apocalyptic tone recently adopted in philosophy', *Oxford Literary Review*, 6(2) 1984: 3–37.

—— (1984) 'Déclarations d'indépendance', in J. Derrida, *Otobiographies: L'enseignement de Nietzsche et la politique du nom propre*, Paris: Galilée.

—— (1985) 'Préjugés: Devant la loi' in J. Derrida et al., *La Faculté de Juger*, Paris: Minuit. Eng. trans. Avita Ronell and Christine Roulston, 'Before the law', in Derek Attridge (ed.) *Acts of Literature*, London: Routledge, 1992.

—— (1986a) *Mémoires for Paul de Man*, trans. Cecile Lindsay, Jonathan Culler and Eudardo Cadava, New York: Columbia University Press.

—— (1986b) 'Admiration de Nelson Mandela ou Les lois de réflexion' in J. Derrida, *Psyché: Inventions de l'autre*, Paris, Galilée, 1987. Eng. trans. Mary Ann Caws and Isabelle Lorenz, 'The Laws of Reflection: Nelson Mandela, in Admiration', in (no ed.) *For Nelson Mandela*, New York: Seaver Books, 1987.

—— (1987a) *De l'esprit: Heidegger et la question*, Paris: Galilée. Eng. trans. Geoffrey Bennington and Rachel Bowlby, *Of Spirit: Heidegger and the Question*, Chicago: University of Chicago Press, 1989.

—— (1987b) *Khôra*, Paris: Galilée, 1993.

—— (1987c) 'Invention de l'autre' in J. Derrida, *Psyché: Inventions de l'autre*, Paris, Galilée, 1987. Eng. trans. Catherine Porter, 'Psyche: Invention of the Other', in Lindsey Waters and Wlad Godzich (eds) *Reading de Man Reading*, Minnesota: University of Minnesota Press, 1989.

—— (1987d) 'Nombre de oui' in *Psyché: Inventions de l'autre*,Paris: Galilée, 1987 Eng. trans. Brian Holmes, 'A number of yes (nombre de oui)' in *Qui Parle*, 2(2): 120–133.

—— (1987e) 'Comment ne pas parler: Dénégations', in *Psyché: Inventions de l'autre*, Paris, Galilée, 1987. Eng. trans. Ken Frieden, 'How to Avoid Speaking: Denials' in Sanford Buck and Wolfgang Iser (eds) *Languages of the Unsayable: The Play of Literature and Literary Theory*, New York: Columbia University Press, 1989.

—— (1991a) *L'autre cap suivi de 'La démocratie ajournée'*, Paris: Minuit. Eng. trans. Pascale Anne-Brault and Michael Naas, *The Other Heading: Reflections on Today's Europe*, Bloomington: Indiana University Press, 1992.

—— (1991b) *Donner le temps. 1: La fausse monnaie*, Paris: Galilée. Eng. trans. Peggy Kamuf, *Given Time. 1: Counterfeit Money*, Chicago: University of Chicago Press, 1992.

—— (1992a) 'Donner la mort', in Jean-Michel Rabaté and Michael Wetzel (eds) *L'éthique du don: Jacques Derrida et la pensée du don*, Paris: Transition.

—— (1992b) 'Force of law: The "mystical foundation of authority"', in Drucilla Cornell, Michael Rosenfeld and David Gray Carlson (eds) *Deconstruction and the Possibility of Justice*, trans. Mary Quaintance, London: Routledge, 1992.

—— (1993) *Spectres de Marx*, Paris: Galilée. Eng. trans. by Peggy Kamuf, *Specters of Marx: The State of the Debt, the Work of Mourning and the New International*, London: Routledge, 1994.

—— (1994a) 'Apories: Mourir – s'attendre aux "limites de la vérité"' in J. Derrida et al., *Le passage des frontières*, Colloque de Cerisy, Paris: Galilée. Eng. trans. Thomas Dutoit, *Aporias: Dying – Awaiting (One Another at) the 'Limits of Truth'*, Stanford: Stanford University Press, 1994.

—— (1994b) *Politiques de l'amitié*, Paris: Galilée. Eng. trans. George Collins (London: Verso, forthcoming); partially translated as 'Heidegger's ear, philopolemology (*Geschlecht* IV)' in J. Sallis (ed.) *Reading Heidegger*, trans. John P. Leavey, Jr, Bloomington: Indiana University Press, 1991.

Descartes, R. (1641) 'Méditations', in *Oeuvres Complètes*, Paris: Pléiade, 1953.

Dews, P. (1987) *Logic of Disintegration: Post-Structuralist Thought and the Claims of Critical Theory*, London: Verso.

Dworkin, R. (1977) *Taking Rights Seriously*, London: Duckworth.

Eagleton, T. (1990) *The Ideology of the Aesthetic*, Oxford: Blackwell.

Ferry, L. and Renaut, A. (1988) *Heidegger et les modernes*, Paris: Bernard Grasset.

Frank, M. (1984) *Neo-Strukturalismus*, Frankfurt: Suhrkamp.

Fynsk, C. (1986) *Heidegger: Thought and Historicity*, Ithaca: Cornell University Press.

Freud, S. (1913) 'Totem and Taboo', in *The Standard Edition of the Complete Psychological Works of Freud* (SE), London: Hogarth Press, 13, 1.
—— (1923) 'The Infantile Genital Organisation' in SE 19, 141.
—— (1925) 'Negation' in SE 19, 235.
Gasché, R. (1979) 'Deconstruction as Criticism', *Glyph* 6: 177–216.
—— (1986) *The Tain of the Mirror: Derrida and the Philosophy of Reflection*, Harvard: Harvard University Press.
Gutmann, A. (1985) 'Communitarian critics of liberalism' in *Philosophy and Public Affairs*, 14(3) Summer, 308–22.
Habermas, J. (1981) 'Modernity – an incomplete project' in Hal Foster (ed.), *Postmodern Culture*, trans. Seyla Ben-Habib, London: Pluto Press, 1985.
—— (1988a) *The Philosophical Discourse of Modernity*, Cambridge: Polity Press.
—— (1988b) *Martin Heidegger: L'oeuvre et l'engagement*, French trans. Rainer Rochlitz, Paris: Cerf.
Hegel, G. W. F. (1798–9) 'Der Geist des Christentums und sein Schicksal' in *Frühe Schriften (Werke*, 1), Frankfurt: Suhrkamp, 1971. Eng. trans. T. M. Knox, 'The spirit of Christianity and its fate', in *Early Theological Writings*, Philadelphia: University of Pennsylvania Press, 1971.
—— (1801–2) *Faith and Knowledge*, trans. H. S. Harris and Walter Cerf, Albany: State University of New York Press, 1977.
—— (1802–3) *Natural Law* essay, trans. T. M. Knox, Philadelphia: University of Pennsylvania Press, 1975.
—— (1803) *System der Sittlichkeit*, Hamburg: Felix Meiner, 1967. Eng. trans. H. S. Harris and T. M. Knox, *System of Ethical Life*, Albany: State University of New York Press, 1979.
—— (1807) *Phenomenology of Spirit*, trans. A. V. Miller, Oxford: Oxford University Press, 1977.
—— (1812–16) *Science of Logic*, trans. A. V. Miller, Atlantic Highlands, NJ: Humanities Press International, 1989.
—— (1821a) *The Philosophy of History*, trans. J. Sibree, New York: Dover, 1956.
—— (1821b) *Hegel's Philosophy of Right*, trans. T. M. Knox, Oxford: Oxford University Press, 1967.
—— (1975) *Hegel's Aesthetics*, 2 vols, trans. T. M. Knox, Oxford: Clarendon Press.
Heidegger, M. (1924) *The Concept of Time*, trans. William McNeill, Oxford: Blackwell, 1992.
—— (1926) *Sein und Zeit*, Tübingen: Max Niemeyer, 7th edn, 1986. Eng. trans. John Macquarrie and Edward Robinson, *Being and Time*, Oxford: Blackwell, 1967.
—— (1929) *Kant and the Problem of Metaphysics*, trans. James S. Churchill, Bloomington: Indiana University Press, 1962.
—— (1933) 'The self-assertion [self-affirmation] of the German university', trans. K. Harries, *Review of Metaphysics*, 28(3): 470–80.
—— (1935) *Einführung in der Metaphysik*, Tübingen: Max Niemeyer, 1958. Eng. trans. Ralph Manheim, *An Introduction to Metaphysics*, New Haven: Yale University Press, 1959.
—— (1946) 'The Anaximander fragment', in David Krell (ed.) *Early Greek Thinking*, trans. David Krell and Frank A. Capuzzi, San Francisco: Harper, 1984.

—— (1951–2) *What is Called Thinking?*, trans. J. Glenn Gray, New York: Harper & Row, 1968.

—— (1953) 'Language in the poem: A discussion on George Trakl's poetic work', in *On the Way to Language*, trans. Peter Hertz, New York: Harper & Row, 1971.

—— (1957–8) 'The nature of language', in *On the Way to Language*, trans. Peter Hertz, New York: Harper & Row, 1971.

—— (1959) *Gelassenheit*, Pfullingen: Neske. Eng. trans. J. M. Anderson and E. H. Freund, *Discourse on Thinking*, New York: Harper & Row, 1966.

—— (1962) 'Time and Being' in *On Time and Being*, trans. Joan Stambaugh, New York: Harper & Row, 1972.

Kafka, F. (1988) *Collected Short Stories of Franz Kafka*, Harmondsworth: Penguin.

Kant, I. (1781) *Critique of Pure Reason*, trans. Norman Kemp Smith, London: Macmillan, 1929.

—— (1785) *Fundamental Principles of the Metaphysics of Morals*, trans. T. K. Abbott, New York: Prometheus, 1987.

—— (1788) *Critique of Practical Reason*, trans. Lewis White Beck, New York: Macmillan, 1956.

—— (1790) *Critique of Judgement*, trans. James Meredith Creed, Oxford: Clarendon, 1952.

—— (1791) *Religion within the Limits of Reason Alone*, trans. Theodore M. Greene and Hoyt H. Hudson, New York: Harper, 1960.

—— (1793) 'On the common saying: "This may be true in theory but it does not apply in practice"' in Hans Reiss (ed.) *Kant's Political Writings*, trans. H. B. Nisbet, Cambridge: Cambridge University Press, 1970.

—— (1795) 'Perpetual peace: A philosophical sketch', in Hans Reiss (ed.) *Kant's Political Writings*, trans. H. B. Nisbet, Cambridge: Cambridge University Press, 1970.

Kierkegaard, S. (1843) *Fear and Trembling*, trans. Alastair Hannay, London: Penguin, 1985.

Lacoue-Labarthe, P. (1986) 'La transcendence finie/t dans la politique' in P. Lacoue-Labarthe, *L'imitation des modernes: Typographies II*, Paris: Galilée.

—— (1987) *Heidegger, Art and Politics: The Fiction of the Political*, trans. Chris Turner, Oxford: Blackwell, 1990.

Levinas, E. (1961) *Totalité et infini: Essai sur l'extériorité*, The Hague: Martinus Nijhoff. Eng. trans. Alphonso Lingis, *Totality and Infinity: An Essay on Exteriority*, Pittsburgh: Duquesne University Press, 1969.

—— (1963) 'La trace de l'autre' in *En découvrant l'existence avec Husserl et Heidegger*, Paris, Vrin, 4th edn, 1988.

—— (1971, 1979, 1980) 'Sionismes' in *L'au-delà du verset*, Paris: Minuit, 1982. Eng. trans. Roland Lack, 'Zionisms', in Sean Hand (ed.) *The Levinas Reader*, Oxford: Blackwell, 1989.

—— (1974) *Autrement qu'être ou Au-delà de l'essence*, The Hague: Martinus Nijhoff. Eng. trans. Alphonso Lingis, *Otherwise than Being or Beyond Essence*, Dordrecht: Kluwer Academic Publishers, 1991.

—— (1975) 'Dieu et la philosophie' in *De Dieu qui vient à l'idée*, Paris: Vrin, 1986, pp. 93–127. Eng. trans. Richard A. Cohen and Alphonso Lingis, 'God and Philosophy', in *The Levinas Reader*, Oxford: Blackwell.

—— (1976) 'De la déficience sans souci au sens nouveau' in *De Dieu qui vient à l'idée*, Paris: Vrin, 1986.

—— (1982a) *L'au-delà du verset*, Paris: Minuit, 1982. Eng. trans. (1971 only) Roland Lack, 'Zionisms', in Sean Hand (ed.) *The Levinas Reader*, Oxford: Blackwell, 1989.

—— (1982b) 'Ethics and politics: Interview with Schlomo Malka', in *The Levinas Reader*, Oxford: Blackwell

—— (1988) *A l'heure des nations*, Paris: Minuit.

Lévi-Strauss, C. (1963) *Tristes Tropiques*, Paris: Union Générale d'Éditions.

Lyotard, J.-F. (1979) *Just Gaming*, trans. Wlad Godzich, Manchester: Manchester University Press, 1985.

—— (1983) *The Differend*, trans. Georges Van Den Abbeele, Minnesota: University of Minnesota Press, 1988.

—— (1987) *Heidegger and 'the Jews'*, trans. Lesley A. Boldt, New York: University of New York Press, 1988.

—— (1988) *The Inhuman*, trans. Geoffrey Bennington and Rachel Bowlby, Cambridge: Polity Press, 1991.

—— (1993) *Political Writings*, trans. Bill Readings and Kevin Paul Geiman, London: UCL Press.

MacIntyre, A. (1981) *After Virtue*, Notre Dame: Notre Dame University Press.

—— (1988) *Whose Justice? Which Rationality?*, London: Duckworth.

Marx, K. (1843a) 'Critique of Hegel's Doctrine of the State' in *Early Writings*, trans. Rodney Livingstone and Gregor Benton, Harmondsworth: Penguin, 1975.

—— (1843b) 'On the Jewish Question', in *Early Writings*, Harmondsworth: Penguin, 1975.

—— (1843c) 'A contribution to the critique of Hegel's philosophy of right', in *Early Writings*, Harmondsworth: Penguin, 1975.

—— (1845–7) *The German Ideology* in *Collected Works*, Volume 5, trans. Clemens Dutt, W. Lough and C. P. Magill, London: Lawrence and Wishart, 1976.

—— (1858) *Grundrisse*, Harmondsworth: Penguin, 1973.

Nancy, J.-L. (1986) *La communauté désoeuvrée*, Paris: Christian Bourgois.

Nietzsche, F. (1887) *'On the Genealogy of Morals' and 'Ecce Homo'*, trans. W. Kaufmann, New York: Vintage Books, 1967.

Norris, C. (1982) *Deconstruction: Theory and Practice*, London and New York: Methuen.

—— (1987) *Derrida*, Fontana Modern Masters, London: Fontana Press.

Nozick, R. (1974) *Anarchy, State and Utopia*, Oxford: Blackwell.

Plato (1956) 'Meno', in *'Protagoras' and 'Meno'*, trans. W. C. Guthrie, London: Penguin.

Ronell, A. (1989) *The Telephone Book: Technology, Schizophrenia, Electric Speech*, Lincoln: Nebraska Press.

Rawls, J. (1972) *A Theory of Justice*, Oxford: Oxford University Press.

—— (1980) 'Kantian constructivism in moral theory', *Journal of Philosophy*, 67(9): 515–72.

Rose, G. (1981) *Hegel Contra Sociology*, London: Athlone.

—— (1984) *Dialectics of Nihilism: Post-structuralism and Law*, Oxford: Blackwell.

—— (1992) *The Broken Middle: Out of our Ancient Society*, Oxford: Blackwell.

—— (1993) *Judaism and Modernity: Philosophical Essays*, Oxford: Blackwell.

Rousseau, J.-J. (1762) *Le contrat social* in *Oeuvres complètes*, Paris: Pléiade, 1959–69.

Salanskis, J.-M. (1995) 'Die Wissenschaft denkt nicht', trans. George Collins, *Tekhnema: Journal of Philosophy and Technology* 2: 57–84.

Saussure, F. de (1915) *Cours de linguistique générale*, Paris: Payot, 1973. Eng. trans. Wade Baskin, *Course in General Linguistics*, New York: McGraw-Hill, 1959, 2nd edn 1966.

Stiegler, B. (1993) 'Questioning technology and time', trans. Richard Beardsworth and Arielle Sumits, *Tekhnema: Journal of Philosophy and Technology*, 1: 31–46.

—— (1994) *La technique et le temps, 1: La faute d'Epiméthée*, Paris: Galilée. Eng. trans. Richard Beardsworth and George Collins, *Technics and Time, 1: The Fault of Epimetheus*, Stanford: Stanford University Press (forthcoming).

Taylor, C. (1979a) *Hegel and Modern Society*, Cambridge: Cambridge University Press.

—— (1979b) 'Atomism', in Alkis Kontos (ed.) *Power, Possessions and Freedoms: Essays in Honour of C. MacPherson*, Toronto: University of Toronto Press.

Index

alterity 103, 118, 121, 128, 133–7, 151–2
American Declaration of Independence 98–102
Antigone 84–91, 115–18
aporia 5, 31, 112, 117; and Aristotle 31–3, 107; and decision/judgement xiv, 5, 31, 33, 37–40, 43; and dialectic 50, 78, 84–92; of law xvi, 31–40, 78, 84–96, 98–104, 122–44; and promise 36–7, 145–57; and responsibility 68–70, 132–7, 139; of space 114–18; of time xvi, 33, 49, 59, 91, 98–104, 104–22, 145–57; *see also* limit
arche-writing 7–8, 12–18, 20–5, 155
arrivant 121, 145–6
Athena 81, 84
avoidance, logics of 153–6

Baudelaire, C. 49
Bennington, G. 3, 26, 158

Caygill, H. 50, 54
contradiction: and aporia 59; contradictory logic 11–12, 62

death 28, 60, 66, 71, 78, 82, 84, 111–14, 130–2
deconstruction 10–11, 61; fates of 2–4; and history 24, 27–31, 34–5, 56–61, 92–5, 96–7, 99–102, 105, 123–4, 141–3, 154–6; of horizon 6, 19, 40, 64, 67, 109–10, 132; and literature 1–4, 25–7, 34–45; 'method' of 4–6

(*see also* empirico-transcendental difference); and modernity 46–7; politics of xi–xvi, 1, 3–4, 6, 10, 12, 18–20, 21, 24, 32–45, 37–45, 46–9, 50–1, 66–8, 74, 78, 92–5, 97–102, 102–4, 105, 109, 114–18, 120–2, 141–4, 146–57, 158 n. 1 (*see also* democracy; promise)
Deleuze, G. xiii
democracy 42, 66, 92; 'democracy to come' xvi; *see also* promise
Derrida, J.: *Aporias* 4, 31, 36, 110, 111, 118–19, 130, 133; 'Before the Law' xv, 3, 24–45, 132; 'Déclarations d'Indépendance' 98–102, 132; *Dissemination* 2, 4, 15, 149; 'Donner la mort' 139–40; 'Force of Law: "the Mystical Foundation of Authority"' 44–5, 99, 132; *Glas* 19, 23, 48, 59, 60, 78, 81, 82, 84–92, 97; *Of Grammatology* xiii, xv, 2, 3, 4, 6–25, 36, 56–8, 149, 155; 'How to Avoid Speaking: Denials' 19; 'Invention of the Other' 101, 149; 'The Laws of Reflection: Nelson Mandela in Admiration' 99; *Ltd. Inc.* 15, 19; *Margins of Philosophy* 4; *Mémoires for Paul de Man* xvi, 33, 36, 99; 'A Number of Yes (Nombre de oui)' xvi, 19; 'Of an Apocalyptic Tone Recently Adopted in Philosophy' 48; *The Origin of Geometry* 7, 15, 16; *The Other Heading* xvi, 36, 42; 'Ousia and Gramme' 27, 32–3, 105, 110; *Politics of Friendship* 36, 110,

115, 122, 133, 152; *Specters of Marx*
36, 42, 110, 111, 122, 129, 132–3,
145–6, 147, 148, 150, 155; *Speech
and Phenomena* 10, 15; *Of Spirit:
Heidegger and the Question* xvi, 18,
36, 103, 120, 153–4, 156; 'Violence
and Metaphysics' 13, 15, 67, 124,
134, 136, 138, 141, 155; *Writing and
Difference* 2, 4, 149
Dews, P. 46
différance 17, 22, 43, 58, 59, 64, 67,
72, 88, 90; of law 29, 35–42; of time
100, 111, 118, 148, 150
disavowal xvi, 48, 118–20, 158; of
inscription 10; of originary technicity
151–2, of the other 127–8; of time
54, 69, 77, 92, 100–1, 106, 109; of
violence 69 (*see also* institution and
violence)
disjointure 99, 101, 116, 132, *see also*
time
Dworkin, R. 51

Eagleton, T. 46
écriture xiv–xv, 2, 37, 57
economy 24–5, 84, 88, 96; *see also*
stricture; violence
empirico-transcendental difference 6,
7, 10, 14, 16, 18, 19, 20, 23, 49,
146
enlightenment 49, 64
Eumenides 80–82
event 28–31, 37, 92-95, *see also*
American Declaration of
Independence
exemplarity: logics of 40, 104, 124,
141–4
ethics 3; ethico-theoretical, the 11–12;
ethical orientation 64, 66; ethics
and knowledge 56, 61–2, 66; fate of
the ethical 61–9 (Kant), 122–44
(Levinas)

Ferry, L. and Renault, A. 46
Feuerbach, L. 49
fate 71–2, 82–4; *see also* ethics;
inscription
freedom 49–51, 55–6; idea of 51–6
Freud, S. 29–31, 33–4, 158 n. 2
Foucault, M. xiii, 47
Frank, M. 46

Gasché, R. 3

genealogy 28–31, 98, 104; *see also*
deconstruction and history
God 28, 55, 70, 99–102, 136, 140,
141

Habermas, J. 46
Hegel, G. W. F. 46–61, 70–95; and
contemporary philosophy 49–51,
57–61; and deconstruction 29, 46–8,
57–61, 70–2, 95–7; Hegel/Kant
difference 51–6, 70–2
Heidegger, M. xv, 102–22, 151–6; and
Nazism 103, 105, 109, 117, 120,
144, 152–6
holy will 65, 71

impossibility 26, 31–3, 36, 38, 42–4,
60, 68, 87, 111, 132, 137
inscription 5, 6, 7, 8, 10, 16, 17,
18–20, 20–5, 95, 146, 149; *see also*
empirico-transcendental difference;
matter
institution xv, 19, 46, 50, 90, 95;
thinking of, through linguistics 3; and
violence 6–25, 62, 98–102; *see also*
aporia of law; inscription
invention xi, xii, xiv, 25, 26, 31, 41,
44, 46, 47, 61, 68, 78, 92, 95–7,
98–102, 105, 125, 146, 149–51, 157

judgement xv, 24–45, 61, 78, 87, 92,
99, 100–1, 104, 107; in Kant 54, 63,
64, 66, 160 n. 7
justice xvii; and time 132–3 (*see also*
disjointure); *see also* ethics; promise

Kafka, F. xiv, 25–9, 35–44
Kant, I. xv, 61–70; *see also* Hegel

Lacoue-Labarthe, P. 37, 115
law: of contamination and repetition
17–18, 20, 154 (*see also* fate); of
contradiction 80–2, 83, 86–8; of law
23–4, 27–31, 58–61, 90, 100, 120–2,
123; and literature 25–7, 34–7; and
singularity 41–5; and time 98–102;
see also aporia of law
Lévi-Strauss, C. 20–3, 82
Levinas, E. xv, 64, 102–4, 122–44
liberalism and communitarianism 50
limit: as axis of modernity 47–8, 51–61;
between ethics and knowledge 61–9;
Heidegger's thinking of 111–14;

inversions of 23, 67, 93, 135–6,
  141–4; prior to Kant and Hegel 78
literature: literariness of 25–7; and
  politics 37–41; *see also* deconstruction
  and literature; law and literature
logic: and time 53–4, 59, 68, 91–5,
  109–10, 122, 141, 148–57; *see also*
  aporia; law; limit
Lyotard, J.-F. 37, 52, 63, 64

Macintyre, A. 51
Marx, K. 28, 49, 74, 94, 147, 163
  n. 2
matter 95–8, 154
middle ground 17, 19
modernity xv, 46, 49–51, 51–61, 78;
  fates of 84–93
metaphysics, xiii, 101–2, 106, 117

Nancy, J.-L. 37, 119
Nietzsche, F. 28, 49
Nozick, R. 51
negative theology 19

ontology 48, 50, 52, 58, 59, 69, 77–8,
  87–8, 90, 91, 92, 94–5, 102, 104–6,
  109–10, 122, 124, 128, 134–6, 141–2
other 118–19, 125–30, 133–7, 139–41
organization: logical, technical and
  remainder xiii, 109–10, 148–57

phantasm 59, 77, 84, 119–20, 149,
  151
Plato 8; Platonism 15
political, the 6, 18–20, 158 n. 1
politics: *see* deconstruction and politics
promise xvi, 6, 36–7, 42, 46, 60, 68–9,
  85, 101, 145–57; and aporia 36–7; of
  democracy 42, 44, 46–98 *passim* (esp.
  46–7, 50–1, 64, 69–70, 95), 143,
  145–6; the messianic and messianism
  64, 101, 143, 145, 150; and quasi-
  transcendentals 36, 156; and technics
  150–3, 155–6
proper name 24; politics of 121, 141–4

quasi-transcendentals 19, 58, 68, 154

Rawls, J. 51
recognition 70–4, 81–91, 159 n. 2

religion 55–6, 127, 141, 152, 154–6; *see*
  also God
rights: and violence 50, 82
remainder xiii, 91
revolt and revolution 69–70, 92–5
Rose, G. 47, 57–61, 71, 77, 97

Salanskis, J.-M. 39
Saussure, F. xiv, 8–18
singular 25–45, 58, 74, 75, 85–7, 86,
  90, 91, 95, 146; and particular and
  universal 41–3, 68–9 (*see also* law
  and singularity); politics of 141–4
Sittlichkeit 47, 50, 57, 75–9
space 111, 114, 118, 143; *see also*
  aporia
spectral, the 83–4, 90, 129, 146–8
Stiegler, B. 145, 151
stricture 19, 23, 60, 78, 87–92, 95; *see*
  also violence
sublime, the 84

Taylor, C. 51
technics xvii, 96–7, 104–5, 109, 120,
  146–57
'there', the 105, 110, 111, 113, 117,
  119, 121, 123, 124, 136, 140, 141,
  151
time xiv, 31–4; delay of 100, 110, 122,
  130, 132; *différance* of 98–102,
  110–11, 150; excess of 91, 111, 129;
  and the human 49, 86, 96, 147–51;
  and the singular 43, 94–5; temporalization of 103–4, 109, 119, 121–2;
  see also aporia of time; technics
trace 6–25, 42, 100, 134, 155
tragedy and politics 78–84 (Hegel),
  114–18 (Heidegger)

violence 6–25, 47, 49–51, 67–8, 69–70,
  99–101, 155; economy of 12, 13, 14,
  17, 23–5, 40, 91, 134; in Heidegger
  103, 109, 120, 152; lesser xiv, xvi,
  12, 20, 24, 46, 61, 63, 68–9, 101,
  134, 154; originary 6, 12, 18, 20, 22,
  23, 24, 50; tertiary structure of 20–5
Volk: in Hegel 75, 78–81, 84; in
  Heidegger 103, 109, 120, 152

'we', community of 42–3, 145–6